Schooling for the People

Schooling for the People

Comparative Local Studies of Schooling History in France and Germany, 1750–1850

Mary Jo Maynes

HM
HOLMES & MEIER
New York London

First published in the United States of America 1985 by
Holmes & Meier Publishers, Inc.
30 Irving Place
New York, N.Y. 10003

Great Britain:
Hillview House
One Hallswelle Parade
London NW11 ODL England

Book design by Deborah England

Manufactured in the United States of America

Library of Congress Cataloging in Publication Data

Maynes, Mary Jo.
Schooling for the people. Comparative local studies of schooling history in France and Germany, 1750–1850.
Bibliography: p.
Includes index.
1. Education—France—Vaucluse (Dept.)—History.
2. Education—Germany—Baden—History. 3. Comparative education. I. Title.
LA713.V34M39 1985 370′.943 84-10929
ISBN 0-8419-0966-0

Contents

TABLES

FIGURES

MAPS

Preface

THE RESEARCH ON WHICH THIS BOOK IS BASED was begun as a dissertation project at the University of Michigan. Michigan was a superb place to study European social history, and the influence of those years remains with me. I would particularly like to acknowledge my tremendous intellectual debts to Charles and Louise Tilly, my teachers, mentors, and friends. But there were many others, too—especially David Bien, a fine teacher and advisor and a careful critic since my first days at Michigan, and Raymond Grew who offered help and criticism based on his own expertise in the social history of education.

When it came to revising and restructuring that massive and cumbersome dissertation material into a book, both Harvey Graff and John Modell volunteered to read the original version, and they have offered me valuable advice throughout the revision procedure. For that I am exceedingly grateful. Among the others who have offered help and support at various moments during the writing of this book, I'd also like to thank Ron Aminzade and John Merriman.

Because this project is a comparative one, I seem also to have relied on the help and resources of at least twice the usual number of institutions and their staffs. The research on which this book is based was supported by grants from the Horace G. Rackham School of Graduate Studies of the University of Michigan, the Social Science Research Council, and the McMillan Travel Fund and Graduate School of the University of Minnesota, all of whom, naturally, accept no responsibility for its contents. In Paris, I availed myself of the services of the Bibliothèque Nationale, the Musée Pédagogique, and the Archives Nationales, whose staff members usually got me what I needed. In Avignon, the staff of the Archives Départementales de Vaucluse made my time in the Midi pleasant as well as productive. I would particularly like to thank Michele Tilloy, Monique Tyron, and R. B. Leminor for their friendship and service beyond the call of duty. In Karlsruhe, the staff of the Generallandesarchiv was always friendly and efficient. Herr Weber, in particular, helped me to make the most of my time there. I would also like to thank the directors and staffs of the city archives of Mannheim and Heidelberg, and Herramtsvorstand Mergenthaler of the Mannheim Standesamt. Finally, the cooperation of the staffs of the various Catholic and Evangelical Archives of Baden facilitated my work with parish registers.

I would like to thank the publishers of *Comparative Studies in Society and History* and *Historical Reflections/Reflexions Historiques* for permission to use materials previously published in those journals.

This book is dedicated to Ron, who has been a companion and source of constant intellectual and emotional support since before I finished my own schooling, and to Daniel, who has taught me a lot.

Schooling for the People

CHAPTER 1

Introduction to the Comparative History of Educational Change

THE HISTORICAL MOMENT OF SCHOOL REFORM

PROPONENTS OF SCHOOLING HAD WON THE DAY in most of Western Europe by the last quarter of the nineteenth century. By that time, parents had chosen to send their children into the classroom, or had been coerced into sending them, to spend a considerable portion of their young lives. The timing and pace of the migration of children into the classroom varied from place to place. In some regions, the process was well under way by the end of the eighteenth century, while in others it began later and intensified only in the middle of the nineteenth century. But the end result was the same everywhere in the West: the process of "schooling society" brought schooling into the prominent position it holds today as a virtually universal phase in the individual life course, and as the basis for collective socialization. And despite the recent challenges by radical pedagogues, most Westerners find it difficult to conceive of a world without schools.[1]

Furthermore, the same historical epoch that produced the rise in school attendance also changed the very character of schooling. Elementary schools began as institutions rooted in an uneven local demand—usually on the part of artisans or better-off peasant families—for the rudimentary instruction they regarded as useful for a variety of religious and secular purposes. But the reform campaign of the late eighteenth and early nineteenth centuries transformed these schools into local expressions of a new program sponsored by sectors of the local and national governing classes to change not only the skill levels, but, perhaps more important, the very nature of "the people." This study will explore the transformation of schooling from a peripheral and casual experience to one of the central and most politically and socially charged routines of growing up. Conceived of in the most general terms—as an effort to understand how and why schools came to hold the place they now do in Western society—the account that follows is nevertheless based on the concrete experience of two small regions, one in southern France and the other in southwestern Germany. The comparative case study method was chosen to illustrate a general phenomenon even while examining local variations in it. The quasi-experimental design of the research behind this analysis serves to highlight the impact upon the schooling process of differences in the political contexts in which it occurred. And although the account is historical in nature, the suggestions about schooling as a social and political process that emerge from it speak as well to the educational dilemmas we continue to face today.

Elementary schools have existed in Europe since at least the High Middle Ages, but until the nineteenth century they were haphazard affairs, catering to a clientele of mixed ages and social characteristics. They were run by freelance teachers who, out of undisguised pecuniary motives, practiced the craft of imparting skills and knowledge to pupils whose attendance in their classes was voluntary and sporadic. Perhaps the church-run schools of northern Europe may be considered as exceptions. Certainly they were difficult to evade, and more elevated moral claims were made about them. But even in these, pedagogic goals were modest—to teach familiarity with the Scriptures and the language necessary to read them. The actual time children spent in them was small, since schooling hours had to be fitted in after more urgent demands on children's time were met.[2]

All of this began to change in the late eighteenth century. Many of the educational reforms which then began to appear had been anticipated earlier, to be sure, but it was only toward the end of the old regime that the new vision of schooling began to affect the lives of great numbers of European children. Schools became school systems. State agents began to reform or create the bureaucracies necessary to bring under state control the array of existing and newly created educational facilities. In the classrooms, more homogeneous gatherings of pupils heard lessons based on curricular plans. Routes of entry into and departure from the schools, formerly as numerous as the pupils themselves, dwindled into a few well-worn paths. Curricula were redesigned according to the tenets of a scientific pedagogy to insure their propriety for explicit goals. Enrollments crept and then bounded upward toward the ambitious universality sought by reformers. By the middle of the nineteenth century, the main features of the modern school system were in place.[3]

An account of these changes in the nature of schooling, changes that occurred throughout much of the Western world in the later decades of the eighteenth century and the early decades of the nineteenth, needs to be set in the peculiar historical moment in which the transformation took place. Of special significance for the history of schooling was the social and economic dislocation that accompanied the transition from commercial to industrial capitalist production techniques, on the one hand, and the political changes that resulted from the consolidation of nation states in the climate established by the French Revolution, on the other. Schooling proponents saw education both as a solution to the structural disruptions generated by social and economic change, and as a political necessity in an age of ascendant mass politics.

The increasing demand for a disciplined urban labor force began to make obsolete the values and lifestyles of the self-employed, often rural and part-time workers of the commercial capitalist era. As rural and artisanal industries were first challenged and then undermined by competition from urban factories and sweatshops, unemployed peasants and artisans fed into the streams of migrants flowing into the developing regions of Europe. Often young, unattached, unemployed, and sometimes unskilled, these migrants appeared as a threat to property owners and public authorities concerned with the preservation of order even as they offered the promise of labor power to those in need of it. And if there was talk, toward the end of the eighteenth century, of the need for places for these people to learn skills, educational writers as often as not simply emphasized the moral and intellectual traits demanded of a modern people. Schooling campaigns spawned in this era bear the mark of fear, of the need to moralize and manage the poor.[4]

It was not only the means by which people made their livelihood that was changing;[4] their very nature seemed to be changing as well. Maxim Pazzis, author of one of the regional statistical yearbooks so popular in the early decades of the nineteenth century, noted with approval the surging population growth in the French département of Vaucluse in the first decade of the century. But he also pointed with dismay to the rising rates of illegitimacy, the high levels of out-migration, and the apparent inability of the people to provide for and control their large families. "One can observe in the poorest classes of the people," he noted, "children who are more unconstrained, bolder than ever before, more irreverent toward their parents, nourished on vice, and stammering, as their first words, horrible oaths, obscene phrases and inconceivable blasphemies."[5] Pazzis' comments reflect a commonplace shared, it seems, by many observers of popular manners—that popular morality was endangered. Although complaints about moral decay are virtually a historical constant, the volume of such complaints reached a crescendo in this era. Middle-class and aristocratic observers often claimed that the growing savagery and immorality of the poor was a problem of unprecedented scope. And insofar as illegitimacy statistics are a measure of the problem they identified, their claims are indeed borne out by the findings of historians.[6]

Young people seemed especially out of control. Church inspectors felt that part of the blame lay in the growing distance of the youth from the churches, and in the new occasions for unsupervised sociability which new customs and conditions offered. An Evangelical inspection report for the village of Handschuhsheim in southwestern Germany for the year 1839 offers but one illustration:

> . . . left to themselves and their peers from nine o'clock in the morning [on Sunday], from the end of religious services throughout the whole day, the young people will be led into moral corruption one after another, like sheep or deer. . . . Given a leisure period this long, the young go to dances held every other week in [the nearby village of] Neuenheim, wherein lies the source of their corruption.[7]

In the growing cities, pastors were not even able to keep records of all their young parishioners, let alone regulate their behavior.

Not all of the educated observers of popular behavior were alarmists, of course. The late eighteenth and early nineteenth centuries did, after all, also produce the Romantic elevation of the popular classes to a position of moral and cultural superiority. Whether regarded as a backlash against the Enlightenment or as an outgrowth of its contradictory ideas about nature and the human conquest of it, the Romantic adulation of "the people" nevertheless rests upon the same social distance from "it." Virtually all the commentaries upon popular morality written in this era of "discovery of the people" were the products of upper-class observers who spoke of the people as an alien species, as exotics.[8] And this conscious or unconscious assumption of a barrier between "the people" and those who wanted to observe, define, manipulate, or transform them needs also to be kept in mind in any interpretation of the educational reforms of the era.

The political events of the French Revolution can only have reinforced the often stated opinion that the people were out of control. The break with tradition the revolution brought to France left all political institutions open to challenge. The revolution itself became a tradition of sorts, rooted in popular culture and in elite fears, producing a necessity for governments in France to contain popular dissatisfaction, to cement the loyalties of the people, continually to secure the status quo. Even outside of France, where the impact of the revolution was less direct, the years of revolutionary upheaval, the constitutional crises they provoked, the ideologies they spawned, the social conflict they unveiled, all made popular sentiment a concern for statesmen to a degree foreign to the Europe of the ancien régime.

But it cannot be denied that these were decades of optimism as well. The first glimpses of the potential productive capacity of an industrial economy and of the political possibilities inherent in alternatives to monarchy had demonstrated to some that human malleability so central to the Enlightenment revision of history. Although conservatives read only catastrophe in the changes which the period brought, liberals were quick to see a demonstration of the capacity to progress. To be sure, everyone acknowledged that social problems invariably accompanied change, but liberals saw these problems as in part the result of the intellectual or political immaturity of the people, who were felt nonetheless to share in the inherent human potential for improvement. According to the educational reformers who began to play an increasingly important role in many European governments in the postrevolutionary decades, the surest road to progress lay through popular enlightenment.

The promise of the future rested with the children, whose capacities needed only to be brought out. A wall poster published in the southern French town of Bollème, announcing the opening in 1831 of the new monitorial school there, captured this sense of excitement:

> It no longer suffices to know how to babble a few words in a lamentable tone or to trace a few lines. It is necessary that children who are entering this era of equality, of industry and of emulation be capable of gaining

> knowledge extensive enough to get out of the rut in which they unavoidably find themselves with the old methods of instruction. . . .[9]

Children raised solely by intellectually deficient or morally backward parents, or exposed only to inept and old-fashioned teachers, were doomed to grow up in ignorance of their own and society's best interests. But this could all be changed in the course of a generation if the children were supplied with a proper alternative environment in their formative years. The schools could provide such an alternative.

This, then, was the atmosphere in which school reformers set to work. Perhaps the best-documented effort was that of the English-speaking school reformers who appeared on both sides of the Atlantic in the early nineteenth century. But the reform community was an international one, with members on the Continent as well, who kept in touch with one another and shared ideas and observations. The international exchange of visits and information contributed to the common vision of an enlightened humanity that schooling zealots shared. But perhaps more crucial to the formation of the reformist spirit was the fact that these observers witnessed, from similar social perspectives, an increasingly similar social reality. Without disregarding differences of deep significance, one can nonetheless detect a common thread in the fears and aspirations shaping school reform throughout the West in this epoch. School reformers everywhere began to promote schooling as a necessary supplement to deficient family upbringing, as a preventative against moral decay and social instability, and as a prerequisite for the full exercise of civic, economic, and moral responsibilities and rights. That similar ideas about reform through schooling took root in ruling-class milieux all over the West in this epoch suggests that their historical origins need to be traced to profound and general transformations. Still, these reform ideologies and the movements they spawned did occur in specific contexts, and the shape that reforms took depended on local conditions. And an account of the meaning and impact of the school reform in any region needs to be set both in its specific local context and in the context of more general processes that influenced developments in any locality.[10]

State officials, entrepreneurs, and other men of property and respectability were not the only participants in and observers of social transformation. "The people," toward whom their reformist energies were directed, had their own perspectives on the world, their own problems with social dislocation, their own concerns about their children. The years of early industrial growth were years of crisis for the small shops, the family farms, the cottage industries. The decline of a system of production based on family enterprises had far-reaching implications for procedures available to families for supervising their children and for securing their children's futures. The crisis in putting-out industry, rural overpopulation, the emergence of new industries and new types of jobs, often away from home, and the commercialization of agriculture all interfered with the usual means of transmitting skills and capital from one generation to the next. The excess children of the villages, who were the product of the population rise of this period, were a burden on the fragile economies of many villages and a challenge to the mechanisms of family and community control that had operated in the past. The promises that schooling proponents held out—that schooling was a route out of poverty, backwardness, youthful unruliness—no doubt appealed to many peasant and artisanal families who were no longer sure that their own resources were sufficient to assure their children's future. Still, the people could not help reacting to the schools and their promise with ambivalence, suspicion, and sometimes hostility. State officials and other sponsors of reform were clearly bent on using the schools for their own ends, and there was no reason to assume that these corresponded with the popular interest.[11]

The history of schooling, then, can be understood only as the history of interactions among a number of interested parties, proponents of school reform acting on behalf of the state or of ambitious local and national elites, as well as those families of peasants, artisans, proletarians, and paupers ("the people") toward whom the reforms were directed. These interactions were loaded in favor of the dominant classes. One clear feature of the reform of the schools in this period was that it was undertaken without reference to, indeed often despite, the desires of the families concerned. The reforms were not popular in any sense of the word. Those who wanted to impose their vision on the schools did not consult the parents of the children they hoped to transform. And even if they soon found out that they could not arbitrarily impose their vision, they could nonetheless alter the institutions, like schools, that helped to set the options open to these families. Certainly the historical record reflects the viewpoints of the dominant classes most clearly. And up until the recent past, historians have been slow to detect that bias in the records and to interpret schooling history accordingly. The voices of the people who were the focus of so much concern have left little imprint on the historical record, but to ignore those voices is to misunderstand the historical process. For the popular response to the grand schemes of the state and other reformers shaped the manner in which those schemes were embodied in institutions and, in turn, the manner in which those institutions shaped people's lives.

For these reasons, records that shed light on popular attitudes about schooling are also of concern here. Given the scarcity of direct evidence, the analysis of popular strategies for education relies more heavily on inference from behavior and observations than does the discussion of elite ideologies. This evidence is suggestive if indirect, and points to the possibility of arriving at very different views of schooling history by proceeding from the popular point of view.

Still, it is important to note that it is the study of institutions and not attitudes that is the focus here. The logic of the argument presented here about the evolution of schooling hinges on the changing interests behind and constraints upon investment in formal schooling on the part of states, communities, and parents. As such, it offers an alternative to many earlier studies, which simply examined the history of pedagogic ideas or school legislation. It is not that attitudes about schooling are uninteresting; the relationship between the changing institutions and changing attitudes is problematic and important to understand. But people neither developed their ideas about schooling nor acted upon them outside of an institutional context. Schooling is a complex phenomenon rooted in socioeconomic and political, as well as cultural, history. It is instructive to find out how the constraints on people's actions were indeed constraining, whatever their ideas (and this was the case for reformist elites as well as for the popular classes). It is this constraining structure, this slowly evolving institutional base, that forms the prime focus of attention in the following study.

The deliberate focus on educational institutions also means that several historical phenomena closely linked with the evolution of schools—in particular the history of literacy, the history of the family, the history of local government—are treated only when they cast light upon schooling. They are always regarded as peripheral to the main subject. The distinction between schooling history and the history of literacy is especially important to underline, since the two are so often confounded. In the late twentieth century, we tend to assume unproblematically that schools are the places where children learn basic skills, especially literacy and numeracy. The current (and perhaps perennial) reexamination of how well the schools are serving this presumed function underscores the power of our association between schooling and skills. The whole point in attempting to dissociate, in this historical study, the complex of social and cultural values that define the place of literacy from the institutional history of schools is to illuminate the historical process whereby schools took over the task of transmitting skills, and to raise the issue of what difference it makes that these skills are taught in places like schools rather than in the many other contexts in which they have been taught and learned in different historical epochs. Perhaps such an approach will also help to cut into that set of unspoken assumptions and myths about schooling that befuddles so much of the contemporary debate as well.[12]

COMPARATIVE LOCAL HISTORY

The study of schooling history presented here is also, by design, comparative. Indeed, all historical study is at least implicitly comparative. The historian attempting to recreate the world of the past begins with his or her own historical moment as reference point and inspiration for questioning. Comparison along the dimension of time is inherent in the historical venture. The emphasis on what is unique, distinctive, or revelatory about a particular state of affairs assumes that some baseline has been established or understood. Still, for some endeavors it is useful to make this comparison explicit; arguments about the impact of a variety of societal characteristics upon specific historical trends seem particularly likely to be clarified through comparison.

In her discussion of comparative history, Sylvia Thrupp has outlined several types of comparative studies suited to the historical method.[13] One of these involves the comparison of two societies that are alike in many regards but present contrasting features in areas of interest to the investigator. Careful comparison of such societies can be suggestive of the important sources of historical variation. The similarities and contrasts that emerge from the comparison of case studies point to likely areas of valid generalization and put a damper on speculations along less fruitful paths. This is the method chosen for this historical study of educational change. As will become apparent, the two regions of France and Germany here considered were similar in many respects, but presented striking contrasts in their educational histories. The comparison will highlight those aspects of political development that were of most significance in creating this contrast. Perhaps comparative studies of this sort are no more than a systematization of the procedure that many historians have followed; the detailed case study pursued with a view toward generalization has long been a part of the historian's repertoire. But by stating clearly what is often only implicit in historical inquiry, by building into the research effort what is often left to chance or afterthought, by providing a built-in test for claims of generality or distinctiveness, comparative study allows more clarity and a new kind of rigor in historical argument.

A comparison of Franco-German schooling history seemed interesting for a number of reasons, but primarily because it allowed an assessment of the possible effects upon popular education of central state policies and patterns of political development that were in some regards dramatically different. Early modern church-state bureaucracies made energetic attempts to provide school facilities and insure attendance in many German states, at a time when in France no central educational bureaucracy yet existed. Even when state involvement in schooling became serious in France, at the time of the revolution, actual enforcement of school attendance was a short-lived pipe dream of a few reformers. The impact of central state bureaucracies on local schools began to be felt only in the 1820s and 1830s.

The impact of administrative differences such as these should suggest the effects and limits of state policy in the realm of education in this historical context. More generally, insofar as the history of schooling is influenced by the evolution of national and local political institutions and political ideologies, the comparative study of schools should add insights useful for current questioning about the "special" character of political development in nineteenth-century Germany, as measured by a presumably more "normal" developmental sequence followed in the Western democratic states.

The rationale for local study was different. The various perspectives from which schooling history will be viewed—state, community, family—entailed a search for evidence that went beyond the repositories of the national bureaucracies. Certainly the administrative perspective reveals itself in these, and the documents produced by the increasingly complex state educational agencies are invaluable for schooling history. But a look at the local records allows both an assessment of the actual impact of state policies and an analysis of what evidence there is about community and family strategies with respect to schooling. In order to facilitate the study of local conditions, then, two small regions were chosen for intensive study: part of the département of Vaucluse in southern France, and a section of the Unterrheinkreis of Baden in southwestern Germany. These particular regions were selected for several reasons: first, archival collections were relatively complete and accessible; second, these regions were similar in several significant respects (notably their geographic character and their religious and socioeconomic composition), allowing, as it were, a degree of control over these complicated and important variables.

While some types of evidence were available at a regional level, the assembly of information precise enough for an analysis of the important changes in the schools entailed the selection of a group of sample communities in each region, communities for which as complete as possible a picture of schooling history could be drawn.[14] The educational histories of these local communities form the core of the comparison, both between regions and among the various communities and families within each region. The results of this comparison will, it is hoped, by highly suggestive of the connections between schooling history and broad social, economic, and political transformations.

Some broad similarities will emerge from the comparison: the common fears of middle-class observers in both areas of actual or potential moral degradation of the popular classes, their faith in the schools as an effective influence upon the human personality and as a substitute for the apparently deficient family life of the people. Similar as well was the evolution in both regions of mechanisms that allowed for universal schooling without threat to the social status quo.

But there were also important differences in the nature and timing of the schooling process in the two regions—in, for example, the involvement of local political bodies in the creation and administration of schools, in the nature of public resources available for schooling, also apparently in the degree to which local people regarded school reform as an imposition from outside or on high. These differences point out how the particular political contexts helped to determine the form school reform took, and consequently the impact of that reform. In other words, the local comparison will suggest not only the general problems and interests that fed into the school reform movement, but also the constraints that affected the implementation of educational plans and the social character of reform. It also suggests the degree of autonomy with which institutions like schools could operate. What follows, then, is a study of educational history, but it is a study that holds implications as well for more general questions about the role of social interests, material determination, and political process in historical change.

THE STATES AND THE SCHOOLS

The states chosen for comparison were different in size and political character. In the middle of the eighteenth century, France was the wealthiest and most populous state of western Europe. French dominance on the Continent had been secured and defended through a centuries-long accumulation of territory and population, and rested on the strength of the largest army and most powerful state apparatus Europe had seen since the days of the Roman Empire. To be sure, the power of the state hinged on social and political compromises that undermined its ultimate effectiveness. Particularly troublesome were customs like aristocratic tax exemption, which displaced the largest part of the fiscal burden onto the shoulders of the oppressed peasantry, and venality of office, which extracted wealth and support from the commercial and financial bourgeoisie at the cost of bureaucratic dependability. Such pressure points became all the more obvious as state military debts accumulated throughout the eighteenth century, and as inflation and economic crisis made the situation of the peasantry and artisanal class even more precarious. The burdensome state survived on sufferance; armed resistance to it on the part of peasants and aristocrats had been effectively crushed in the middle of the seventeenth century, but all indications suggested that state demands were still resented. Peasants still withheld taxes as far as possible, still made efforts to keep their grain from going to the support of the army and the court in the capital. They still defended local customs, local prerogatives, and local culture in the face of growing national claims. But the question of popular loyalty to the state was not a pressing one during the ancien régime; popular compliance with state directives was assumed, and assured, when necessary, through recourse to arms. Only with the revolution would this change; only with the destruction of the ancien régime did the problem of popular integration become a central one for the French ruling classes.

The problem of relations between the state and the people was somewhat different in Baden. Beginning with a territorial core on the boundary of France and the Holy Roman Empire, the state of Baden was assembled from a myriad of splinter states typical of the Upper Rhine region. Here the political traditions of enlightened despotism had taken root; the rulers of the tiny principalities strove to make the most of the economy of small farms that served as a source of livelihood for their peasant tenants, of rents for the rentier aristocrats, of labor for the merchant capitalist industries so common by the end of the eighteenth century. The paternalistic states of the region often sidestepped popular opposition, protected peasant communities from the more devastating effects of the intrusion of market relations, and encouraged and even imitated the industrial and commercial enterprises of the urban *Bürgertum.* A small state with a well-organized bureaucracy and an effective police system, Baden absorbed the various territories it acquired without too much difficulty. The paternalistic grand duke, entrenched in his tower in Karlsruhe, simply became father to a growing population.

Still, even the well-run state of Baden could not escape the touch of the revolution. When, as a result of carefully conducted relations with Napoleon and careful compromise with indigenous progressive movements, the Badenese state fell heir to the entire southwestern corner of Germany, the problem of popular incorporation took on a new urgency. The revolution had touched the Badenese people, too, and the issue of popular loyalty was one that was important in the new state on the Rhine.

The two states in question thus emerged from different political traditions, were governed by somewhat different interests, and faced different administrative problems in the era of school reform. Furthermore, within each state the persistence of distinct regional traditions and regional economies meant that the particular process of school reform would vary in each locality. The small districts of these states chosen for intensive analysis cannot be viewed as microcosms. Nonetheless, it is only within the context of a small region and of individual communities that the precise dynamics of state intervention in schooling emerge. A comparison based on the study of individual communities in small regions of the two states will illuminate the interplay of the national and local components of school history.

VAUCLUSE

The département of Vaucluse, or, more particularly, the two arrondissements of Avignon and Apt, formed the political and cultural northern boundary of Provence. The region included in the study extends from the foothills of the Alps in the east, westward into the Rhone plain. (See Maps 1 and 2.) Within this region there is a great deal of geographic variation. The most significant topographic contrast is the distinction between the eastern highlands and the western plain. Although the climate is mild and the growing season long enough to allow the production of olives, wine, and silk, many villages, particularly those at higher elevations, were subject to the ravages of occasional devastating frosts.

The rivers that flowed through the département and into the Rhone, especially the Durance and the Sorgue, were important channels of communication before the improvement of roads in the mid-nineteenth century. In fact, the southeastern part of the arrondisse-

Map 1 VAUCLUSE on the Map of France

Map 2 VAUCLUSE, Main Topographic Features

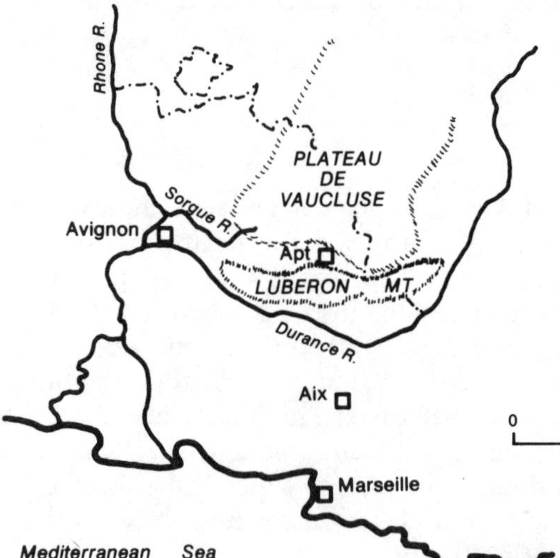

ment of Apt was more naturally linked, by way of the Durance valley, with Aix and the region to the south than it was with the western part of the département. The general east-to-west mountain ranges, particularly the narrow Luberon to the south, split the département into distinct subregions and further isolated the southeastern part from the Rhone plain. Trade routes, seasonal migration patterns, and traffic in general bowed to geographic pressures, following river valleys and circumventing the barriers of the hills.

Historical frontiers reinforced geographic ones. The rugged terrain that became the arrondissement of Apt at the time of the revolution had been, during the ancien régime, included in the bailliage of Aix-en-Provence in the French province of Provence. The arrondissement of Avignon, on the other hand, was created from territory that belonged to the papal state and the independent Comtat Venaissin until the time of the revolution. The administrative boundaries of the département, as drawn in 1802, are presented in Map 3. Map 4 indicates the location of the twenty sample communities in Vaucluse selected for detailed study.[15]

As the northern boundary of Provence, the département of Vaucluse was located in one of the most distinctive cultural regions of France. Here, a variation of the so-called "language of the troubadours," Provençal, was the everyday tongue of the people. French officials often viewed the popular refusal to speak French as a manifestation of that particularism so subversive to national sentiment, and as a constant symbol of the broader hostility toward all that was national, progressive, new. In the words of one frustrated official from Paris, "everything that bears the mark of progress is received with defiance, sometimes fought with ferocity."[16]

Like dialects spoken throughout the Midi, those of Vaucluse were derived from a *languedocienne* tongue whose roots were Latin and whose structure and vocabulary distinguished it from the northern *langues d'oil.* In the middle of the eighteenth century, the northerner de la Brosse resigned himself upon arriving in Avignon to "neither understanding the people nor being understood by them."[17] A Polish count traveling in Provence at the end of the century thought the language sounded like a mixture of French and Italian.[18] By the time of their observations, however, Provençal was much closer to French than it had been in its medieval heyday. Borrowing from French had become the common manner of expressing what the patois could not. By the end of the eighteenth century, generations of borrowing from the politically dominant French language had left the medieval language much altered and brought it closer to French.

Map 3 VAUCLUSE, Arrondissements of Avignon and Apt

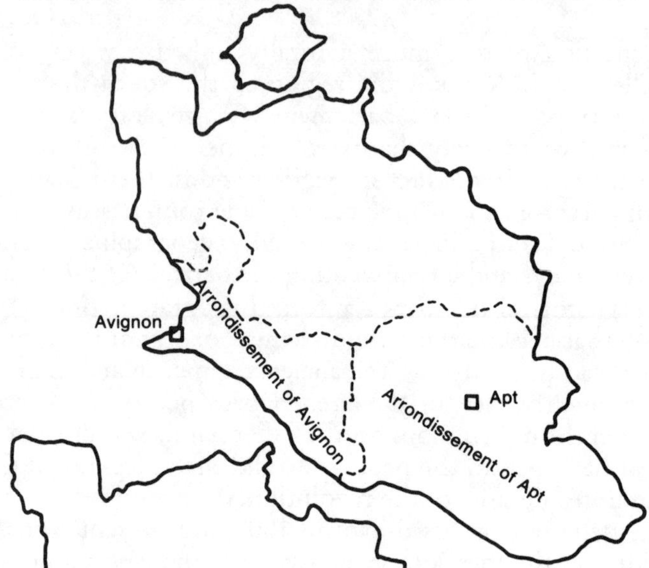

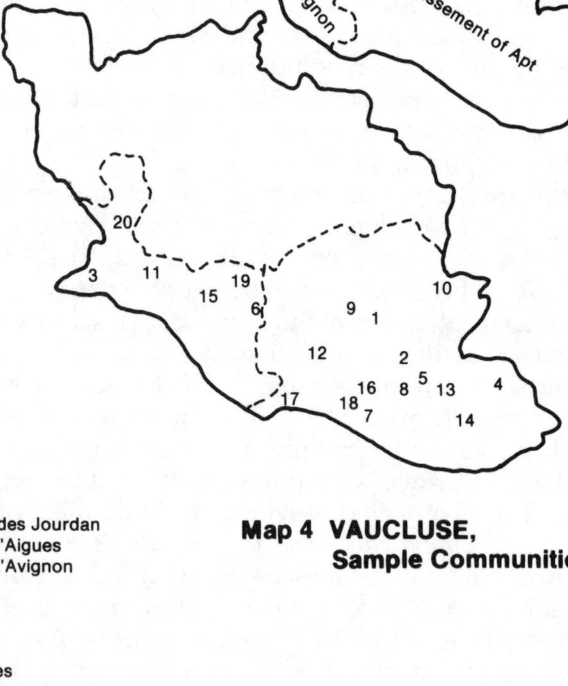

1. Apt
2. Auribeau
3. Avignon
4. La Bastide des Jourdan
5. Cabrières d'Aigues
6. Cabrières d'Avignon
7. Cadenet
8. Cucuron
9. Gargas
10. Gignac
11. Jonquerettes
12. La Coste
13. La Motte d'Aigues
14. La Tour d'Aigues
15. L'Isle-sur-la-Sorque
16. Lourmarin
17. Merindol
18. Puivert
19. Saumanes
20. Sorgues

Map 4 VAUCLUSE, Sample Communities

Nonetheless, Vauclusans still had trouble with French. At the time of the French Revolution, when for the first time it became a political necessity to communicate effectively with the French population, the government undertook a program to translate important decrees into the major patois and to attempt to reform the linguistic habits of patois-speaking citizens. Popular societies often served as linguistic as well as political intermediaries. At a meeting of one such group, the Club Patriotique of Apt, in 1791, it was decided that since the members had difficulty pronouncing the words of the oath of allegiance the secretary would recite it and the candidate merely reply in French, "I do swear."[19] While the revolution certainly added a large number of French words to the patois, many of its local activities were nonetheless carried out by necessity in patois.

During both the revolutionary period and the Napoleonic era, there were various government programs and surveys aimed toward linguistic unification. The major outcome of these preliminary efforts, however, was the production of a body of evidence attesting to the variety and vitality of patois. According to Maxim Pazzis,

> patois . . . is the language of the people in the village and in the countryside. French is little used even in the city by the common classes, and if those who have been educated would prefer to speak only French, continual relations with workers, artisans and countryfolk often necessitate speaking patois. Magistrates, especially criminal justices, are obliged to use it and even to understand all of its subtleties. Ministers of religion all too often believe themselves obliged to use patois.[20]

Patois throve, then, if susceptible to continual alteration, but it would be a mistake to take the persistence of patois speaking as a sign that Vaucluse was a backwater. In the era of the revolution, the people of Vaucluse were enmeshed in intense social and economic networks centered on the bourgs so characteristic of the region.[21] Toward the middle of the nineteenth century, nearly 50 percent of the population was living in urban communes (that is, of 2,000 or more residents), and this pattern of urbanism was an old one. The proportion of the population living in the *villes-chefs-lieux,* the more important urban communities, had risen only slightly in the first half of the nineteenth century—from 20 percent in 1806 to 23 percent in 1836.[22]

Still, within the département regional differences in population distribution were striking, as were differences in growth rates. (See Table 1.) The western arrondissement of Avignon contained a population of some sixty thousand at the end of the eighteenth century, dispersed in twenty communes. The eastern arrondissement of Apt,

TABLE 1
Population Change in the Territory of Vaucluse and in the Arrondissements of Avignon and Apt

Location	*1760*[a]	*1806*[b]	*1836*[c]	*1852*[d]
City of Avignon	28,000	23,789	31,786	35,890
Arrondissement of Avignon		61,853	69,820	78,384
City of Apt	6,500	5,374	5,958	5,770
Arrondissement of Apt		53,666	55,199	55,916
Département of Vaucluse	196,033	205,832	246,071	264,618

[a] Expilly, *Dictionnaire géographique* . . . and M. Pazzis, *Mémoire statistique sur le département de Vaucluse* (Carpentras, 1808), pp. 178–179.
[b] M. Pazzis, pp. 178 ff.
[c] France, Bureau de la Statistique Générale, *Statistique de la France* (Paris, 1837).
[d] France, Bureau de la Statistique Générale, *Mouvement de la population* . . . (Paris, 1856).

which comprised a territory twice as large as that of the Avignon district, held a slightly smaller population distributed among fifty communities. Changes over time only accentuated these regionally distinctive patterns: the sparsely populated arrondissement of Apt experienced only a slight increase in population during the late eighteenth and early nineteenth centuries, and then entered into a long period of demographic stagnation; in contrast, the western half of the département continued to grow throughout the period. Many communities in the arrondissement of Avignon grew by 50 percent or more in the first few decades of the nineteeth century. Growth in the eastern communities was modest (less than 15 percent generally), and some even lost population.

As in most of Europe at this epoch, agriculture was the greatest employer of human energy in Vaucluse, even if by the turn of the nineteenth century the impact of industrialization was already perceptible. It has been estimated that at the end of the ancien régime, fully 80 percent of the work force of Vaucluse was employed at least part time in agriculture. As smallholders, Vauclusan peasants typically combined subsistence production of wheat, wine, and sheep with production of oil, wine, silk, and other products for the market.[23] In the late eighteenth century there was also a well-established textile industry based on putting-out; in fact, even at the beginning of the nineteenth century "industrial production was as completely alive in the countryside as in the city." As late as 1830, a quarter of the textile weavers of the département were living in rural communities.[24] Production of silk thread was perhaps the most common rural industrial occupation, but linen and wool production also persisted. Pazzis claimed that the rural wool industry was already in a state of decay by the time he wrote his statistical memoir in 1808, but it still survived in some villages. Future trends were apparent to him as well:

> Several cotton filatures have been in existence for a few years. This sort of industry, which offers sure and substantial profits to the entrepreneur, usefully employs the popular classes in the towns—girls, women, even children of both sexes who from the age of eight years are capable of earning fifty centimes a day. This employment was needed for a long time to replace the work which the (domestic) filature and manufacture had provided in the old days.[25]

The département of Vaucluse was never to become an important industrial center. On the contrary, the once flourishing regional textile industry eventually foundered in the face of competition from the factory- and urban-based manufacturing of more developed regions. Nonetheless, certain communes did become factory centers, and the effects of industrialization were felt even where the new technology did not reach. By the middle of the nineteenth century, part of the population had left agriculture. Overall in the département, agricultural work still employed two-thirds of the active population, but the age-long opposition between the mountain and the plain had become more emphatic. An analysis of the economic structure of the canton of Apt revealed a classic pattern of deindustrialization and depopulation already apparent by the middle of the nineteenth century. Most noteworthy was the disappearance of the weaving population, but there was a simultaneous withdrawal in the early nineteenth century of nearly all industrial activities with the exception of those directly related to agriculture and the extraction of raw materials.[26]

In contrast, the Rhone and Sorgue valleys were relatively prosperous. Changes in the occupations of brides and grooms marrying in the town of Sorgue are illustrative: at the turn of the nineteenth century, fully 70 percent of the grooms indicated that they were working in agriculture; brides generally did not indicate an occupation. Forty years later, only 50 percent of the men marrying in Sorgue were peasants. The change in the brides' manner of describing their occupations was even more striking: nearly 40 percent of them indicated that they worked in industry, usually textile industry in the town. The number who were reported as daughters of peasants without other occupation was only 40 percent.[27] This more striking change in the employment patterns of women is not surprising; as textile manufacturing, especially silk, moved from the countryside

Map 5 UNTERRHEINKREIS of BADEN on the Map of the German States

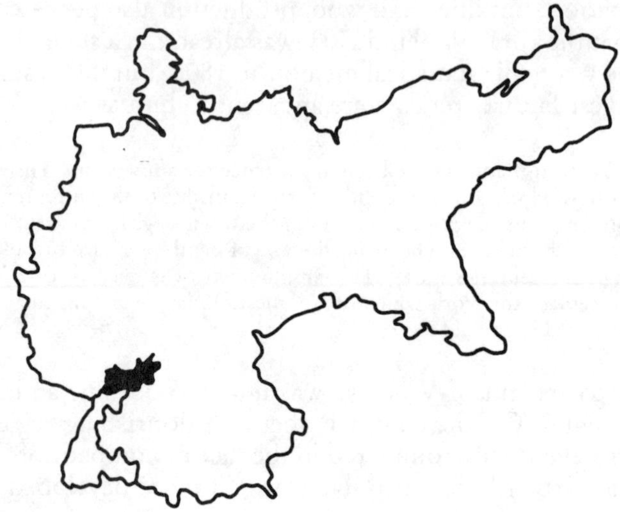

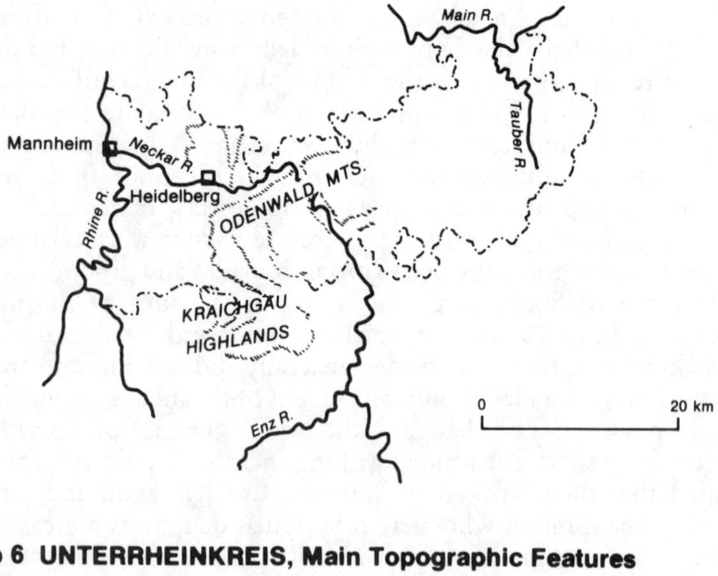

Map 6 UNTERRHEINKREIS, Main Topographic Features

into the city, it was the female labor force that was most affected. The peasants' daughters who once were employed with by-occupations on the farm now had to look to the growing factory towns for work. So, even though Vaucluse was by no means at the forefront of economic development, the impact of the new system of production had positive and negative repercussions that were perceptible throughout the département in the early decades of the nineteenth century.

BADEN

Like Vaucluse, the Unterrheinkreis of northern Baden is dominated in the west by a grand river plain. The Rhine valley is a distinct geographic area, including the administrative Kreise of Mannheim and Ladenburg, and quite different from the hillier and more wooded Kreise of Heidelberg, Wiesloch, and Sinsheim to the east and south. (See Maps 5 and 6.) Although the climate of the Unterrheinkreis is not as warm and dry as that of Vaucluse, it is nonetheless among the mildest of Germany. In the early nineteenth century the region was noted for its agricultural productivity, and many of the products upon which the Vauclusan economy was based were also important here, most notably wine and mulberry leaves. As in Vaucluse, intraregional traffic of all sorts tended to follow the river valleys that led into the Rhine.

The administrative history of the Unterrheinkreis is even more complex than that of Vaucluse. Much of the western part of the Kreis had been included in the territory of the elector of Pfalz until the time of the Napoleonic consolidation in the early nineteenth century; other parts had been under the rule of religious and lay nobility. In fact, this region typified that hodgepodge of splintered sovereignties so common in early modern Germany.[28] With consolidation, however, the entire area was incorporated into the state of Baden. First called the Neckarkreis, the area under consideration later became part of the larger unit known as the Unterrheinkreis.[29] Map 7 shows the boundaries of the Unterrheinkreis. Map 8 indicates the locations of the twenty sample communities studied here.

The consolidation of these small states into Baden was, it appears, a remarkably smooth process. Perhaps this was a consequence of the relative homogeneity of the populations involved. To be sure there were religious differences, but rulers in this confessionally troubled region had long since worked out formulas for living with religious pluralism. Each locality also had its cultural peculiarities, including a

Map 7
UNTERRHEINKREIS, Landkreise Boundaries of Western Half

1. Stadtkreis Mannheim
2. Kreis Ladenburg
3. Kreis Heidelberg
4. Kreis Wiesloch
5. Kreis Sinsheim

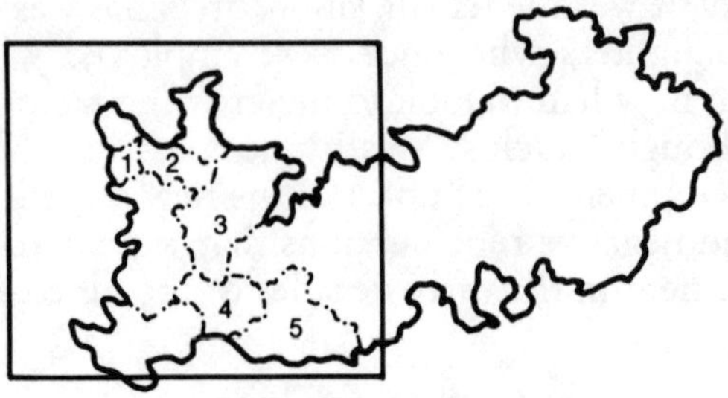

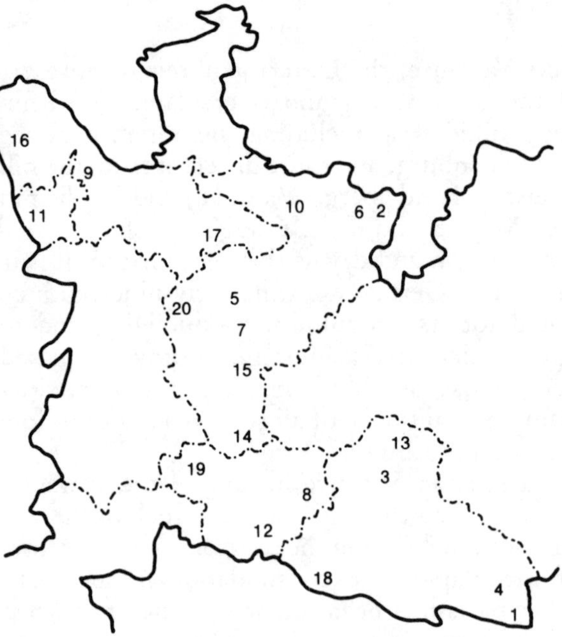

1. Bockschaft
2. Brombach
3. Daisbach
4. Ehrstädt
5. Handschuhsheim
6. Heddesbach
7. Heidelberg
8. Horrenburg
9. Käferthal
10. Lampenhain
11. Mannheim
12. Mühlausen
13. Neidenstein
14. Nussloch
15. Rohrbach
16. Sandhofen
17. Schriesheim
18. Waldangelloch
19. Walldorf
20. Wieblingen

Map 8 UNTERRHEINKREIS, (Western Half) Sample Communities

0 20 km

dialect. In contrast with France, however, and even other German states, there is little evidence in Baden of attempts forcefully to stamp out dialect speech. Bilingualism was accepted, perhaps even encouraged in some official circles. Children had long been expected to learn *Hochdeutsch* and to read and speak it in school, but there is no evidence of attempts to keep them from learning or speaking dialect. Awareness of local peculiarities, such as they were, and willingness to tolerate them and take them into account in policy formation in Baden contrast with the universalist assumptions beneath much of the contemporary French legislation. No doubt the source of this difference is located in the type of political compromise that created the Badenese state. Since the state was a creation of the Napoleonic consolidation drive, its absolutist political institutions and corporatist social structures were left intact to a surprising degree. The concerns of *Stand*, region, religion, and corporation continued to influence policy in a manner that would have been impossible in postrevolutionary France. Linguistic policy is a case in point. The use of standard German was encouraged for administrative purposes, but knowledge of German did not seem to have the same significance for statesmen in Baden that use of the national tongue had for the French. School laws and practices recognized and expected variety. The school ordinance of the Reformed *Kirchensektion* of 1797 specified that, "given the great variety in our country in speech, type of land, and customs, and since schoolteachers have to live on the same footing as their fellow citizens and need their undivided trust even more than other civil servants," no teacher was to be assigned to a post in a province other than that in which he was born.[30] Teachers knew of their responsibility "to teach political instruction . . . and the German language," but it is only rarely, usually in cases involving forced assimilation of Jewish people, that one finds evidence of conflict over linguistic policy.[31] In any case, the persistence of dialect speech was not defined as a state problem, nor viewed as an obstacle to popular political integration.

The Unterrheinkreis was quite a prize for the Badenese government. It was economically the most developed region of the state and precociously urban, with around 30 percent of its people listed as urban dwellers in the middle of the nineteenth century. The weight of this legally defined urban sector remained steady during the population growth of the period, and, as in Vaucluse, rates of population change in the early industrial epoch varied dramatically across the region. (See Table 2.) Between 1780 and 1871 the population of the economically backward Odenwald (north and east of Heidelberg)

TABLE 2
Population Change in the Unterrheinkreis in the Regions around Heidelberg and Mannheim

Location	*1780*	*1818*	*1852*
City of Heidelberg	13,500	15,712	22,975
Landkreis Heidelberg	37,500	52,826	75,252
City of Mannheim	25,000	28,334	36,642
Landkreis Mannheim*	43,000	56,389	77,287

*Actually, there was no Landkreis Mannheim during the late eighteenth and early nineteenth centuries. The population referred to is that of the region, which was a separate administrative unit; this territory was largely included in the Landkreis Ladenburg during the century under consideration.

Source: Staatliche Archivverwaltung Baden-Württemberg, *Stadt- und Landkreise Heidelberg und Mannheim* (Mannheim, 1966).

doubled. In the Kraichgau highland (to the south of Heidelberg) population increase was on the order of 150 percent. In the Neckar valley itself population grew around 200 percent, and in the booming Rhine plain to the west increases of up to 300 percent were noted in some communities.[32] The stagnation of the legally defined urban sector may mask the fast growth in the suburban "villages" of this area, which were becoming centers of industry and commercial agriculture. Mannheim suburbs like Sandhofen and Käfertal, Heidelberg suburbs like Handschuhsheim and Wieblingen doubled or tripled their populations in the course of a few decades, while in some cases retaining their rural legal status.

The economic profile of the population is hard to draw, given the absence of routine censuses. Nonetheless, it is clear that the labor force composition in this region was not too dissimilar from that of Vaucluse. Until well into the nineteenth century, most families made a living through a combination of subsistence agriculture and production for the agricultural market or cottage industry. Alfred Heunisch, a contemporary statistician, calculated that in 1830 about 120,000 Badenese families were propertied peasants and an additional 38,000 families were landless agricultural workers. This is, about two-thirds of the labor force was engaged in farming.[33] By 1849, again according to Heunisch, the agricultural work force had declined to 43 percent of the total. At this latter date, 37 percent of the people were engaged in manufacturing exclusively, and an additional 6 percent were classified as industrial workers with agricultural holdings *(Ackerbautreibende Gewerbeleute)*.[34] A recent economic history of the period notes a less dramatic rate of movement out of agriculture, but essentially substantiates Heunisch's observations. (See Table 3.) According to Wolfram Fischer, the period between 1829 and 1848 was the period of fastest factory growth in Baden before the last quarter of the nineteenth century. In the course of those twenty years, the factory labor force increased some 300 percent.[35] Still, it must be noted, that factory workers represented only a small fraction of the total labor force. But the economic impact of the changes brought with the introduction of industrial imperialism was dramatic for domestic and artisanal workers in certain industries.

The state-level trends were paralleled in changes in individual communities, as illustrated by evidence from a few of the sample communities for which population lists from this period have survived. Neidenstein had 50 peasant families and 20 artisanal families in 1797; by 1825 there remained only 29 peasant households, while the number of families of industrial workers had risen to 59.[36] Schriesheim, an agricultural market town at the end of the eighteenth century, was predominantly industrial by the middle of the nineteenth; by then there were a larger number of artisanal and manufacturing heads-of-household (190) than there were agricultural (135).[37] In north Baden, then, probably to an extent more notable than in Vaucluse, even if the bulk of the population continued to rely upon agricultural activity for at least part of its income, the rise in part-time and full-time industrial employment was significant in the early decades of the nineteenth century. And the growth in the nonagrarian sector was a subject of note. But here too, even in the context of important economic transformation, many communities remained or actually became exclusively agricultural; manufacturing jobs were often created in the cities at the expense of rural workers,

TABLE 3
Change in the Occupational Structure in Baden

Proportion of the total labor force employed in		*1810*		*1844*	
Agriculture		52%		40–44%	
Home	Industry & commerce	2%	36%		36–40%
Artisanal		33%		31–34%	
Factory		1%		5–6 %	
Day labor				4–6 %	
Other		12%		7–11%	

Source: W. Fischer, *Der Staat und die Anfang der Industrialisierung in Baden, 1800–1850* (Berlin, 1962), pp. 277–297.

forcing outmigration because of underemployment. Industrialization, or, more aptly, the move of industry from shops and homes scattered throughout the region in communities of all sorts into factories and cities, was a gradual and uneven process. In both of the regions studied, the growing "developed" regions were distinguishing themselves from rural hinterlands destined to become more exclusively agricultural in character.

THE CHURCHES AND SCHOOLING

In both regions, then, in this early industrial era, indications of change abounded—in the establishment of the first factories, in the growth of the agricultural market, in the crises affecting artisanal and domestic production in industries susceptible to competition, in the new patterns of demographic growth and intensified migration. Local observers watched these trends and wrote awed descriptions of the signs of economic vigor, even while expressing dismay at the effects these changes seemed to work upon the popular character. And these changes, coupled with the dramatic political challenge to the established order which the revolutionary years had brought, also affected the usual routines of interclass relations and political domination. Older forms of national and local domination, rooted in the beliefs and institutions of the estate society, no longer could be counted on. Furthermore, events also undermined the position of the established churches, once so central to both popular cultural life and the perpetuation of popular deference and resignation.

In earlier days, it seemed, people had taken their religion more seriously. Religious institutions, including many of the little schools of the ancien régime, had played a major role in community life and had been a central element in the popular account of how the world worked and how things should be. To be sure, there were times when religious visions had buttressed popular rebellion. This was especially marked during the early decades of the Reformation. Popular gains wrested then from social and political superiors had left their mark on local institutions, and many of the regional differences in the local endowment of schools and other religious institutions date back to this era. But between the time of the political resolution of the age of social, religious, and political conflict that the Reformation had launched and the late eighteenth century, the churches had for the most part acted as reliable allies of the ruling classes throughout

Europe. But, like so many other aspects of the popular existence, popular religiosity was also changing in the late ancien régime.

Because of the centrality of the churches to popular cultural life, and because of the common argument that regional differences in educational patterns in Europe are somehow reducible to confessional differences, it is important to consider the changing role of the churches in schooling history. Again, the regions and sample communities studied were chosen with this consideration in mind. In both regions there were Protestant and Catholic communities. In both regions the changing institutional position of the churches, and their changing hold over the popular mind, influenced local schooling history.

In Vaucluse, as recently as the seventeenth century, the cause of religion had served as a rallying point for the challenges of the Midian peasantry to the French state. The mountains of southeastern Vaucluse had sheltered Protestant dissidents during and after these religious wars. Despite rigorous and often bloody repression, communities of Protestants survived in the Aigues valley and in scattered mountain villages in the eighteenth century. (See Map 9.) But among Protestants and Catholics alike, adherence to the religious practices and beliefs showed signs of weakening late in the century of Enlightenment. In the secularization apparent from many signs, Vaucluse was in step with much of the rest of France.[38] Still, even if the hold of the church over the population of Vaucluse was weakened by the cultural evolution of the eighteenth century and further by the attack on church property that the revolution brought, the role of religion in schooling history cannot therefore be discounted. In the era following the revolution, a religious revival closely connected with the legitimism that found strong support in some parts of the département had educational ramifications as well. To be sure, the strong remnants of popular religiosity particularly apparent in peasant communities would be transformed in the course of the nineteenth century, but in the early era of school reform, religious opinion closely intertwined with political sentiment continued to influence popular response to state educational plans.[39]

In Baden, where the churches were more securely entrenched and people were at birth required to be registered with one of them, membership in a religious community was apparently of greater significance for the population as a whole. In the Unterrheinkreis religious affiliation was distinctly regional in character. Catholics comprised slightly more than half of the population overall,[40] but

Map 9 Protestant Communities in Vaucluse in the Early Nineteenth Century

Source: E. Baratier *et al*, Atlas historique de Provence (Paris, 1969).

Map 10
Religious Adherence in North Baden, Landkreise of Ladenburg, Heidelberg, Wiesloch, and Sinsheim, Stadtkreise Mannheim, c. 1800

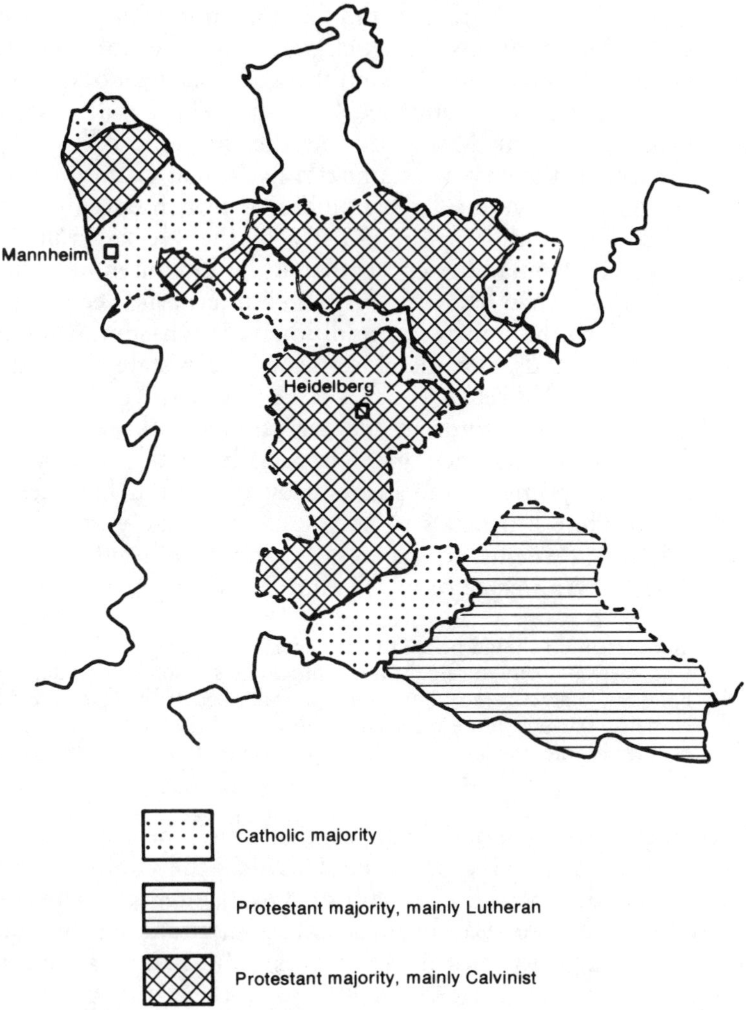

Source: Stadt und-Landkreise Heidelberg und Mannheim; GLA: 313/2816.

there were regions and communities of Protestant domination. (See Map 10.) The Landkreis Heidelberg was predominantly Calvinist, although there were Lutheran and Catholic minorities in many communities. The Landkreis Wiesloch was split; the northwestern half was mostly Calvinist, but the southeast, formerly a possession of the diocese of Speyer, had remained Catholic. The Landkreis Sinsheim was largely Lutheran. Many communities in the Landkreis Landenburg, as well as the city of Mannheim itself, had Catholic majorities. In addition there were a large number of Jewish communities scattered throughout the region, mostly in the Neckar valley. These churches in Baden had better weathered the Enlightenment and revolutionary epoch than had their French counterparts. Secularization in Baden involved the transfer of traditional church-administered properties to state hands, but the close ties between state and church and the rights of the churches to tithes were not dissolved.

Still, there were signs in the early nineteenth century that the churches were losing their grip. Especially in the rapidly growing cities, reports point to the inadequacy of church facilities, to the inability of church officials to keep tabs on a highly mobile population. Again it seems to have been the youth who were most troublesome. An inspector in the Amt Wiesloch warned in 1811 that

> more attention should be paid to servants, apprentices and journeymen who keep company during the hours of religious lessons on Sundays and holidays, [a practice] so contrary to the established order. This should be curtailed through more stringent supervision. . . . The wilder these people become, the lower should be our tolerance of their absence from religious services.[41]

Even in the orderly grand duchy on the Rhine, there were portents of moral chaos for those who feared it. Unless the youth subscribed to the moral code, social life was doomed to disintegrate. The churches, the old regulators of youthful socialization, could hardly be ignored in any campaign to reform that process. But it is clear that in both France and Baden, as elsewhere in Europe, there were powerful secular interests at play in the issue of education by the end of the eighteenth century. Education was increasingly believed to serve vital purposes like economic prosperity and the security of the state, in addition to serving the end of moral training. It was too important to leave to the churches. This, then, was the context in which reformists turned their attention to the schools.

CHAPTER 2

The Schools of the Ancien Régime

THE EDUCATIONAL LEGACY OF THE ANCIEN RÉgime was, despite contemporary denigration, far from negligible. Western Europe was well endowed with schools by the end of the eighteenth century. Local school facilities were unequally diffused, but even in a relatively backward area like Vaucluse all but the smallest communities were likely to have raised a public subsidy for a teacher.[1] Of the fourteen Vauclusan sample communities included in a budget survey conducted by the French government in 1780, fully twelve were allocating funds from the communal fisc for a *maître d'études* or *régent de'école.* The two exceptions were Auribeau, with only 24 families, and Gignac, with a total population of 160.[2] In relatively well-endowed areas like northern Baden, there would be a community-subsidized school even in the smallest village. Of the twenty Badenese sample communities, all but one had at least one such school by the 1780s. The one exception, the tiny village of Bockschaft with a population of only eighty, actually founded a school in 1790.[3]

The broad availability of publicly subsidized elementary instruction suggests a collective commitment to education in the ancien régime that was more serious and general than has often been assumed. The existence of a variety of private schools—designated as *Winkelschulen, Nebenschulen, petites écoles*—also attests to the vitality of popular instruction. These latter schools, especially common in urban areas, were often run as much for the convenience of working parents as for the enlightenment of their children, but they nonetheless added to the array of institutions imparting elementary instruction. Because they generally escaped official notice, the full importance of these schools is difficult to evaluate. But when authorities had cause to investigate them, they turned up in large numbers. In mid-eighteenth-century Mannheim, according to a complaint of the public schoolteachers, there were at least seven *Nebenschulen* competing for pupils with the official schools. One of these was run by an innkeeper named Althof in his inn, where, the complaint was, "the schoolchildren entrusted to him were led into disorder so hateful to God and into a shameful wildness," which made the civilizing task of their later teachers all the more difficult.[4] Whatever the character of the instruction imparted in them, the existence of a large number of these schools attests to a strong popular demand for schooling.

Still, not all communities were able to provide for schooling, and not all families had access to it. Regional differences in the provision of schooling during the ancien régime had an impact apparent even in later epochs; as similar as the simple public schools of the ancien régime were in terms of what was taught and how it was taught, administrative differences already apparent in the late eighteenth century meant that the tasks faced by educational reformers were also quite different.

Although one can detect arrangements—usually originating between the fifteenth and seventeenth centuries—for schooling in the records of communities all over Europe, these varied markedly from one region to the next.[5] In Vaucluse, as in much of Mediterranean Europe, it was decidedly the political community and its officers who played the most active role in the hiring of teachers and in the supervision of their activities. Even in the Comtat Venaissin with its strong papal ties, "the primary school appears to owe its creation as much to municipal initiatives as to the inspiration of the clergy . . . it was from the municipal budget that it drew its principal means of support."[6] Typically the village *syndic* or council would allocate a fixed yearly salary—the *gages* or *honoraires*—out of local revenues. The contract drawn up with a schoolmaster also specified the *mois*, the monthly payment made by the parents of children attending school. Often the teacher was obliged to teach a specified number of indigent children without payment, but only in rare cases, generally in the larger towns, was the fixed salary set at a high enough level to allow the teacher to do without tuition payments. The earliest recorded contracts, dating from the fifteenth and sixteenth centuries, often made provision for the nourishment of the teacher during the period of service, and some made allowance for lodging. For example, the "rolle de ceux qui doivent nourrir le Mtr. d'Eschole pour cette première année 1682 commençant à la St. Michel" from the community of Bedarrides listed the families responsible for feeding the teacher. One or two families together took charge of a month's repasts in exchange for lowered tuition for schooling for their sons.[7] There is little evidence of nourishment clauses of this sort for the eighteenth century, although the practice may have continued unremarked. Most communities, however, seem to have been paying their schoolmasters fairly generous cash salaries by this time. The teacher at Saignon, for example, was paid 100 livres in 1769 and was allowed to charge between 5 and 10 sous a month for each pupil, with these fees rising as the pupils advanced from reading to writing to arithmetic.[8] In Caumont the fixed salary was 150 livres in 1788; in addition, the teacher was authorized to charge between 3 and 6 sous per pupil.[9] At the end of the ancien régime, salary allocations ranged between 50 and 200 livres; the most common allocation was 150 livres, a not insubstantial sum for what was generally seasonal work, in an economy where manual laborers earned the equivalent of between one-half and one livre a day.

Smaller and poorer communities apparently found it difficult to raise this salary. Although fixed salaries were generally smaller in the villages, per capita assessments for them weighed more heavily. In the viguerie of Apt, communities of fewer than two thousand residents paid nearly four times the amount per capita that larger communities paid for teachers. Small communities were further disadvantaged in that they included fewer school-aged children at any one time, which made it unlikely that the teacher could supplement his salary by a large amount in *mois.* As a result, the smallest communities were unable to assemble incomes high enough to attract schoolmasters; of the twenty-one communities of fewer than five hundred residents in the viguerie of Apt in 1780, only twelve were subsidizing schoolteachers.[10]

Larger communities, on the other hand, could afford larger salaries; many even subsidized schools run by teaching orders, who taught the popular classes free. In the first half of the eighteenth century free schools run by the Brothers of the Christian Schools were established in several Vauclusan communities, including Avignon, Apt, and Pertuis. Several towns also established free schools for girls, these generally run by the Ursulines. In addition to their communal subsidy, these teaching orders usually relied on help from pious endowments, which defrayed their cost to the public. For example, the eight brothers who were teaching in the city of Avignon until the revolution were paid just over 1,000 livres throughout most of the eighteenth century. Of this amount, 320 livres was drawn from a perpetual *rente* established by private gift in 1703; an additional 300 livres a year came from a later papal endowment; the city of Avignon allocated 400 livres each year from its municipal budget. These types of arrangements presented difficulties after decades of inflation; the brothers complained continually in the latter decades of the century that they could no longer live on their income.[11] Still, the comparative wealth of the urban communities in terms of educational endowments and resources is clear.

But whether it is a question of these well-endowed urban schools or the villages' subsidies for schoolmasters, the provision of schooling was primarily in the hands of the local community. The services of teachers were largely paid for in *monnaie de France.* The market in schoolteachers, like that of the other services and commodities exchanged in the numerous fairs and marketplaces of Haute Provence, was a cash market in the latter decades of the eighteenth century.

An examination of the numerous records pertaining to school finance in late-eighteenth-century Kurpfalz and its vicinity suggests some striking differences. As in Vaucluse, smaller communities were not as able as the towns and cities to raise attractive salaries for their schoolteachers, but they could all offer some sort of living. Drawing from an incredible variety of sources, they were able to assemble incomes large enough to support a teacher and maintain low tuition fees. A school budget from Neidenstein is illustrative. Neidenstein, including a population of around six hundred at the end of the eighteenth century, supported several schools. An especially detailed account has been preserved of the revenues of the Reformed schoolteacher at the end of the ancien régime. He received:

1. For the clock—from tithe funds . . . 30 Kr.
2. At Eppenbach, on account of the clock, from tithes . . . 30 Kr.
3. For washing the church linens yearly . . . 30 Kr.
4. From the poor fund, yearly at Martinmas, for carrying around the collection plate . . . 30 Kr.
5. For playing the organ . . . 10 Fl.

6. For each child who attends school, in addition to the log which the children bring, quarterly . . . 15 Kr.
7. From the gracious lordship, every year . . . 3 *Malter* wheat
8. From tithes, idem . . . 1 *Simri;* 1 Fl.
9. From each peasant . . . 1 *Garbe* wheat, one *Garbe* barley, one *Garbe* oats; from each peasant with a plow . . . one *Garbe* of mixed produce and one *Garbe* of oats
10. From each citizen and resident . . . a sexton's loaf, the same for each child who goes to school, a loaf of bread in addition to the above tuition
11. One *Morgen* of meadowland in the valley under the sheep bridge
12. A garden plot such as the other citizens use (from the commons)
13. A free dwelling in the lord's house besides the attached cook's garden and orchard and also the use of the barn
14. Wood, from his gracious lordship, such as each citizen receives, kindling, which, however, the schoolteacher must have cut
15. Personal freedom
16. For each burial of a communicant . . . 1 *Simri* wheat
17. For each baptism . . . 1 of loaf bread
18. For each wedding . . . 1 measure of wine, a piece of meat and 1 loaf of bread or 30 Kr. to buy it
19. For the funeral of a child not yet confirmed . . . 1 loaf of bread.[12]

This account is unusually detailed, but it is typical in other respects. Most schoolteachers in the region received income in all these forms and from all of these sources. Of the twenty Badenese sample communities, there were at least fourteen that provided their schoolteacher with a plot of land in the late eighteenth century, and virtually all teaching positions were paid partly in kind. Old customs like the *Wandertisch,* the practice of feeding the schoolteacher on a rotating schedule in the homes of the parents of his pupils, still persisted in the smallest communities. Payment in grain and wine was still also common, an especially troublesome form of payment to the teachers, who had to travel a few times a year to haul large quantities of wine from central depots. Complaints about the inconvenience came from Catholic schoolteachers in Heidelberg in 1786, and in Käferthal a decade later.[13] Late-eighteenth-century registers from the dioceses in the north Badenese area indicate, in fact, that cash salaries of more than 20 or 30 florins out of livings totaling between 200 and 300 florins were unusual; only in the larger towns were teachers likely to collect more than 30 florins in cash.

Another part of the "living" of the schoolteacher in many Badenese communities was the schoolhouse. In addition to classroom space, this generally included rooms for the teacher and his family.

Figure 1
Plan for the Reformed School in Handschuhsheim, 1767

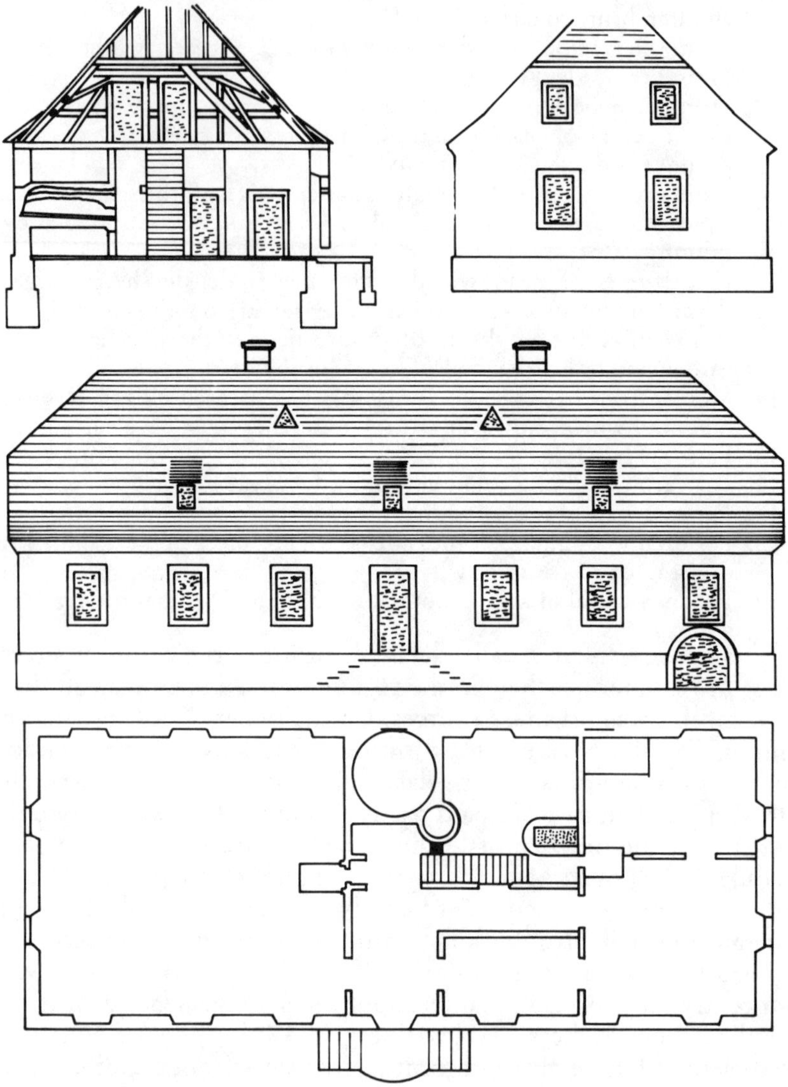

Source: GLA: 229/38401.

(Figure 1 illustrates the ground plan of a typical Badenese schoolhouse, that of the village of Handschuhsheim.) Occasionally classrooms or teachers' accommodations were simply carved out of existing buildings, but the most common arrangement was for a special building to be raised at the expense of the religious community. In Vaucluse, in contrast, the schoolhouse was almost totally unheard of in the eighteenth century. Larger towns sometimes built them, but in the villages the teachers had to bargain over whatever space was available and often ended up holding classes, and sometimes sleeping too, in an old attic or stable.

The availability in Baden of communal resources for the support of schooling alleviated the material obstacles to schooling provision encountered by many of the smaller Vauclusan communities. Furthermore, whereas per capita expenditures for public schooling were naturally higher in both regions, large enough subsidies in land and kind could be assembled in rural Badenese communities to allow the cash salary and tuition fees to remain low. In this region, tuition fees were usually lower in villages than in urban areas—the reverse of the situation in Vaucluse.

This comparison of the means of financing primary instruction in the two regions during the ancien régime suggests significant differences in the political economy, which would persist to some extent through the period of reform as well. In Vaucluse communities established schools and financed them through the same decision-making process that determined all communal expenditures. The cost of the teacher's salary had to be weighed against other pressing needs for cash. Where communities were small or poor, the expenditure was often out of reach. But complaints about the high cost of paying a teacher may sometimes have been no more than dodges contrived by municipal councils dominated by interests opposed to public schooling. This can be seen quite clearly in the case of Apt, whose council justified a vote taken in the 1780s to withdraw support from the Christian Brothers' school on the grounds that schooling "tended to take a great number of workers away from agriculture."[14] But teaching could be discontinued for other pragmatic reasons; the town of Sorgues interrupted the teaching subsidy between 1771 and 1777 while funds were diverted for the reconstruction of the church. In Vaucluse public schools were contingent upon the fiscal situation of the local government and the political opinions of the municipal council.

In Baden teachers' livings were less tied to annual allocations of public revenues and less linked with formal political processes. The financial institutions that supported schools in Baden bore the mark of a political economy centered on the communal tenure of property; the availability of communal lands to which teachers could be granted usage rights, and the persistence of communal claims to part of the surplus extracted by outside claimants in the form of rents and tithes, meant that the teacher's salary could be assured without undue strain on the communal fisc. And this income was shielded from the power of the politically influential in a period when such influence could easily have meant an end to schooling subsidy.

The importance of these kinds of communal resources to Badenese schoolteachers is apparent from their *Kompetenzen*—periodic summaries of income. Not only did communities draw upon communally owned lands to supplement cash salaries; they also could grant full citizenship rights, entailing access to common meadows and woods, to teachers foreign to the community. Personal freedom—that is, exemption from dues that could be construed as vestiges of servitude in the old manorial system—was also part of the bargain made with teachers. In addition, even that part of the teacher's salary that was paid in cash often originated, not from the budget of the political community, but from either the Catholic or Protestant ministry, which in turn drew its funds from locally collected tithes. As was true elsewhere in Europe, part of these tithes were diverted into secular hands, but communities still saw part of them return in the form of support for clergy, teachers, and church and school buildings. A survey conducted in the 1790s to determine the proceeds from tithes and their application suggests the extent to which church and school still relied on this income. The proceeds from the town of Wieblingen, for example, were split roughly equally among four main beneficiaries: the *Hofkammer*, the central religious ministry, the Freiherr Wembold zu Mainz, and the local pastor and schoolteacher. In Walldorf, the main recipients were the Catholic pastor, the central religious ministry, and the cathedral and convent of a nearby town, which in turn returned part of their share as a contribution to the costs of the Catholic and Reformed schools and churches of Walldorf.[15]

This channeling of tithe income into the schools contrasts with the disposition of the *dîme* in Vaucluse. In the South of France in general, both tithe collector and landlord were typically urban rentiers who had little contact with or responsibility toward parishioners and tenants. Money that flowed out of the community in the form of tithes rarely brought anything in return except for an inadequate salary for the *vicaire*, which represented only a small portion of the total amount collected. Scattered tithe reports suggest that some titheholders returned as little as a quarter of their revenues in the form of *charges* like clerical salaries and church upkeep. For example, one M. de Nadaillon, receiver of the tithe for the region around Thor in western Vaucluse, collected revenues valued at around 4,500 livres at the end of the ancien régime. Out of the proceeds of the sale of his rights he paid salaries to the *curé* of Jonquerettes, the chaplain at his own castle at Thouson, two additional sacristains, and an abbot, which totaled 1,115 livres. His net proceeds were nearly 3,400 livres from a tax that was nominally collected for the support of religious institutions. In the village of Lacoste the abuse was less dramatic. Nonetheless, of the 1,936 livres the tithe netted, only 973 went for the payment of the *curé* and the vicar and the costs of the collection and sale of the tithe.[16]

The regional comparison suggests that schooling arrangements were linked in important ways with the political economy of the community, the history of which followed a decidedly different course in Baden and in Vaucluse. Why Badenese villages were more successful than those in Vaucluse at preserving communal resources during the early modern period remains open to question. The history of communal interactions with churches, landlords, and state authorities since the sixteenth century left its imprint on community life even at the dawn of the industrial era. Community actions during the religious reform period of the sixteenth and seventeenth centuries altered the disposition of tithes thenceforward. To be sure, French peasants too took part in *grèves des décimables.*[7] Reformed communities defied the church and state and hid away in the mountains in Vaucluse and elsewhere. But the political failure of the reform in France left preexistent abuses largely intact. In Baden, on the other hand, the regional success of the Reformation in an era of massive peasant revolt against both economic and religious overlords had an impact on the political economy of the community that would be as significant for the history of schooling as for its effect on people's minds. Indeed, many of the chunks of land that became part of the teachers' salaries were formerly possessions of Catholic clergy and monasteries. Tithes continued to be collected, but communal claims on their proceeds were subsequently taken more seriously.[18]

The different conditions of communities in Baden and Vaucluse had roots in other political and economic developments as well. The failure of villages in Vaucluse to maintain their communal properties is symptomatic of trends resulting from the advanced commercialization of agriculture. Although economic transformation was primary in this process, it seems likely that the political relationship between villages and the state also had some bearing. Despite the sporadic efforts of various French kings and *intendants* to defend communal properties, the relentless commercialization of agricultural exchange, which brought in its wake the alienation or division of such properties, actually fed on the drive of the huge French state for cash revenues.[19] The impact of market constraints upon the provision of schooling was already apparent in the late ancien régime. Village propertylessness and the need to make public transactions of all sorts in cash only exacerbated the problem of school finance, so formidable in the absence of the right to church wealth.

The central role of tithe income in financing the Badenese school system persisted alongside a generally more active involvement of church bureaucracies in school supervision. But informal connections between school and church were taken for granted in both regions. In both Baden and Vaucluse the lay teacher was expected to act as a sort of junior partner to the village pastor. Many of the minor perquisites of the office were connected with religious duties: bell ringing, care of the sacristy, witnessing at religious rituals, and the like. *Kompetenzen* routinely listed some income attached to *Uhr* or *Glocken* responsibilities in the Badenese villages. Often the teacher received some income as *Mesner*, sexton. In Vaucluse and the surrounding region a similar relationship held; the teacher often doubled as *chantre* or *bedeau*.[20] Sometimes contracts for *régents d'école* spelled out these duties and their remuneration. The teacher at Sorgues, for example, was paid 24 livres as *conducteur de l'horloge*, in addition to the 90 he received for teaching during the year 1783/84.[21] The instruction itself had a religious character. According to one historian of Haute Provence, "schooling was immersed in a religious aura," a characterization that applied equally well to Baden. Teachers in both regions were expected to teach catechism, psalms, and Bible reading, and to take children to religious services and to begin and end each day with prayer. The texts children read were generally religious. Still, despite the informal religiosity that pervaded the instructional atmosphere in both areas, the formal links between church and school were stronger in Baden than in Vaucluse. This claim has been demonstrated in the realm of finance, but it was true of supervision as well.

Pastors in Baden were supposed to make frequent visits to the school and to report to their superiors on the results of their inspections[23] and their examinations of the schoolchildren. As in much of northern Europe, there were in the communities of the Kurpfalz yearly public examinations that tested children not only for their competence in religious doctrine and moral questions, but also in the mundane subjects of spelling, arithmetic, and writing from dictation.[24] Such exams were routine in the eighteenth century, at which time they were organized and conducted by the *Dekanat* of each diocese.

In France a similar annual examination of the schools was included in the prescribed duties of the bishop. Although some reports from these inspection tours have survived and suggest that some bishops took this duty seriously, it is clear that many were neglecting this aspect of their pastoral charge. With one or two exceptions, the bishops of the Comtat and Haute Provence were among the negligent. There is little evidence of active church involvement in the typical rural school. In the absence of systematic visitations from outside authorities, communities in the Vaucluse were much more independent in schooling matters than were their counterparts in Baden.

What actually went on in these schools—a central issue—is not easy to recapture. Again, the more highly structured Badenese system has left more records. In Vaucluse the whole project of teaching was, during the ancien régime, imbued with a spirit of transiency and contingency that was not conducive to permanent record. Even the teachers themselves were often transients, seasonal migrants drawn from the Alpine communities, where peasants cultivated reading and writing skills in order to supplement the meager income derived from the cultivation of crops during the brief growing season.[25] Many of the Alpine bourgs held annual *foires aux maîtres d'école,* where aspiring teachers would assemble to bargain with representatives of communities in need of their services. Each teacher wore a specified number of feathers in his hat: one for those who taught only reading and writing; two for those who could also teach ciphering; three for those who knew Latin. In communities lower down in the plain, teachers would sometimes just show up unannounced, "arriving toward the end of summer, wandering from village to village, wearing the prescribed cap . . . with a feather planted behind the ear."[26] Only in the larger towns was teaching a full-time profession. Recruitment of teachers took a more serious form and generally entailed the distribution of placards advertising the post and a competition among the various applicants for the job.[27]

Part-time teaching was also common in Baden, but with the important difference that teachers were nonetheless year-round residents of the communities in which they taught. Since they generally received part of their income in land, the farming of that land during the growing season provided incumbents with a necessary supplement to their teaching salary.

There are examples in both regions of teachers who pursued other by-occupations. Some were artisans; Catholic officials in the Diocese of Worms complained in 1750 that too many teachers were forced to take up *Nebendienste* because of the inadequacy of their teaching income, and thus neglected their official duties. It was especially difficult for teachers in small communities to survive from teaching alone, and it was in these that by-occupations were most common. In the community of Neidenstein, for example, Catholic schoolchildren were taught by a tailor, and later by one of his sons, a shoemaker. In the villages of Haute Provence there are reports of teachers engaged in a whole gamut of professions: masonry, shoemaking, weaving, tailoring, barbering and hairdressing, surgery, and work as minor officials.[28]

To say that teachers were not professional is not to say that they were incompetent. But just how capable they were, and just what was expected of them in the way of expertise, is difficult to determine. In both regions teachers were allowed to teach only with the authorization of regional officials—the *vice légat* or *intendant* in France, the *Konsistorium* in Baden. Authorizations that were handed out attested to moral character more than to capacity, although by the last decade of the ancien régime the Kurpfalz had established a classification system whereby each aspiring *Schulkandidat* was ranked by the *Konsistorium* as:

1. competent in the necessary school subjects,
2. conversant (in them) but not excellent,
3. knowing no music, and not excellent, or
4. not at all learned.[29]

In the end, however, it was still up to the holder of *Patronatsrecht*—variously the religious community, the lord, the pastor or a representative of the church bureaucracy in Baden, the local *syndic* or council in Vaucluse—to be satisfied concerning the talents of prospective teachers. As long as the teacher had met the minimal requirements for authorization, he could be chosen to fill a post. The only credentials necessary beyond this were the abilities needed to satisfy the clientele. And what that took varied according to the circumstances of the post.

The general quality of teaching in ancien-régime Vaucluse remains mysterious because of the paucity of the record. The system of seasonal hiring certainly allowed the easy replacement of teachers with whom the community was dissatisfied. Bargains were struck, pay rates established on the basis of the teacher's claims of competence, which were ultimately testable. Still, while communities could check on the master's reading and penmanship skills, they were usually less concerned with pedagogic technique. Virtually all teachers practiced the traditional *méthode individuelle,* calling each pupil separately to his desk for recitation or to read texts. The only exceptions were the Brothers of the Christian Schools and the other male and female teaching orders who imitated their simultaneous teaching of large groups of children.

Teachers in Baden seem to have followed the same individual method of instruction. The various encounters among parents, teachers, and church representatives even produced records that are suggestive about the kinds of skills teachers had, or were expected to have. Since most parents were not as directly involved in the hiring decision as those in Vaucluse were, there were in fact cases of conflict stemming from disagreements about pedagogic expectations. When they were dissatisfied with their children's teacher, parent had no recourse but to petition the holder of patronage rights, or the local religious authorities. One example comes from the Catholic community of Schriesheim in 1750. Parents there wrote a petition asking for the replacement of the teacher, who was so incompetent that "after the loss of several years time there [were] children who [could] not even write their name legibly . . . even fewer [who could] cipher."[30] The teacher was eventually replaced, but the process took five years. Other evidence suggests higher levels of competence. When the Catholic post in Sandhofen fell vacant in 1740, a number of teachers applied for it and indicated in their letters their various capacities. Most commanded an easy and elegant *Hochdeutsch* and wrote in clear handwriting. If some were deficient in arithmetic (indeed, two of the applicants even made mistakes in the multiplication exercises they included in their applications!), the teacher who eventually got the post showed competence in all the requisite subject matters.[31] Where the post was a desirable one, the community could choose from a number of qualified candidates.

The inspection reports and records kept by teachers themselves add to our picture of the school of the ancien régime. One teacher's report, that of Johan Hautz, the Reformed schoolmaster of the city of Heidelberg, began with a poem composed for the occasion:

> Praise God! It is behind me now,
> Another whole semester.
> Now, to my superiors,

I owe accounting clear
Of what I've done in all this time,
To show I've done my best.
Dear God, since I've done all I could
With your grace bless me now.

Hautz then went on to list the names of the seventy-five boys and forty-seven girls who were enrolled in his class for that year of 1728, along with their ages, the length of time they had been enrolled, their grades in "diligence" and "obedience" (a simple "good," "average," or "unsatisfactory"), and the point in the psalter or catechism to which they had memorized.[32] Hautz's register is not unique, but such systematic records of schoolchildren and their accomplishments are all too rare for this period.

Still, there are indications, and they are quite consistent, about the program of studies. Children began with the ABCs and spelling, then progressed to reading, then writing (paying a progressively higher fee for the most part). In the more advanced schools, arithmetic was also taught. The organization of teaching in Hautz's class is clearer than most. (See Table 4.) His class subdivisions are also more precise, but the nature of the subjects taught and the progression from one to another were typical. Most Badenese teachers divided

TABLE 4
Class Organization, Heidelberg Reformed School, 1728

Ordnung	*Number of pupils*	*Age range of pupils*	*Length of time enrolled*	*Subjects*
V	14	4½–7	¼–½ yr.	ABCs
IV	23	5½–9	¾–1¾ yr.	Spelling
III	20	6½–11½	1–4½ yr.	Reading in psalter
II	28	5½–14½	2–5 yr.	Memorizing, reading in New Testament, most also writing
I	38	9–14	½–5¾ yr.	Reading Old and New Testaments and letters, writing

Source: GLA: 204/1819.

their pupils into, if not five, at least two groups with different skill levels. The beginning pupils, not yet learning to write, often paid half the amount in tuition paid by the more advanced. The only subjects all attended together were singing and prayers. Hautz's register also indicates the typically wide range of pupils' ages, both within a single *Ordnung* and in the class as a whole. Taught one by one and entering at an age that depended on the familial situation, the pupils progressed at their own pace.

Scattered indications from Vaucluse suggest surprising similarities in learning patterns. There, too, teaching progressed from letters and syllables through reading, writing, and ciphering. There, too, fees increased accordingly, and what each pupil studied was determined by a specific agreement between the parents and the teacher based on the pupil's capacity to learn. In any one class there would be pupils of mixed ages and skill levels as, for example, in the school of Saignon, where in 1672 there were five pupils working on the alphabet, six who were reading the Notre Dame, eight who were learning to write, and ten who studied arithmetic.[33]

If the simple skills taught in the little schools of Vaucluse and Baden were similar, efforts to curtail coeducation, which began in Vaucluse at the end of the seventeenth century, resulted in a divergence there in what was taught to boys and to girls. The moral reform era of the seventeenth century produced both an increased concern for education in Catholic countries and an increased church involvement in questions of sexual propriety. One result was a papal ban in 1680 on the teaching of girls by male teachers in the same classrooms where boys were taught. The proscription was significant, for where communities were hard pressed to provide even one teacher, the impact of the decree could be the destruction of girls' schooling opportunities. Some communities apparently ignored the ban. In Sourges, for example, the contract of the *régent d'école* for the year 1763 specified that the *régent* would "hold classes in the consul house and . . . receive in them girls of a tender age," if not their older sisters.[34] Other communities tried to make arrangements for girls by calling in female religious orders like the Ursulines, or, on rare occasions, even lay female instructors. Where there was a separate school for girls, they were taught a curriculum tailored to their presumed needs; in Caumont the endowed school for girls taught "doctrine, piety, reading, writing, sewing and unwinding silk."[35] The Ursulines often held two types of classes for girls in the towns where they taught, regular elementary instruction and more basic classes emphasizing catechetical instruction for those older unschooled girls who showed up a few months before their *première communion.*[36]

This pattern of special arrangements for girls, of their frequent exclusion from the schools their brothers attended, contrasts with the general norm of coeducation that prevailed in Baden. There boys and girls were taught together, and were generally taught the same subjects. Only in the larger towns were there special schools for girls, taught by female religious orders. And only toward the end of the eighteenth century were connections made between schooling and the vocational future of the child, which undermined the custom of teaching the same subjects to boys and girls.

A quick survey of conditions in the schools of the ancien régime leaves the impression, then, that the process of teaching and learning, the character of the classroom experience, and parental expectations about the skills they wanted teachers to transmit were not radically different in these two regions of Europe. Because Badenese communities were more able to provide a viable living to their teachers, it seems likely that the average village teacher there was somewhat better qualified, a claim perhaps counterbalanced by the greater security of tenure in Baden, which made it more difficult to oust incompetents. Given the greatly divergent community resources for schooling in the two areas, the broad availability of publicly subsidized schools is remarkable. Still, the divergent features of the two systems are clear and important: the relative undersupply of schooling funds in the smaller Vauclusan communities; the expensive tuition fees there, which discouraged attendance; the pattern of development of separate and unequal facilities for girls, which may have reinforced in Vaucluse the female subservience in other spheres characteristic of both regions; finally, the closer links of the Badenese schools with the state-church bureaucracies.

These concrete differences in the organization of the schools of the ancien régime created differences in their susceptibility to change as well. The contingency of schooling arrangements in Vaucluse has already been suggested; even during the ancien régime local political disagreements or unusual demands on the communal fisc could result in a temporary cessation in schooling subsidies. The depoliticized, largely church-administered endowment of schooling in Baden was less open to disruption. It is arguable that, even had both regions experienced similar changes in their political systems at the end of the ancien régime, the consequences for schooling would have been different. But in fact, of course, the end came in very different ways.

The revolutionary upheaval in France that brought down the ancien régime entirely undermined, for a while at least, the usual arrangements supporting the schools. The ideological breakthrough that accompanied the revolution placed the public control of schooling high on the political agenda. But the ruptures in political practice that the revolution brought meant that old routines were no longer usable; everything was open to question. Changes in monetary policy, the nationalization of church lands, reform of taxation procedures all combined to make traditional ways of running schools inappropriate or impossible.[37] This was apparent in Paris, where each revolutionary assembly considered a new set of proposals for the complete overhaul of the schools. It was apparent in each community where old practices were stopped and new ones suggested. In Cavaillon, for example, the municipal council brought in by the revolution decided that the community should provide free schooling for all of its children instead of the old system, where "the teachers [had] hardly any pupils because, in addition to the salary paid by the commune parents [were] obliged to pay a sum each month to the teacher. . . . The result [was] not only that the children [did] not acquire good principles because the schoolmasters [were] not paid enough, but also that most of the inhabitants [could] not afford the cost of an education."[38]

National reforms eventually revised completely the manner of public subsidy. Between An II and An IV (1793–1795), teachers who had been certified by the district administration were paid on a per-pupil basis from district funds. They received 20 francs per year for each *jeune citoyen* and 15 for each *jeune citoyenne.* Fragments of evidence from Vaucluse for these years show that these reforms were enforced, at least for a time. Schoolteaching according to this plan was established in at least ten of the fourteen sample communities in the arrondissement of Apt. Instruction was, for the first time in French history, free for all. Enrollments were high in many communities, markedly higher than before, especially among girls, who had in many cases not had access to schools in the past.[39]

The effects of this reorganization were short-lived, however. Teaching salaries disappeared during the fiscal and political crises of the later years of the revolution, and there were no longer endowments or established practices to fall back upon. Teachers pleaded in vain for their subsidies; the prefects of the First Empire clearly disavowed any central responsibility for financing primary schooling and claimed that communities were charged with it.[40] Communal budgets from these years rarely indicate subsidies for teachers. In Sorgues, for example, the once generous support for schools disappeared in 1792 and, despite the default of the district government a few years later, did not reappear until 1808, when the municipal council voted subsidies of 100 francs each for an *instituteur* and an *institutrice.*[41]

During the first decade of the nineteenth century, teachers in Vaucluse were nearly all dependent on the tuition fees they collected, and few received subsidies. Their fees were perforce high, ranging between 75 centimes and 3 francs a month. Only with the gradual establishment of fiscal stability and political routine did subsidies reappear, but even in 1820 there were fewer communities subsidizing schools than there had been before the revolution.[42]

Baden did not escape the revolution, whose eventual impact on the political character of southwestern Germany was profound if gradual. But the political reforms introduced in the revolutionary epoch and accelerated under the pressures of Napoleonic consolidation left many institutions largely intact. To be sure, the secularization of church properties and the tightened state control over churches did affect school endowments and school administration. But tithes and other resources behind the "livings," the archaic collection system, and the premarket modes of communal finance escaped unchanged. As would be the case with the reform of other feudal holdovers like serfdom, the public takeover of tithes and other religious resources would be done through the gradual process of commutation, a process still incomplete even in the middle of the nineteenth century. As in so many other spheres, the reorganization of schooling in Baden was gradual, quiet, moderate in character, directed "from above" in the spirit that often marked reform in the German states. Already under way during the latter decades of the ancien régime, the state takeover of schools entailed the gradual tightening of control over the church bureaucracies, which in turn took more and more of the control over schools into their hands. The church ministries were enveloped in the powerful *Innenministerium*, but they were already accustomed to ministering in the interests of the state.

The opening decades of the nineteenth century brought an intensification of the state interest in schooling already apparent at the end of the ancien régime. In both France and Baden, reformist ideas resulted in ambitious state reforms of the schools by the 1830s. But the very project of reform was different from the outset, as a result of the legacy of the ancien régime and the manner of its demise.

CHAPTER 3

Schooling for the People
The Reform of School Administration

THE ERA OF POLITICAL REVOLUTION AND REFORM that began in 1789 brought ideological upheaval as well. Many of the heresies spoken in the salons of the *philosophes* and written in their censored tracts found themselves elevated to the status of official policy by the opening decades of the nineteenth century. The new views of human psychology and Enlightenment theories of state began to assert themselves particularly strongly in the area of educational policy. The obscurantism already undermined by the mass political participation and social dislocation inaugurated by the "dual revolution" gave way to a new approach.[1]

Evidence of obscurantist fears of popular education appeared even at the very end of the ancien régime. In the 1780s the *intendant* of Provence added his voice to those opposed to the spread of popular schooling. As he put it, "a peasant who knows how to read and write [will] leave agriculture to learn a trade or become a legal adviser, which is a very great misfortune. . . ."[2] This official antipathy toward schooling was echoed in decisions like that of the municipal council of Apt in 1784 to suppress the town's free school run by the Christian Brothers. The council justified its act by claiming that the school "tended to take a great number of workers away from agriculture" and maintained that in closing the school it was "conforming to the wishes of the government and doing a great service to the country."[3] Although such local opposition to the subsidy of schooling continued to manifest itself well into the nineteenth century, most agents of the central state rejected the obscurantist tradition and began to espouse a more positive view toward mass schooling. Local councils might continue to refuse funds for schools, but they could no longer do so with the backing of the state. By the turn of the nineteenth century, the more commonly held official opinion was closer to that of the Prussian educational reformer von Rochow that "the intelligence of a peasant is not a barrier to his becoming a talented farmer, an industrious worker, a loyal servant and an obedient soldier."[4]

There were already hints in some places in the late eighteenth century of an awakening of official interest in popular schooling. The opening decades of the nineteenth century spawned campaigns all over Europe designed to bring elementary schools under state control and to make them more responsive to state needs. No longer willing to leave so important an institution as the popular elementary school up to the supervision of local church and community, or to leave school attendance to the whim of parents or church administrators to enforce, state agencies undertook more active involvement in the administration of primary schools. Universal schooling became a state goal, and officials took steps to assure that the content of that schooling would take state interests into account and help to forge "the people" into a citizenry appropriate to the postrevolutionary state and the early industrial capitalist economy.

Many of the German states had, in fact, passed laws as early as the sixteenth century that suggested state interest in schooling. Actual efforts to influence teaching, curriculum, and attendance were, however, undertaken only toward the end of the eighteenth century. The Prussian General School Regulations of 1763 provided a model and impetus for reform in other states as well, although it is clear that even in Prussia these early reform proposals remained pretty much a dead letter.[5] Still, these early laws set an important precedent for central direction of schools.

Popular response in Germany to the French Revolution and to the German collapse in the face of the Napoleonic challenge stimulated administrative interest in schooling. A spate of new legislation concerning schooling testifies to the nature of official concern. The Reformed *Kirchensektion* of the Kurpfalz, for example, passed a regulation in 1797 that set out the basic organizational features of the *Trivialschulen* and prescribed the content of the curriculum. The regulation stated that the schools' teaching plans should be oriented toward

> the study of Bible history . . . guidance toward devout rather than mechanical uplifting of the heart to God at the beginning and the end of the day's occupation. . . . With regard to civic life, [the lesson plan] should promote the learning of competent reading and writing of our country's language and of arithmetic. . . . As for morality, it should be of prime concern in the plan, which should take as its goal habituation to constant attentiveness, continual occupation and precise order.[6]

The Catholic elementary school edict of the state of Baden, which was passed a few years later in 1803, required schools to teach

> to the city dweller and the countryman all that is necessary for him to know for his life's calling as a Christian and a state citizen, without pushing him to a level of intellectual development such that [his calling] is neglected or becomes distasteful to him.[7]

Although still showing traces of older expectations about school's purpose, these turn-of-the-century edicts hint at a new one as well—that proper social attitudes and civic virtues could be taught along with reading and religion. By the 1830s it was taken for granted that the schools had important social and political functions to fulfill. The Badenese state law on public school instruction passed in 1832 stressed that teachers were to devote "special care and diligence to political instruction and in particular to the German language."[8] The general recodification of 1834 made explicit state goals with respect to primary education:

> . . . the essentials of civic virtue are to be awakened also, and the children are to be impressed with the duty of loyalty to the Grand Duke, love of fatherland, obedience to laws and ordinances, attentiveness to religious and secular authorities . . . and to their duties toward their fellow citizens.[9]

In France the specific political content of schooling plans was subject to variation with regime. Nonetheless, all of the governments that succeeded one another after the demise of the ancien régime state shared the conviction that some form of civic indoctrination was a necessary component of childhood training. The national assemblies of the revolutionary years set the tone by producing a variety of reform plans. Although not all of these plans granted the state a monopoly over the regulation of primary instruction, they all rested on the assumption that the provision of schools was vital for the security and survival of the state.[10] Even the conservative restoration government, reluctant to intrude into traditional church preserves, found it expedient to make some provision for state involvement in elementary schooling, and hoped to use the schools to its political advantage as well. The restored monarch signed an ordinance in 1816 maintaining that instruction founded "on the true principles of religion and morality [was] not only one of the most fertile sources of public prosperity but also . . .[contributed] to the good order of society, [prepared] the way for obedience to the law and for the performance of duties of all sorts."[11]

Local representatives of the French state echoed this idea. After the passage of the 1816 ordinance, the *recteur* of the Académie of Nîmes wrote to the cantonal committees in his jurisdiction that they were to oversee schoolteachers in their performance of the tasks of "[maintaining] order, religion and good manners and [encouraging] the fulfillment of all the duties of Christians and subjects."[12] The schools could serve as seedbeds of legitimist sentiment according to the same environmentalist principles that once had them producing good *citoyens.* This was clear to the *recteur* as he wrote to the prefect of Vaucluse in 1826: "Instruction wisely directed and supervised cannot fail to inspire [our youth] with religious and monarchist opinions."[13]

The inefficacy and volatility of educational planning under the restoration stemmed not from lack of commitment to schooling as much as from the tension between sensitivity to the political need for schooling, on the one hand, and the commitment to religiously controlled schooling of many of the religious supporters of the regime, on the other. The July Revolution brought an end to this particular kind of tension. The new regime assumed that the state would play the central role in schooling. The assumption that the state could and should act as a "neutral" overseer of the purveyors of that basic knowledge vital to the civic and moral education of the human being and citizen underlay the energetic plans of the 1830s to reform the elementary schools and bring them within the reach of all children. The educational plans developed by the reformers of the July Monarchy period were purportedly nonpartisan, in the best interests of the whole society. Needless to say, however, those virtues considered to be essential for the formation of loyal French citizens, and for the preservation of the social order, were to be a central part of the curriculum. In his exposition before the chamber of deputies of the new school reform plan of 1833, the education minister, Guizot, stated simply and elegantly the aims of the state's intervention in the school:

> through the teaching of reading and writing and arithmetic [the proposed curriculum] provides for the most essential necessities of life; through teaching the legal system of weights and measures and of the French language it implants everywhere, enhances and extends the spirit and unity of the French nation; through moral and religious instruction it provides for another order of needs every bit as real . . . for the dignity of human life and the protection of the social order.[14]

The logic behind the Guizot Law appears even more clearly in a circular address to primary schoolteachers in 1833 and intended to explain the new law to them and to outline their particular duties with respect to it. Guizot explained that the new law had as its goal that

> all Frenchmen acquire if possible that knowledge which is indispensable for social life and without which the mind languishes . . . [but the law is designed] for the state as well, and in the public interest, since liberty is secure and routine only among a people who are enlightened enough to hear . . . the voice of reason. Universal primary education is thus one of the greatest guarantees of order and social stability.[15]

In Guizot's vision, the maximal interests of the individual and those of the state, which acted as arbiter among competing individual interests, were ultimately one and the same. Education produced more individuals enlightened enough to appreciate this convergence. Presumably, with mass education, persistent misconceptions that led to violent conflicts over basic constitutional issues would diminish. In the phase of transition to a constitutional state, the schools were to play a crucial role: they could teach future citizens to accept the new conception of the state even while teachers refrained from explicitly partisan stands. Teachers were cautioned to avoid "opening the schools to the spirit of sect or party and nourishing the children on those religious or political doctrines which put them, so to speak, in revolt against authority." Instead, the teachers should restrict themselves to instilling in their pupils "faith in Providence, the sanctity of duty, submission to paternal authority, respect for the law, for the Prince and for the rights of all."[16]

This was the "nonsectarian" message of the schools. Reduced to its essentials, as in Guizot's instructions to the *instituteurs,* its content is strikingly similar to that suggested by the Badenese law of the same period. The reforms of the July Monarchy did resemble, more than is commonly recognized, school plans originating in the distinctive political traditions of Central Europe (and, for that matter, plans emerging in the United States and England at this same time).[17] Still, despite notable similarities in the phrases used to describe the political content of primary schooling by French officials and their more statist German counterparts, the form that state involvement took in each region was different. This contrast in style (and impact) of state intervention in schooling was both the result and the expression of the different patterns of political development characteristic of France and Baden.

A significant difference in educational policy, one that underpinned and exemplified other policy contrasts between the two states, concerned the question of obligation. Baden, like many other German states, had had a long history of *Schulzwang*—laws obliging school attendance. Some German princes had promulgated as early as the sixteenth century laws that required communities to have schools.[18] In the Kurpfalz, there were laws passed on several occasions during the seventeenth and eighteenth centuries requiring children to attend school. The multiplication of such ordinances in the latter half of the eighteenth century, and the imposition of fines for noncompliance with them, suggest both that earlier ordinances were not well enforced and that serious efforts to reform schooling practices were then under way. An ordinance passed in 1751 required Catholic parents to send their children to school until their first communion and to pay school tuition and money for firewood even when their children did not attend class. Truancy was made punishable by a fine of between 1 and 3 florins. The following year the Bishop of Worms, who administered some of the Catholic parishes in the Kurpfalz, published a decree that all Catholic teachers were to hold summer school sessions, which all pupils were required to attend.[19] Over the course of the next few decades, the recurrence of complaints from school inspectors of all creeds about parental failure to comply with the school laws adds credence to the claim of one local historian that it was only with the incorporation of the area into the highly organized Badenese state that these laws began to be enforced. "The takeover by Baden was a great blessing for education," he writes in apparent admiration for the state's reputed efficiency, "unexcused truancy immediately met with punishment."[20] Although he may be exaggerating the effectiveness of the Badenese system, there are nonetheless indications that the *Schulzwang* was being enforced by the early decades of the nineteenth century. Every teacher was required to keep a register noting the excused and unexcused absences of each pupil. The school inspector took this list to the mayor, who, with his police to back him up, could impose fines of between 2 and 12 kreuzer for each day of unexcused absence, or between four and twenty-four hours in jail for parents of repeated offenders.[21]

Coercion was an established educational practice, and it remained an assumption in the reforms proposed and carried out in the early nineteenth century. In fact, many of the reforms were designed precisely to insure that no children would evade the schools. The reform law of 1834, for example, established the *Entlassungschein,* the school-leaving certificate. This certificate was to be granted, upon reaching school-leaving age, only to those pupils who could demonstrate competence in elementary school subjects. Permission to leave school, in other words, was theoretically contingent upon learning. A group of reform-minded teachers from the town of Wiesloch even demanded that this certificate be made a prerequisite for employment. This, they reasoned, would be the only truly effective means of enforcing school attendance laws. The *Entlassungschein,* the teachers felt, had to "have the same value as the vaccination certificate: that is, without it, no boy or girl [could] go into service, take up a handicraft, get a permit to migrate, become a citizen or a master craftsman."[22] Pupils who were truant more than a specified number of days during the course of their elementary schooling could be denied the certificate when they reached school-leaving age. Although it is clear that the school-leaving certificate did not in practice become the passport to adult economic and political status these teachers wanted it to be, at least not by the middle of the nineteenth century, its establishment added one more discouragement to truancy to the already impressive array of coercive measures available to school authorities in Baden. State authorities, school officials, and teachers interested in enforcing universal school attendance were prepared to use force to insure that their goal was reached.

In France, in contrast, with the exception of a brief period during the revolution, primary school attendance remained voluntary until the last quarter of the nineteenth century. The policy of obligation was hardly a practical option, since in areas like Vaucluse only a minority of children were attending school at the turn of the nineteenth century.[23] In the absence of adequate funds for school subsidy and the personnel to enforce attendance, any attempt to force school attendance would probably have met with failure. Although universal school attendance was their goal, French administrators of this period decided to rest their hopes of accomplishing it on the voluntary cooperation of parents, who would be persuaded of the merits of schooling. For example, one Vauclusan inspector sensitive to the preference for a voluntary policy, especially in the South, wrote:

> some people [subscribed] to the principle that it is necessary to do good for a society despite itself, thinking that we in France should pass a law

> similar to those in force in some northern European states which oblige parents to send their children to school, under penalty of fines or imprisonment, until the age of thirteen or fourteen years. But would this measure, which has succeeded in a country where the people are accustomed to respecting the law and those who enforce it, have the same success here? I do not believe so, at least not as far as our population of the Midi is concerned . . .[24]

The southern people, he went on, were for better or worse devoted to liberty, to local custom, to the preservation of individual rights. Coercive measures would only backfire because they would be unenforceable. The net result would be a decrease of respect for state institutions. Universal primary schooling, however desirable a goal, would have to be accomplished gradually through the persuasive powers of its own demonstrated worth. This cautious reluctance to risk outright coercion to fulfill the goal of universal schooling would only be abandoned in the early days of the Third Republic, by which time the radical republican interpretation emphasizing the egalitarian promise of schooling had enough support within both the educational bureaucracy and the population at large to counterbalance the political liabilities raised by compulsory-attendance legislation.[25]

In France, then, in part as a result of the political heritage of the ancien régime, and in part as a consequence of the political link between state school reform and laissez-faire liberalism, coercion was both impractical and politically indefensible for most school reformers. Incorporation of all of the children of the people into the schools was still the goal, but the means had to be more subtle; the appeal to reasoned self-interest had to dominate over outright coercion. In Baden the legal persistence of absolutist institutions and *Ständestaat* assumptions of social and political inequality and patriarchal political relationships encouraged the enforcement of old, if previously unenforced, policies of obligation. Broadly speaking, educational officials in both areas shared similar goals: "the people" were to be shaped in the schools into the kinds of future citizens the state wanted and social stability required. But the institutional means employed to assure that the schools performed this function were different, and necessarily so, emerging as they did from material conditions and political traditions that were distinct. These differences affected every step on the way to school reform.

The new state interest in schooling led to increased intervention in the administration of schools. If the schools were to be reshaped to meet the new political and socialization functions, it was necessary to change the way they were run in order to make them more responsive to state needs. Proper schools had to be available in every community, and what happened in those schools had to be amenable to state direction.

In Baden school administration was already in the hands of the church administration; state bureaucratic reorganization brought this more closely under the supervision of the secular state. As a result in particular of the reorganization of the state of Baden during the period of Napoleonic consolidation, direction of the state churches was placed under the auspices of the Ministry of the Interior. Special sections of this ministry were established for administering the property and institutions of the three recognized churches—Reformed, Lutheran, and Catholic. This supervisory structure remained essentially unaltered throughout the first half of the nineteenth century, although the two Protestant sections were combined in 1820.

This central *Kirchensektion* held direct supervisory powers over secondary schools, normal schools, and a number of special educational institutions. Supervision of primary education was in the hands of the regional-level *Dekanat* of each Kreis, and school finance was handled through the fiscal apparatus of the Kreisregierung.[26] Schools continued to be subsidized through tithes collected from religious communities, and the active role of the state churches in the administration of schools was more or less taken for granted. To be sure, the subject of secular control over the schools was raised in the consolidation period.[27] One proposal considered was to unite all educational institutions under the control of a single secular authority, and to make provision for the churches to teach only religious lessons separately. Such a plan, its proponents felt, would make schooling less costly and should present religious people with no difficulties, since "the ABCs, grammar and arithmetic do not have to be taught in a Catholic, Reformed or Lutheran style."[28]

But even if there was support in the enlightened circles of the state bureaucracy for this sort of arrangement, the final compromise worked out in the process of consolidation between the Grand Duke Karl Friedrich and his churches left the *Kirchensektionen* responsible for the administration of schools, and every public school had to be affiliated with one or the other of these churches, even as every child had to be assigned to a religious community at birth or migration into the state. Despite continued opposition to clerical control over the schools, a movement that accelerated until the 1840s, officials of the state churches held onto their strong position in the school system until the 1860s. But the persistence of church involvement in schooling should not be interpreted as a sign of state weakness. Indeed, the subsumption of the churches into the state bureaucratic system insured state involvement in school administration as well.

The situation was quite different in France. Educational officials of the revolutionary and postrevolutionary period consistently confronted more serious obstacles in their efforts to reorganize the school system and bring existing institutions into the sphere of influence of the state. The ancien régime state had by and large ignored the schools, and control over them remained decentralized. Church efforts to organize schooling at a level higher than the parish, or occasionally the diocese, were similarly unenergetic. And the heritage of local control was a powerful one.

The first short-lived attempts to centralize school administration followed the passage in 1792 of the Bouquier Law. According to its provisions, licenses to teach school were to be granted only to certified good citizens, whose work would be supervised and paid for by the district rather than the individual community. The law was enforced for a short time, but the central dispensing of teaching salaries had disappeared by 1795.[29] Napoleonic centralization, culminating in the establishment in 1808 of the Université, brought the state into the schools permanently. The Université was a state-controlled, bureaucratically organized corporation granted a monopoly over the licensing and regulation of institutions of higher education. France was divided into académies comprised of several départements each; within each académie, the *recteur* appointed by the Université supervised all educational institutions. During the first two decades of the Université's existence there were countless skirmishes about the so-called *écoles clandestines*—schools taught by teachers who were evading the certification procedures, teaching fees, and per-pupil taxes imposed by the Université. But eventually most teachers began either sending in the high fees or going out of business because of them. More and more of the local collèges dutifully began reporting about financial conditions and enrollments.[30]

Significant state intervention in primary schooling began only during the restoration. Earlier concern was limited to periodic surveys of the state of existing subsidies and the number of practicing teachers. A royal ordinance of 1816 created a system of local committees, headed by the *curé* of the parish and comprised of local notables, charged with the supervision of elementary education. These committees were in turn responsible to arrondissement-level committees that also examined and licensed teachers. Finding the volunteer personnel needed to staff these committees proved to be a problem for Université authorities. On the one hand, they sought clerical cooperation with the educational plans of the restored monarchy, but at the same time, many Université officials were committed to increasing the role of the state in schooling as well, and needed to find local supporters for that cause. To counterbalance clerical influence on these committees, the minister of public instruction directed that the choice of committee members should insofar as possible fall on "enlightened persons disposed impartially to examine new methods rather than rejecting them out of hand."[31] These committees were assembled quickly; by the end of 1816 all of the cantons in the two arrondissements of Avignon and Apt had submitted lists of committee members. Along with the local pastors, these committees were comprised of property owners, local officials, and a scattering of tradespeople.[32]

The uneasy alliance between the church and the restoration state was twice upset, and each administrative change had ramifications for the personnel of these local administrative committees. In 1824 the clerical party assumed control over the national bureaucracy, a few years after its local triumph in areas like Vaucluse. In 1828, national policy again emphasized the power of the secular state in education, and by 1830, the time of the fall of the Bourbon monarchy, secular control over the local committees supervising education was established as a firm principle. Reforms in 1830—among the first to be passed by the "bourgeois monarchy" that came into power in the July Revolution of that year—also gave to the representative of the central state more authority; the prefect now had the right to choose the majority of the local school commissioners. The new directive of 1830, which outlined procedures for the establishment of local committees of supervision, stated that committee members should be selected from among "elite citizens, who besides their title to esteem and public consideration, are avowed friends of popular education and disposed to make sacrifices of time and even small sums of money . . . to improve this education. . . ."[33] The July Monarchy government also promptly established a regular inspection system for the primary schools, recruiting inspectors who were charged with annual tours of all the schools in their district. According to the terms of the 1833 directive, they were supposed to "break the tendencies toward autonomy of the cantonal committees, push instructional methods towards uniformity, and strengthen the influence of the Royal Council over all of primary instruction."[34]

In theory, then, local supervision of schooling was in the hands of secular appointees of the central state. Still, establishing the theory and implementing it were two different things. In contrast with the state of affairs in Baden, where early compromise with church officials had allowed the establishment of a centralized and professional school bureaucracy responsive to the demands of the state and the state churches, French educational officials continually confronted the problem of negotiating with the church, with its vested interest in educational institutions. The recruitment of the volunteer local administrative personnel, so crucial in the French situation to the implementation of national policy, was continually hampered by the mésalliance or outright conflict between church and state. And the problem was especially severe in areas like Vaucluse that were centers of organized legitimist and ultramontane opposition to the July Monarchy state.[35]

School reformers could not simply proceed from an institutional "clean slate." Their options, when they sought to make the schools produce the kinds of pupils they sought, were constrained by the material present and the historical past. The actual educational institutions they inherited presented them with both a starting point and a set of constraints; perhaps more subtly, their sense of the possible bore the imprint of their own political experience and that of their predecessors. The differences in both institutional starting point and political sensibility, which existed alongside an essentially similar set of goals held by educational authorities in Baden and Vaucluse, are well illustrated in an examination of the actual operation of school reforms in local communities. The ways in which school officials in the two regions handled real teachers in real classrooms, the impact they were able to have on conditions in the schools in different kinds of communities, their persistent frustrations, all attest to both the ideal image of schooling held by reformers and the very real problems they faced in trying to transform existing institutions to match that image. The task was a large one, clearly more formidable in Vaucluse than in Baden. Teachers had to be made into worthy functionaries of the state. Schoolrooms and school buildings had to be rebuilt as appropriate greenhouses for the nurturance of civic and moral sentiment. The curriculum and the materials used in teaching had to meet specifications set by officials with a new sense of mission. The records of encounters between agents of the central state and the local schools testify to the immensity of the endeavor.

CHAPTER 4

Schooling for the People
The Pedagogic Reform

SCHOOLTEACHERS WERE THE LOGICAL FOCUS OF reformers' attention. As state functionaries, with a mission defined in ever more grandiose terms, teachers had to command the respect of parents and maintain a style of life compatible with the new dignity of office. School officials and, as they became more professionally self-conscious, schoolteachers themselves began to see contradictions between the expectations associated with their new roles and the characteristics of the traditional teacher of the old regime. Early inspection reports and communications from teachers, records of salary transactions and the like, are filled with references to problems connected with the redefinition of the teacher's image and role.[1]

Salaries were a troublesome issue. In order for teaching to become a respectable profession comprised of independent lay family men, teaching posts had to pay enough to support a teacher and his family too. That the new breed of teacher would be male was an unspoken assumption behind official policy; that went along with the effort to upgrade the job and to turn the teacher into a minor functionary of the state.[2] Furthermore, as a minor notable, the teacher had to be distinguishable from the people to whom he ministered on behalf of the state. Meager support for a seasonal incumbent would no longer suffice. The teaching reforms of the 1830s in both Baden and France made provision for minimum incomes in even the smallest communities. Examination of actual salaries in communities suggests that the problem of providing adequate salaries remained severe in Vaucluse; nonetheless there is in both areas evidence of improvement in teaching incomes in the early nineteenth century, improvement resulting at least in part from the pressure from the state government, and its aid.

The financial position of teachers in Vaucluse had been especially precarious at the turn of the nineteenth century in the wake of the fiscal disruption of the later revolutionary years. Teachers' incomes, comprised largely of tuition fees, rarely surpassed a few hundred francs a year. The securely endowed teaching posts in Baden present a contrast; reforms and secularization there had left most *Schulpfrunde* intact. Still, the position of schoolteachers in Baden was far from ideal. Collecting what was due them often involved struggles with the families they served, and what was due them was often inadequate because of inflation and because more and more of the teachers had families to support. Increasing complaints from teachers about their salaries and the manner of their payment attest to the incompatibility of the old system of support and the new image of the teacher.

Wandertisch and other forms of payment in kind came under attack. The practice of feeding the teacher on a rotating basis in the homes of his pupils' parents was a source of contention. Many teachers found the custom demeaning and impractical. It certainly interfered with the family life many teachers were beginning to expect. In 1804 the community of Horrenburg debated switching from the *Wandertisch* arrangement to a payment of *Kostgeld.* Some of the villagers were apparently unhappy with the older custom, but decided they preferred "to give the schoolteacher food to [giving him] money, since money is rare these days and food for one man at the family table doesn't strike them as being as valuable as money."[3] The switch was, however, made a decade or so later, at a time when many other communities were also abandoning traditional means of supporting their schoolmasters.[4] *Schulbrod* and *Glockenbrod,* loaves of bread given in exchange for teaching and bell ringing, went the way of the *Wandertisch.* The community of Waldangelloch voted overwhelmingly in 1815 to retain the *Glockenbrod;* by the 1830s it had disappeared. In Walldorf, money was substituted for bread in 1826. Payment in wine was particularly troublesome to teachers, and there were numerous complaints on the subject, but even as late as 1836 schoolteachers' complaints show that the practice continued.[5]

Counterbalancing the teachers' complaints about payment in kind were their fears of the danger of inflation where payment was made in cash. Complaints about the inadequacy of salaries in inflationary years were numerous, beginning in the 1790s. Requests for subsidies from the state for firewood and tuition multiplied. Ironically, the very conversion to cash payments usually made at the request of the teachers made their situation more precarious. Teachers from Mannheim complained that prices that prevailed at the time when their salaries were converted to cash had become so inflated that subsistence was no longer possible.[6] As teachers in Baden began to form professional organizations in the first half of the nineteenth century, salary reform was high on their agenda of interests. Teachers organized petition drives and lobbied for the abolition of customs like the *Wandertisch;* they wanted minimal salaries for all teaching posts; some even demanded the abolition of tuition fees and the substitution of a simple salary instead.

State officials were sensitive to the need to improve teaching salaries and could hardly quibble with teachers' demands for higher incomes. In the 1830s the French and the Badenese governments began programs of regular subsidies to augment the salaries of the most poorly paid teachers. In 1832 the Badenese government allocated 55,000 florins to this end, enough to raise teaching salaries 15 percent.[7] A French government grant in the same year allocated 10,000 francs to the primary schools of Vaucluse. About 1,000 francs of this were applied to teaching incomes. By the end of the 1830s, seven of the twenty sample communities in Vaucluse were receiving state grants of between 120 and 250 francs annually to pay their teachers. Among the recipients were four of the five communities of fewer than five hundred residents, communities that had been in the recent past unable to support teachers at all.[8] Although small, these subsidies represented the first material evidence of the seriousness of state intentions to transform schoolteaching and schooling.

Because of the complexity of the systems for reimbursing teachers, it is difficult to estimate trends in teaching incomes, but the evidence does suggest that they were rising steadily and perceptibly during the first half of the nineteenth century. Table 5 summarizes these trends for the sample communities in Vaucluse and Baden. In Baden fixed income rose little between the late eighteenth and the early nineteenth centuries, but increasing enrollments brought rising tuition incomes. Advances were apparently more noticeable in the north Badenese sample communities than in the country as a whole. Heunisch reported in 1833 that the average teacher's income overall

TABLE 5
Average Incomes of Public Schoolteachers by Size of Community, Sample Communities in Baden and Vaucluse, 1800–1836

	Baden (florins)				*Vaucluse (francs)*			
Communities	*c. 1800*	*(n)*	*1836*	*(n)*	*c. 1800*	*(n)*	*1836*	*(n)*
<2,000	160	20	191	16	283	6	389	14
>2,000	370	31	487	38	315	12	622	33
All	287	51	399	54	304	18	553	47

Note: During the early nineteenth century, average incomes of the general population have been estimated at around 275–300 florins a year in Baden and around 450–500 francs in Vaucluse at full employment; at the same time, the wages of agricultural laborers were around 110–120 florins and 250–350 francs respectively in Baden and Vaucluse.

Source: See Appendix II for the variety of archival sources that contain evidence about school finance.

was just over 200 florins a year. By 1857 the Badenese average had risen to about 240 florins, substantially lower than the amount urban teachers in north Baden received, but higher than rural salaries.[9]

In Vaucluse the rise in teaching salaries during the first half of the nineteenth century was more dramatic, in part because of the decided setback that occurred between 1789 and 1820 or so. In the sample communities the turn-of-the-century average of around 300 francs had nearly doubled by the middle of the nineteenth century. Inspectors reported higher incomes especially in the arrondissement of Avignon. Teachers there averaged nearly 800 francs a year in the 1830s, as compared with the average of around 500 francs in the poorer arrondissement of Apt.[10]

At these rates, village teachers in both regions earned an income somewhere between that of an unskilled laborer and that of a fully employed artisan. In both regions, urban teachers were substantially better paid. In addition, a post as teacher began to offer a security rare in the early industrial period. Come what may, the teacher's income was secure and brought a modicum of security for the future in the form of a pension. Teaching salaries were moving toward the levels that the new status of teaching required.

Salary improvements also helped to release teachers from the necessity of resorting to the by-employments that educational officials regarded as unprofessional and undesirable. The days when teachers were part-time artisans, innkeepers, or gravediggers approached their end. By the middle of the nineteenth century, the only common and acceptable source of outside income was work as a communal secretary or public witness. These services were, in fact, commonly linked with teaching posts. In 1826 the Catholic community of Neidenstein requested that the office of public clerk *(Gerichtschreiberei)* be formally attached to that of the Catholic schoolteacher, since "the income of that office [was] so little that [the community could not] attract a learned schoolteacher."[11] In Vaucluse the practice of combining the posts of teacher and *sécrétaire de commune* became quite common during the second and third decades of the nineteenth century as the option of hiring a part-time teacher was disappearing. Although the income from either post was meager in small communities, the combined income was respectable. A report of 1859 indicated that twenty-nine of the lay public schoolteachers in the département were deriving some income from their service as communal secretary.[12] As earlier makeshift solutions to the problem of providing income for teaching fell into disuse and disfavor, the new option provided an alternative acceptable to state authorities.

The traditional expectation that the schoolteacher would serve as a junior partner to the local pastor was harder to shake loose. Again, the association had had income implications, since there were perquisites attached to offices like that of sexton or bell ringer. Especially in Baden, where ties between school and church were stronger and more pervasive, minor church functions and their reimbursement formed a part of nearly every *Kompetenz,* or account of a living. As explicit secular concerns impinged more and more on the vague but very real religious character of the post of teacher, the assumed subservience of the schoolteacher to the clergyman became increasingly problematic. Some teachers continued to welcome the additional income and accepted their religious status. But for many others religious duties and expectations were becoming onerous, and they shared with some school authorities the desire to overturn the compromises embodied in official regulations, and to work for a complete separation of the schools from religious control. In both regions teachers were among the leaders of movements for the secularization of education, movements whose goals were compatible with the drive to create a teaching corps that was more professional and committed to service to the state. Indeed, the marginal and fluid status of schoolteachers in both areas in this reform era—they were caught between state and local community, between church and state, between their own professional ambitions and their instinctive sympathy for the needs of the modest social classes from which they were recruited—

goes a long way toward accounting for their proclivity to involvement in the political activities that eventually fed into the revolutionary movements of 1848.[13]

The reform of the teaching profession entailed more than the upgrading of salaries and the transformation of teaching into an autonomous full-time profession. In order for the new expectations about schooling to be fulfilled, access to teaching posts had to be regulated and candidates shaped to be the kind of emissaries the state needed. In Baden the right to appoint the teacher belonged traditionally to the holder of the *Patronatsrecht,* a right that often went along with the financial endowment of the post. Originally the holder of the right was often the lord of the community, but by the late eighteenth century the church bureaucracies had already asserted their claim to this right in many cases. At the time of the appointment of a schoolteacher to the Reformed school of Mannheim in 1759, for example, Reformed officials pointed to the "vexation, conflict and disorder" that usually arose on the occasion of a vacancy, which they felt justified appointment by the church hierarchy.[14] Although the local Reformed community fought back, the bureaucracy had the force of the state government behind it. After this date, appointments seem routinely to have been made by church officials after they received applications from prospective candidates. When a community was dissatisfied with its teacher, its only recourse was to petition the *Dekanat* or the *Konsistorium,* who came to hold the ultimate power of hiring and firing. The *Kirchenrath Instruktion* of 1797 codified existing practices for the certification and placement of *Schulkandidats.* According to these ordinances, in the case of a vacancy in a teaching post local and *Oberamt* officials, would submit to the appropriate *Konsistorium* a list of candidates, and the *Konstitorium* then made the appointment. *Patronatsrecht* was invoked from time to time, for example at the time of the creation of a Jewish post in the 1820s, but the Badenese Ministry of the Interior denied such patronage procedures any role in the hiring of teachers.[15]

In Vaucluse, in contrast, local community councils and notables retained their traditional responsibility in the hiring and supervision of teachers. During the restoration, when the national government made its first attempts to encourage public instruction, hiring was assigned to the local committees. These were, however, to choose teachers from among individuals licensed by arrondissement committees. The government of the July Monarchy did little to impinge upon the local selection of teachers, although by the late 1830s a new requirement specified that teachers be approved by the Université to teach in a specified locale. Furthermore, the new system of inspection opened the way for state evaluation of a teacher's performance. Central state involvement in hiring remained largely advisory throughout the first half of the nineteenth century, but mechanisms for a more direct role were established. Still, the retention of local prerogatives contrasts with the bureaucratic centralism so typical of Baden.

What was really at stake in the hiring and supervision of teachers, of course, was a degree of control over the character and behavior of the teacher. The simple assurance that there was a teacher in every community was not enough; that teacher had to meet the new performance standards that state representatives were setting. Despite constant complaints on the subject of teachers' qualifications, there was apparently no shortage of practicing teachers in either Baden or Vaucluse. Most communities had teachers in the later years of the ancien régime, and the towns and cities had them in abundance.

In Vaucluse the newly created public subsidies for teaching made available during the early years of the republic were claimed by a large corps of *instituteurs.* Despite the interruption of communal subsidy brought by the revolution, the number of individuals who plied the teaching trade remained high. A survey conducted in An X (1802) uncovered seventy-five teachers practicing in the arrondissement of Apt alone, even though many communities that formerly supported schools were reportedly without them at the time.[16] By the end of the second decade of the nineteenth century, when juries were established to review and certify teachers, there were sixty-five teachers who received certification in the arrondissement of Apt. Although numerous, these teachers were distributed unevenly; only about half of the fifty communities in the arrondissement had teachers. In the arrondissement of Avignon, nineteen of twenty communities had teachers at this time.[17] The number of female teachers was also surprisingly large. Between 1819 and 1831, more than 150 women received either brevets or letters of obedience to a religious order that entitled them to teach in the département. By the mid-1830s there were thirty-five *institutrices* teaching in the arrondissement of Apt and twenty-six in that of Avignon, but virtually all of these women were either members of religious orders or teachers in private schools. At this time there were more than a hundred male teachers authorized to teach in the two arrondissements, and men held a monopoly over lay, public posts.[18]

In Baden the number of teachers was larger, and they were more widely scattered. There were at least fifty-five publicly subsidized teachers working in the twenty sample communities at the turn of the nineteenth century. All of these were men, but a few had wives who shared classroom responsibilities with them. In addition, there were an unspecified number of private teachers concentrated in the towns and cities, teachers who survived despite official harassment. By the late 1830s there were sixty-five public schoolteachers and a few dozen private schoolteachers tolerated and regulated according to the provisions of the new laws of the 1830s.[19]

If teachers were by no means in short supply, inspectors and administrators were nonetheless skeptical of the competence of many of them. Much of the surviving evidence on the question reflects disdain of the inspectors—themselves often products of the elite classical schools—for the local, rural, and unprofessional character of many teachers. By the time of the first systematic inspection reports in the 1830s, village teachers in Vaucluse were often deemed inadequate. The inspectors criticized them for a variety of offenses. Some were accused of negligence: M. Taubert of Cavaillon was "immoral, quite ill-kempt" and had purportedly taught only five or six of his twenty-five pupils how to read and write; Villard of Cabrières d'Avignon allegedly "completely neglected his duties as *instituteur*" despite the fact that he was well educated enough to have taught Latin to his son. Others were incompetent on all scores: M. Germain of Roussillon was charged with "complete absence of order and of method," which produced the terrible reading, ill-kept notebooks, and lack of understanding of arithmetic exhibited by his pupils.[20] Some teachers inspired lengthy diatribes on the part of the inspector—M. Bernard of St. Saturnin d'Apt, for example, who elicited this reaction at the time of the inspection of 1838:

> Never has incompetence more pronounced, rusticity more brusque, filth more repulsive . . . been combined in one teacher and in one class. . . . After an hour and a half of interrogation, the sole response that we (M. the Mayor and I) were able to get from the pupil designated as the smartest was that "the first letter of the alphabet is 'a.' "[21]

Still, Bernard was not the worst teacher in the arrondissement. The inspector reserved that distinction for Armand of Cabrières d'Apt. Old, ill, and untrained, this teacher taught pupils "bad reading, detestable handwriting . . . and arithmetic limited to the first two rules." Their exercise books were "filled with spelling errors," and they had "no sense of grammar."[22] These were not scattered complaints. By the late 1830s, when inspectors rated teachers separate on their *moralité, capacité,* and *zèle,* teachers in Vaucluse fell short of

TABLE 6
Teachers' Competence in Communities of Different Sizes, according to the Inspection Report of 1836–1837, Vaucluse

Arrondissement of Avignon *Size of community*	*Number of teachers categorized as* "*Assez*" *or better*	"*Mediocre*" *or worse*
Less than 2000	3	13
More than 2000	26	18
Arrondissement of Apt *Size of community*	"*Assez*" *or better*	"*Mediocre*" *or worse*
Less than 2000	11	36
More than 2000	14	23
Total	54	90

Source: ADV: T, FIA, 207.

inspectors' demands. Most were sufficiently zealous, and there were few complaints about morality, but the vast majority were judged incompetent. (See Table 6.) This was especially true of teachers in the rural communes, and more pronounced in the relatively backward arrondissement of Apt, where three-quarters of the rural *instituteurs* received negative evaluations of their intellectual and pedagogic capacities.[23]

Badenese teachers were subject to charges of incompetence as well. The inspector of the Reformed school of Waldangelloch complained in 1810 that "even the pupils in the highest division [could] not read fluently, correctly and with expression."[24] A Catholic deacon reported on the occasion of his visit to Sinsheim in 1817 that the teacher was neglecting to maintain a truancy register and that "children who have attended the school for two years [could] not even syllabicate and others who were enrolled since All Saints' of the [previous] year [did] not have any knowledge of the first letters of the alphabet. . . ." The deacon also commented on the arithmetic abilities of the pupils: only ten of the sixty-seven pupils in the lower division could count to a hundred; in the upper division, only two knew how to divide, and many did not know their multiplication tables.[25] The general tenor of complaints in Baden suggests, however, a higher level of expectation concerning teachers' abilities. And there were a large number of applicants looking for teaching posts during the first half of the nineteenth century; a vacancy in a lucrative post would bring a swarm of applications. There were about two dozen applicants for vacant posts in Heidelberg and Handschuhsheim in the 1820s. The Evangelical post in Schriesheim was apparently considered a plum; there were dozens of applicants for it on the several occasions it fell vacant.[26] This very competition suggests that school officials had a large number of options when selecting teachers for the more desirable posts, and so could afford to be particular. There is, nonetheless, a likelihood that the less desirable, poorly endowed rural posts were filled by candidates who might not have qualified in a more competitive situation.

Aside from alleged incompetence among teachers, inspectors were bothered by problems of occasional immorality or insubordination. Teachers were supposed to behave in a manner appropriate to their status as servants of the state and the moral order. And often they did not. Charges of drunkenness surfaced with some regularity. The schoolteacher Arnaud of Rustral was "accused of beating the children and giving himself over to drink."[27] In Kohlhof, authorities learned in the 1840s, parents were refusing to send their children to the schoolmaster because of his drunkenness.[28] Teachers were chided for undue violence of temperament; the *instituteur* Ducros of Sorgue, for example, appeared in one report as "a violent man with the very serious vice of losing his temper with the children."[29] In short, despite the large number of teachers who held classes in the communities of Vaucluse and North Baden in the early decades of the nineteenth century, state school officials continually argued the need for closer training, placement, and supervision of public schoolteachers. Teachers had to satisfy the increasingly rigorous standards of performance applied by central authorities and inspectors. The political and moral mission for which the teachers were being groomed entailed behavior of a certain kind; teachers had to be sober, strict without being brutal, disciplined, submissive to political authority, and respectful of the established religion of the community they served. Many of the teachers discovered in the inspection tours fell short on one or more of these criteria.[30]

To alleviate the problems of incompetence and indiscipline among teachers, and to regulate access to the teaching profession, state authorities began to intervene in the training and licensing of teachers. The precedent for state certification of teaching was old; as early as the seventeenth century, candidates for teaching posts in the Kurpfalz had been required to sign a pledge before taking up a post. In the pledge, the teacher promised to teach correct religious doctrine, to conduct the pupils to services, to respect the customary rules of behavior, and "to remain loyal and gracious toward the Pfälzisch Elector as his ordained higher authority."[31] By the end of the eighteenth century teachers were prohibited from practicing without a license from one of the state churches, and most public posts were filled by certified *Kandidaten,* many of whom had received their training in the new state normal schools scattered throughout the upper Rhine region. There had been a seminary for Protestant schoolteachers in Karlsruhe since 1768. Many Catholic teachers attended the *Lehrseminar* in Mainz until the opening of one in Mannheim in 1787. At the time of the consolidation of the Badenese state, official seminaries were established in Karlsruhe and Rastatt. Unauthorized teachers faced increasing repression in these decades, as evidenced in the controversies over the so-called *Winkelschulen.*[32]

Licensing of teachers came later to France. In theory, even during the ancien régime teachers were supposed to obtain authorization from the bishop. During the revolution, teachers had to arm themselves with certification of their civic-mindedness, but it was only during the restoration that state agencies claimed the authority to judge the teachers' competence and reserved the right to deny permission to teach. Despite the new legislation, clandestine teaching and teachers' evasion of bureaucratic regulation continued to be a problem for the Université. The debate over the freedom to teach without state interference remained politically salient throughout the whole of this era, since the church in particular was prepared to defend its right to run schools independently of the state.

Still, precedents were set. French authorities combined their new claim to the right to license with efforts to influence teacher training as well. Efforts to open normal schools during the restoration met with little success, but when départemental funds became available in 1832, the first state normal school in the département opened in Avignon.[33] The two-year course of study had modest aims. Besides applying themselves to the same basic elementary subjects they were going to teach, *élèves-maîtres* studied pedagogical technique, bookkeeping, elementary science, history, geography, and music in addition to the French civil code and government ordinances. State policy specified a limited education for *normaliens,* one that would be appropriate for their modest social origins and future expectations, even if the Ministry of Education was somewhat embarrassed by the forthrightness in this respect of the director of the normal school of Avignon, who wrote to the ministry in 1840 that

> if [normal school] education is not to be a dangerous instrument and is to be responsive to the needs of families and of the government, if it is to be in all respects proportionate to the needs of the schoolmasters who receive it and to the classes to which they will transmit it, such an education, we do not shrink from saying it, must be above all eminently Christian . . . because our young men, educated and poor, thrown into a society where the ideas of ambition, independence and revolt are so prominent, will be more susceptible than everybody else to the evil influence of the disrupters of order.[34]

The establishment of the normal schools, and the more forceful assertion of the state's right to grant and withhold permission to teach, soon began to have an impact on the composition of the teaching corps. *Normaliens* were more likely than other applicants to be granted brevets, certificates of competence to teach. There were sixteen candidates for the brevet in Vaucluse in 1837, and of them all seven non-*normaliens* were judged inadequate. One particularly promising candidate who had not had normal school training was given a scholarship to study in the normal school. All the graduates of the normal school passed muster, with the result, the inspector happily noted, of encouraging a rise in the number of applications to the normal school in response to "the severity shown by the commission in its examinations of applicants for the brevet."[35] When vacancies in teaching posts appeared, school administrators encouraged local communities to select normal school graduates. Université officials regarded this influence over the selection of new teachers as essential to their goals, since, as one inspector put it,

> it is essential that the teaching personnel be composed only of men who through their conduct and their knowledge can have influence over the populace and bring them to welcome instruction by making them aware of its advantages.[36]

In their inspections reports, inspectors applauded the progress they saw in the quality of teaching "principally in the areas where [they] had been able to place pupils of the normal school."[37] And for those teachers already in posts in the département prior to the opening of the school, there were special six-week improvement courses subsidized by the state. Several Vauclusan teachers took advantage of these courses and were rewarded accordingly. Simon of L'Isle-sur-la-Sorgue won several of the gold and silver medals awarded annually by the département to the best teachers; Meritan of Saignon was offered a post in the local branch of the Education Ministry.

A number of important steps were taken toward the transformation of the teaching corps into a body of professional and respectable state functionaries. A second leg of the program of reforming the classroom environment brought under official scrutiny the physical surroundings in the schoolroom itself and the manner of its organization. The deliberations of the Royal Council of the French Ministry of Public Instruction, which became the official guidelines for educational reform, presented the ideal. Classes were to be held in a large hall with a courtyard attached. There was to be placed "in full view of the pupils an image of Christ and a bust of the King bearing the inscription: DOMINE, SALVUUM FAC REGEM." The teacher's desk was supposed to be mounted on a high platform to facilitate surveillance of the entire class. On the walls there were to be affixed "placards on which were written in large letters the principal duties which the pupils had to fulfill." The classroom had to be swept and aired daily.[38]

The actual classrooms that inspectors entered during their early tours shocked them. The rooms in which children learned lessons appeared disorderly and bustled with many activities, particularly where they were located in a residence or public building, or where the teacher served as a secretary, tax collector, or artisan. The school of St. Saturnin, for example, was attached to the tax collector's office and was crossed continually by residents conducting tax business. In Bedarrides, in order to enter the schoolroom it was necessary to cross the billiard hall. In Gadagne the classroom "was very badly located, in the attic of the city hall with a low ceiling and too few windows and insufferably hot"; in Gignac, too, the classroom was in "a horrible little attic."[39] A survey of 1835/36 revealed that only nine of the twenty communities of the arrondissement of Avignon owned schoolbuildings. Communities in the arrondissement of Apt were even worse off; only six of the fifty communities there had special communally owned buildings for schoolrooms. School officials estimated in the following year that thirty-one of the communities without schoolrooms were either too small or too poor to afford them; seven were deemed capable but unwilling to build them; fifteen had apparently promised to begin construction in the near future.[40] Building the schoolrooms adequate to meet new standards was costly; over half of the communities surveyed estimated that they would need 3,000 francs or more to build or repair a school. The state made grants available to communities in need, but by the middle of the nineteenth century only four of the twenty sample communities in Vaucluse had buildings that the inspectors felt to be sufficient for local needs.[41]

Schoolbuildings and teachers' residences were significantly better in Baden. Many teachers' *Kompetenzen* specified that a house and a classroom were part of the reimbursement for the job.[42] That nearly every community had a schoolbuilding in the early nineteenth century is apparent from Heunisch's statistics for 1833. He indicated that the *Kirchensektionen* of the Interior Ministry administered 1,327 Catholic teaching positions and 1,000 schoolbuildings, and 570 Protestant teaching positions and 570 buildings respectively.[43] The quality of the buildings, particularly in crowded urban areas, was sometimes below standard. A professor of hygiene charged with building inspection in 1810 reported that one school in Heidelberg was "unfriendly, damp, dark and in a bad location" and another "had bad air because of the large number of pig stalls in the vicinity."[44] Still, complaints like this are rare, and available evidence suggests that most Badenese communities owned schoolbuildings that were generally considered to be adequate.

Whatever the condition of the schoolroom itself, the conduct of the classes held within it was more important. Educators were concerned with the orderliness of instruction, methods of teaching, and the content of lessons, more than they were with the character of the building. The stress on order and method only became more emphatic as the growing size of classes enhanced the potential for chaos. The population rise that swelled the numbers of young people in both of these regions, coupled with the measures taken to increase school attendance, produced a veritable flood into the classroom. The pattern of growth of Mannheim's school population suggests the dimensions this trend could take. In 1755 the Catholic pastor estimated that there were probably over a thousand Catholic children in the city, of whom at least four hundred were between the ages of five and twelve. At this time there were only two Catholic elementary teachers in the city, and the pastor was aware of the potential problem of encouraging all the children to attend.[45] As more parents began sending their children to school, complaints by the teachers of overcrowded classrooms became more numerous. The teachers maintained that "if the children [were] to be taught well and in an orderly fashion, there should be no more than sixty, or at most seventy children in one classroom and before one teacher."[46] By their calculations, the community needed six Catholic teachers. The Protestant teachers were no better off. The resignation of one of the city's Lutheran teachers in 1800 left the remaining two with more than a hundred pupils each. In 1811 the Reformed teacher was teaching 111 boys and girls.[47] As late as the 1840s, teachers in Mannheim still faced huge classes; one assistant teacher had 120 pupils, while another had 142—this despite the reform law of 1836, which had specified that 120 pupils was the legal maximum.[48]

Mannheim was an extreme case, but similar patterns were apparent in many other communities. In the town of Schriesheim the Reformed girls' schoolteacher had 120 pupils in his class in 1818, 150 in 1822, and 190 by 1831; he was granted an assistant a few years later.[49] In the Heidelberg suburb of Handschuhsheim, the Reformed teacher saw his class expand from 140 pupils in 1800 to 200 by 1820! At the time of the Evangelical union he was given an assistant, and by 1836 the two teachers had 280 pupils between them.[50] Even in villages like Daisbach, Ehrstadt, Sandhofen, and Wieblingen, classes grew to more than a hundred pupils during the early nineteenth century, when the effects of population growth and the enforcement of *Schulzwang* were not countered by any significant expansion in the teaching corps. The pupil-teacher ratio in the Badenese sample communities climbed from an already high seventy-to-one in 1800 to nearly a hundred-to-one in 1836.

The rising classroom population stimulated both measures designed to alleviate overcrowding and innovations designed to facilitate the teaching of large groups. Many of the larger communities in Baden instituted split shifts and reorganized classes to allow more time to teach the more advanced pupils. In Mannheim, Heidelberg, and Schriesheim, for example, late-eighteenth- and early-nineteenth-century reorganizations created the so-called *Elementarschulen* for six-to-nine-year-olds learning the ABCs and catechism, and the *Knaben-* and *Mädchenschulen* for ten-to-fourteen-year-olds learning Bible reading, writing, arithmetic, history, and geography.[51] Communities that were too small to support more than one teacher often resorted to split shifts. For example, in Mühlhausen the Catholic teacher had 147 pupils in 1813. He noted that even if he allowed each pupil one minute of reading aloud, the reading lesson alone would take two and a half hours, leaving little time for more advanced work. He wanted to institute a double shift, teaching more advanced subjects to pupils in the morning, and reading and spelling in the afternoon.[52] In Heidelberg, where the Reformed elementary school had grown to over a hundred pupils by 1815 and "would have been even larger," local authorities noted, "if [they] had not acted to prevent younger children from entering," the children were divided into two shifts, each attending classes for three hours a day.[53]

The subdivision of classes into groups with homogeneous skill levels was another method of facilitating the teaching of large numbers. The practice of subdivision had been in use earlier, but by the early nineteenth century virtually all Badenese schools had at least three *Abteilungen*, which, even though they met simultaneously in the same room, were pursuing different subjects. With greater regularity of attendance and the emphasis on orderly and methodical instruction, age ranges within each of these subdivisions narrowed as well. Classes were becoming "grades."

The French national directive of 1835 also included prescriptions concerning the organization of the class: each pupil was to have an assigned place; pupils were to be divided into sections according to their accomplishments; each section was to be kept occupied continually. The regulations claimed that "by constantly occupying his pupils' time, even the youngest, the schoolmaster will maintain order and discipline without resorting to too many punishments." The manner of address of the teacher was to be distant, dignified, controlled. The teacher was to refrain from all familiarity with his pupils; *tutoyant*, patois, and the like were outlawed. In fact, the best classroom order and atmosphere would be achieved if the teacher "[refrained] as much as possible from speaking, to give the different orders, instead [replaced] the spoken word with the signal."[54]

The suggestion to use signals calls attention to the sorts of innovations teachers and educational officials developed to create the desired order among the large gatherings of children. As in Baden, many pedagogic innovations served to increase teaching efficiency in a situation where the ratio of pupils to teachers was increasing. Classes in Vaucluse were smaller than those in Baden, but their growth during the early nineteenth century was even more dramatic, from an average of only about twenty-five pupils per teacher in 1800 to around seventy by 1836. As in Baden, the largest classes had 150 or more pupils.

Some of these new techniques had actually been developed during the ancien régime by the teaching orders engaged in teaching special classes for the urban poor. The Brothers of the Christian Schools had perfected the best-known and most imitated methods for teaching and disciplining large classes. Their "simultaneous method," a novelty in the late eighteenth century, involved teaching all the pupils in the class at once. Everyone's attention had to be focussed upon the lesson or recitation in progress, and a strict discipline was practiced to keep the lessons running according to plan. The brothers relied on an elaborate system of signals to maintain this discipline:

> two taps of the signal rod obliges the pupil to begin once again the word he has pronounced incorrectly and which he may say better the second

> time; if he doesn't improve after one or two tries, [the teacher] should then strike a single time with the signal so that the other children look up, and make a sign to one of them who is doing the same lesson to read the word the other has mispronounced.[55]

The use of signals reduced direct communication between teacher and pupils to a minimum; the children could be regimented through their day in school, following a strict schedule punctuated by the taps and angles of the signal rod. As the regulations cited above indicate, some aspects of the "simultaneous method" were adopted by later secular school reformers faced with the same prospect of large numbers of children in need of taming.

But there was in France a competing method designed for the same end. The monitorial method, known in France as the *méthode mutuelle,* was also developed by pedagogues interested in teaching large numbers of the children of the popular classes. According to this method, the teacher would teach student monitors, who would in turn teach their fellow pupils. Like simultaneous classes, those of the monitorial schools relied on a high degree of classroom discipline and strict order. Several monitorial schools were opened in Vaucluse, at first with apparent success. A. Pascal, who opened an *école mutuelle* in Avignon, reported in 1831 that

> the school in Avignon has grown since its opening last February to nearly 200 pupils; the classes are in constant activity; they are learning to read books and manuscripts, writing, arithmetic, French grammar, analysis, linear design, catechism, prayers and Christian doctrine. More than seventy of those who entered two months ago without knowing anything are beginning to read phrases and to write under dictation.[56]

Despite the enthusiasm reflected in the initial high enrollments in the monitorial schools, they quickly began to decline. Part of the cause for this was the political controversy they generated; the church was opposed to them because of their secular orientation and origins.[57] Still, the social and pedagogical concerns they addressed were persistent ones. The monitorial method does seem to have had a more lasting impact on the teaching methods used in other schools, and even the *Frères* adopted some of the techniques used in the *mutuelles.*

Thus as enrollments grew and classrooms were becoming more crowded than ever, pedagogic innovations were developed to meet new contingencies. The new forms of classroom discipline were strict and differed in character from the sporadic, largely corporal punishments of the traditional classroom. Educators of this period made strenuous efforts to limit the use of corporal punishment even while they insisted on the maintenance of order. Simultaneous response to

Figure 2
Lesson Plan of the Reformed School of Waldangelloch, 1811

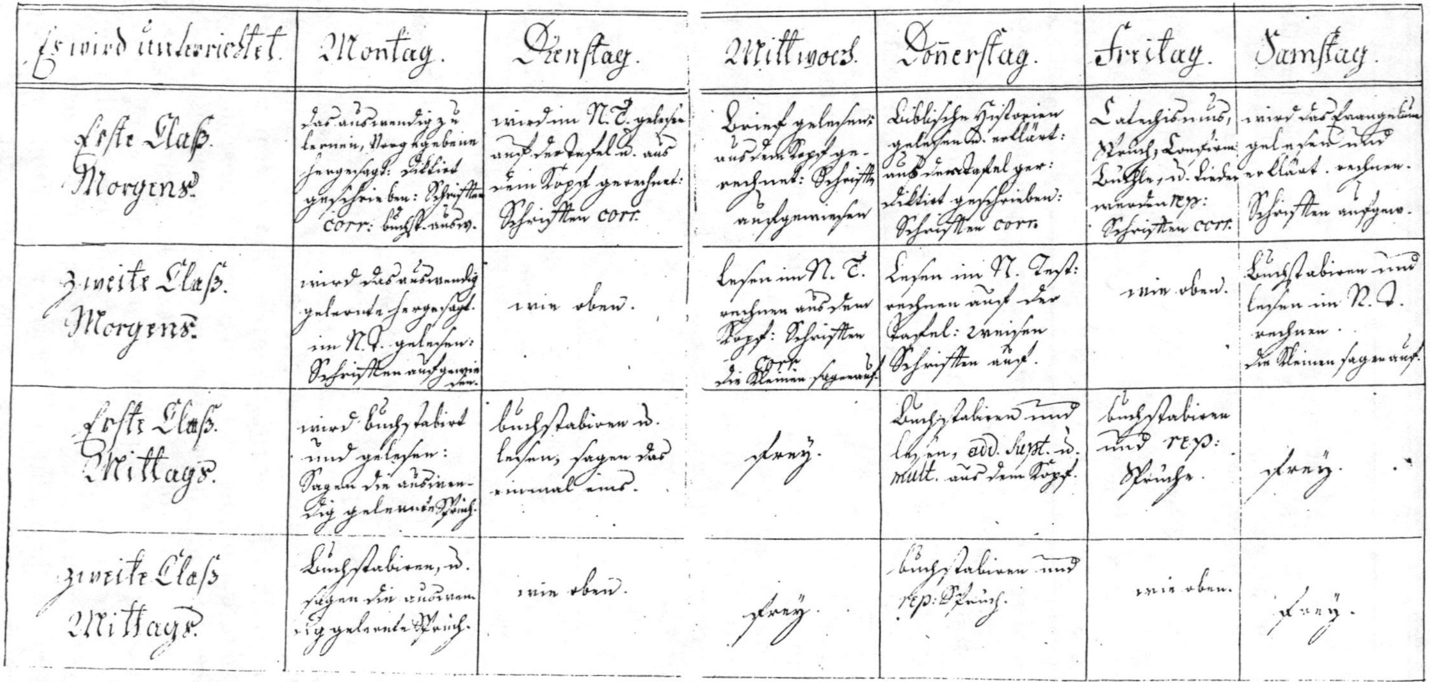

Es wird unterrichtet.	Montag.	Dienstag.	Mittwoch.	Donnerstag.	Freitag.	Samstag.
Erste Claß Morgens.	[illegible]	[illegible]	[illegible]	[illegible]	[illegible]	[illegible]
Zweite Claß Morgens.	[illegible]	wie oben.	[illegible]	[illegible]	wie oben.	[illegible]
Erste Claß Mittags.	[illegible]	[illegible]	frey.	[illegible]	[illegible]	frey.
Zweite Claß Mittags.	[illegible]	wie oben.	frey.	[illegible]	wie oben.	frey.

Source: GLA 229/109025

preestablished signals was becoming the rule of classroom conduct. The increasing size of classes, the crowded conditions in an atmosphere permeated with the new sense of seriousness and purpose ascribed to schooling, encouraged more and more teachers to adopt the new methods of regimentation. Unruly crowds of children whose wildness was tamed by random strokes of the cane violated the image of the school taking shape in the minds of reformist pedagogues and officials. But whatever the intention behind their introduction, the new methods must have meant that ever increasing proportions of the child population spent time in an environment governed by strict rhythms and formal rules.

But for all of their attention to the form of instruction, to enhancing their control over the classroom environment and over the teaching corps, state officials did little in this period to alter the content of primary education. Evidence about the subjects taught in the primary schools suggests that little had changed. The *Trivialschulordnung* of Baden for the year 1803 specified that "the subjects of instruction in the [elementary] schools must be a) spelling, b) reading, c) writing the German language, d) arithmetic, e) singing, f) Bible history, g) religious instruction."[58] Lesson plans show that these subjects were indeed taught in most classes. As in the eighteenth century, pupils progressed from spelling and syllabicating to reading and then writing. Commitment to memory of sections of the Old and New Testament remained an important part of learning. Existing lesson plans (see Figure 2, for example) indicate the number and spacing of hours devoted each week to various subjects. In Vaucluse instruction also continued to proceed from reading to writing to arithmetic, and the amount of tuition continued to rise with the pupil's progress. The reform laws of the 1830s attempted to establish a more uniform pattern of progression through these subjects and added grammar, history, and geography to the curriculum. Reformers also advocated the abandonment of progressive rates of tuition. But the inspection records indicate that in the 1840s this practice still persisted. Furthermore, even though all of the suggested subjects actually were taught in the more advanced schools, most teachers still offered instruction only in the basics of reading, writing and arithmetic.[59]

If the skills imparted in the schools were little changed, some administrative energy was applied to altering textbooks and other teaching materials. Books and other printed materials had been available in every community, but reading material considered appropriate for classroom instruction was rare. In part, the official concern with teaching materials resulted from the use of new methods. As long as teachers used the individual method, the actual text used for teaching each child could be different. Parents traditionally supplied their children with whatever texts were available. Simultaneous or monitorial teaching demanded identical texts. Books had to be uniform and available in large numbers. Paper and writing materials, as well as the array of new teaching aids like wall charts, maps, and blackboards, had to be provided somehow if the new techniques were to be successful. The teacher in the monitorial school in Avignon, for example, complained that "a number of pupils [were] frustrated to the extent of abandoning their education by the lack of the modest sums necessary for the purchase of paper, pens, ink and books . . ."[60]

But in addition to the simple practical problem, there was the issue of appropriateness. Inspectors condemned the practice of parents who "not wanting to buy readers for their children, gave them instead the sole volume that has perhaps been in the family for generations."[61] Books had to be up-to-date, geared to the pedagogic design of the school, and appropriately moralistic and patriotic. The French regulations of 1835 stipulated that children's reading materials should be things "that would be useful to them to know in the course of their lives like leases, bills and contracts," and examples of writing "should contain only those things useful to children, notably religious dogmas and precepts, the most essential rules of morality, aspects of French history most likely to inspire love of our country . . ."[62] In both Baden and Vaucluse, official readers began to replace or supplement the generally religious materials like Bibles, New Testaments, and devotional literature, once the mainstay of reading instruction. Church officials in Baden had long been involved in the publication of catechisms for use in the schools. By the turn of the nineteenth century, church bureaucracies began to organize the publication and distribution of ABC books and readers as well. The centralized printing and distribution of texts helped to bring about the desired uniformity. A rule passed in 1837 by the Evangelical *Kirchensektion* prohibited from classroom use all but the two authorized ABC books.[63] By the 1840s, school authorities were providing readers geared to meet the presumed learning capacities of different age groups. These readers were in use in the larger schools in the cities, although lesson plans suggest that the New Testament still dominated classroom reading assignments in the average class.

In Vaucluse, the teaching orders engaged in teaching the poor had set the precedent for centralized publication and distribution of texts, even as they had introduced pedagogic innovations. In Avignon at the end of the ancien régime, the Brothers of the Christian Schools made available syllable books for 1 sou, small catechisms for 2 sous, and copies of the *Devoir du Chrétien* for 13 sous.[64] Materials provided by the French state during the revolution followed this model to some extent. Revolutionary catechisms were the reading materials of many of the short-lived schools of the First Republic. For the next two decades, state efforts to influence the content of instructional materials were sporadic. Proponents of monitorial education were eager to provide the books and other teaching devices necessary for the method, but it was only under the July Monarchy that the state began its active intervention in the production and dissemination of texts. In 1831 state grants were distributed to each département for the purchase of textbooks. Arrangements were made with private publishers (most notably Hachette) to produce inexpensive texts and wall posters. Hachette's catalogue of 1831 included:

Alphabet et premier livre	at	50 F. for 500 copies
Tableaux de lecture		100 F. for ten sets
Arithmetic de Vernier		50 F. for 100 copies
Petit catechism de Fleury		62.50 F. for 100 copies[65]

The government itself purchased and distributed large numbers of these editions. In 1831 the minister of public instruction approved the distribution of five hundred thousand copies of the *Alphabet et premier livre* at government expense. This book was supposedly the most essential to classroom instruction because of its useful moral lessons and the uniformity that would allow teachers to make use of the new methods. In this most common of children's readers, French schoolchildren could read "prayers used by Catholics," essays about "the progress of civilization in modern times" and about "the advantages of our present condition." The latter essay told children that

> peace and tranquility are the desires of all France. It is they which have brought us the progress in our prosperity. Our fields no longer lie fallow. They are usefully employed by agriculture. The plowman and the artisan are as free as the *duc et pair.* They subject to the same laws. . . . Canals, bridges . . . schools have been built in all communities. . . . Man is more enlightened, happier. . . . Crimes are also less frequent.[66]

The département of Vaucluse received fifteen hundred copies of the new *Alphabet* . . . and three hundred copies of the catechism, which the prefect subsequently distributed in the communities of Avignon, Cavaillon, and L'Isle-sur-la-Sorgue. In 1837 the département received an additional two thousand copies of the *Alphabet* . . . along with reading charts, catechisms, arithmetic books, and one hundred copies of *Robinson Crusoe.*[67]

It should be noted that at the time of the 1833 inspection, that is, even before the massive distribution of reading materials by the state, twenty-four of the thirty-two schools inspected in the arrondissement of Apt reportedly used schoolbooks that were "uniform and sufficient." This would suggest that, even if some schools lacked books, the majority did not. The problem state authorities were trying to solve in their involvement in textbook distribution was not so much one of scarcity as unacceptability of existing resources. Local schools had teaching materials, but they were not adequate for the purposes of the state educational officials. And in order to supplement or replace existing resources, state authorities, particularly in France, had to put pressure on local communities to adopt innovations.

A pattern then emerges in the educational changes of this epoch. Local educational resources did exist in the early decades of the nineteenth century in many communities, but these were deemed inadequate by the new standards. They were more adequate in Baden than in Vaucluse, and more acceptable to inspectors with a new vision of what the schools were supposed to accomplish. But in many respects—in the recruitment and training of teachers, in the alteration of teaching methods and classroom materials—schooling in both regions came to correspond more closely to official expectations. In both regions classrooms were reshaped to some degree into the sort of environment that the new psychological, political, and social expectations for the schools demanded. The burden of school finance still rested on the local community, and that burden grew larger as new regulations concerning teachers' salaries and school attendance and classroom materials began to be enforced. But agents of centralized educational bureaucracies had managed to insert themselves into the processes of hiring, supervision, and training of teachers, had introduced programs of school inspection, and had begun to alter the character of teaching and learning. The side effect, not always intended but explicit in many of the reform measures, of taking the teaching of children out of the hands of parents and communities and putting it into the hands of educational experts increasingly likely to be trained, supervised, and paid by the state, was also apparent by the middle of the nineteenth century. The campaign to reform the schools was not an unopposed campaign, however, and the process of school reform was not one-sided. Teachers and educational officials often found themselves challenged by the communities and families they purportedly served. "The people" neither always approved of the changes nor silently acquiesced to them. And to get the other side of the picture, an examination of the evidence about the meaning of school reform to local communities and parents is in order.

CHAPTER 5

Community and School
Reform and Local Politics

THE IMPLEMENTATION OF THE EDUCATIONAL PLANS of state authorities was by no means automatic. The response of local communities to central plans and directives depended on local political machination, confessional and ideological loyalties, even village feuds. Still, some broad observations can be made about the responses of local communities to state efforts to reform the schools.

Again, regional differences are striking. In Vaucluse the role of the local political community remained important enough, its cooperation crucial enough to the provision of schooling, that local obstruction or alteration of state goals was a possibility and a fact; local political history is an important element of schooling history. In Baden, where the direction of the schools was depoliticized and bureaucratized through its subsumption under the authority of the centrally directed state church ministries, decisions about the schools were out of the hands of local politicians. Furthermore, the methods of financing schools, which remained, as I argued earlier, to a surprising extent continuous with those of the ancien régime, exaggerated the politically contentious character of schooling in Vaucluse, its relative isolation from local political routine in Baden. Schooling in Vaucluse continued to draw support from the local community budget; these funds were continually subject to debate. In Baden, where communities only gradually disentangled themselves from traditional methods of school finance, the burden of school subsidy remained both less tangible and beyond the reach of the usual routines of community finance. Schooling was not one of many competing public expenditures; rather, it was a separate matter altogether, handled by the religious rather than the political community.

In France, a series of laws spelled out community responsibility with respect to schooling. The Guizot Law made clear what the Bouquier Law and subsequent legislation had suggested: the provision of schools was indeed an obligation, and it was an obligation that fell to the local community. And the new kinds of schools envisioned by the state were no small burden. It is not too surprising, then, that school officials met with resistance in their efforts to persuade local municipal councils to allocate the funds necessary for the reform of the schools. This resistance was apparent from the earliest moments of serious reform effort. In 1830 the July Monarchy government passed as one of its earliest measures a law requiring all communes to hold deliberations concerning school finance. They were to report on the amount of funds necessary for proper schools, the amount appropriate for the teacher's salary, the current availability of local school funds, the number of poor children in the community receiving communal subsidy for their tuition payments, and projected charges. The response from Vaucluse was the classic refusal to comply that would become the French administrator's nightmare: communes either refused to see the need for reform of current practices or claimed that reform was impossible. The phrasing of some of these refusals suggests that local governments were experienced at sidestepping the demands of central state authorities. The council of the bourg of Bonnieux decided that

> the wholly paternal intention of [His] Majesty in issuing the above-cited ordinance was to provide the poor classes the means of instructing themselves; but in rural communes, and in this one in particular, any *ad hoc* expenditures would be useless because they would not fulfill [His] Majesty's goal. . . .[1]

Following this line of reasoning, the council claimed that any increase of the existing 50-franc-per-year subsidy of a teacher's rent would be pointless. The council of Mirabeau was no less adept in the exchange, reporting that it

> [recognized] the bounty and solicitude of [their] august monarch for his people, [wanted] to support insofar as communal revenues permit these benevolent intentions, but [considered] at the same time the interests of the taxpayers whose losses from the hail and the freezing weather of last winter have caused local revenues to decrease, [did not want] to resort to the extraordinary taxation [suggested for the support of schools by the new law].[2]

The council decided to vote a subsidy of 100 francs for a teacher who was already in the community, in exchange for his teaching eight pupils free.

These 100 francs voted by the council of Mirabeau were a more generous response than most. In the nine Vauclusan sample communities for which deliberations on this matter have been preserved, councils came up with one excuse after another for local inapplicability of the new law: larger communities usually claimed that existing school facilities were adequate; smaller villages pleaded insolvency or lack of need for schools. The council of Apt, for example, claimed it already had a school and had received a départemental allocation for the establishment of a new *école mutuelle.* Cucuron, Lourmarin, Merindol, and Sorgues claimed to have several well-attended private schools. The villages of La Motte d'Aigues, Cabrières d'Avignon, and Saumanes reported that they had schoolteachers who were acting as secretaries to their mayor and receiving a public salary in the latter capacity. The councilors of Saumanes reasoned further that it would be pointless to subsidize the schooling of the poor, since they would not go to school anyway. Finally, the tiny hamlet of Jonquerettes simply declared that it was impossible for the community to support a school.[3]

Even more annoying to educational officials than the local refusal to recognize the need to support school reform was the suspicious rejection of new educational subsidies offered by the state. In 1831 the académie of Nîmes received a grant of 60,000 francs to be dispersed among the départements in its jurisdiction for the establishment of public schools. The prefect of each département was supposed to collect information about communities still lacking a public school and select from among them a few ideal candidates for state aid. At first prefects were thwarted in the plan "because of the difficulty of obtaining the necessary information from local authorities." The prefect of Vaucluse finally suggested a few communes he considered to be likely candidates, with the commune of Vaugines heading his list. When apprised of its selection and the state's offer of aid in the project of establishment of a school, the municipal council responded:

> 1. there are not enough children here to keep a schoolteacher busy
> 2. people prefer to have their children work rather than sending them to school
> 3. there is no building appropriate to house a teacher
> 4. those fathers who want their children to receive some education . . . send them to Cucuron
> 5. finally . . . all the funds available to the community will be absorbed by the construction of a clock tower and a fountain. . .[4]

The council decided that its only contribution to the undertaking would be a subsidy of 50 francs for the schoolteacher's rent. This whole procedure was duly reported by the incredulous prefect, who claimed that the village had a municipal treasury of 8,000 or 9,000 francs. To him, the whole incident proved that "no one in the region knows how to appreciate the benefits of education and the favors the government wants to grant."[5]

Still, it is clear that some communities in Vaucluse did have financial difficulties. The very style of local finance in France, resting as it did on the combined use of income from communal property and essentially regressive taxes like the *octroi*, complicated public finance in regions like Vaucluse, where many small communities were without much property. The larger and wealthier communities could exploit their tax base for the support of schooling, but smaller and poorer communities could not. Contemporary commentators were not unaware of the problem. Guizot noted in a report written in the early 1830s that

> . . . in those former provinces which conquest or family alliance have most recently united to France—Champagne, Burgundy, Alsace-Lorraine, Franche-Comté—communities have continued to be the proprietors of their communal forests, whereas in the older France . . . these have been entirely lost. For communities in those provinces, [the woods] are a source of considerable revenue. It is with these revenues that they have built schoolhouses and paid the teachers . . . and the taxpayers have had to pay only very low rates.[6]

The fiscal disruptions of the revolution were also especially severe where there was no property to back subsidies. Without traditional procedures or endowments to fall back on, communities often preferred to allow a private teacher to set up shop wherever a livelihood was to be made. Even many good-sized towns let their public subsidies lapse during the revolutionary period and were slow to reestab-

TABLE 7
Number of Sample Communities in Baden and Vaucluse Supporting Publicly Subsidized Elementary Schools, 1780–1840

A. Vaucluse	*Number Having Public School in:*					
Size of Community	*1780*	*(n)*	*1810*	*(n)*	*1840*	*(n)*
Less than 2,000	15	(16)	1	(13)	13	(13)
More than 2,000	2	(2)	3	(4)	7	(7)
Total	17	(18)	4	(17)	20	(20)
B. Baden						
Less than 2,000	12	(14)	16	(16)	14	(14)
More than 2,000	2	(2)	3	(3)	6	(6)
Total	14	(16)	19	(19)	20	(20)

lish them. (See Table 7.) Records for the town of Sorgues, for example, indicate that there was no public expenditure for schooling between 1792 and 1808.[7] Only five of the twenty Vauclusan sample communities were providing for schooling in their annual budgets in the early 1820s, whereas at least fifteen had done so in 1780.[8]

The state's insistence that communities fund schools could not alone overcome these material problems. Implementation of the plan to make a school available to every community of necessity entailed central subsidy of the smallest and poorest. It was only through state subsidy that the minimum salary for an *instituteur* could be provided, and it appears that state intervention eventually brought about the establishment of schools in communities where formerly there had been none. In four of the six Vauclusan sample communities that had begun receiving state educational subsidies by the 1840s, there had been no school a decade earlier.[9] If the cost of community-subsidized schools was not the only obstacle to the success of school reform in Vaucluse, it was certainly a factor.

The stability of arrangements for the support of schooling and the relative abundance of resources in Baden contrast as markedly in the early nineteenth century with those of Vaucluse as they had in the eighteenth. The *Kompetenzen* reports of this later epoch illustrate that sources of support for schoolteachers had changed little since the old regime. A schoolteacher from the village of Waldangelloch calculated in 1802 the proportions of his income derived from various sources and showed that only about a tenth of his income of 230 florins or so came from his cash salary. An additional quarter of his income resulted from tuition fees, but the remainder came to him in the form of land or payment in kind. The value of the land alone accounted for a third of his "living."[10] Even in the middle of the nineteenth century, virtually all of the teaching positions in the Badenese sample communities endowed their holders with a plot of land; most paid part of the salary in kind. As late as the 1830s, cash salaries of more than 50 florins were rare except in the cities.[11] *Kompetenzen* reports and communal budgets also suggest the importance of *Bürgergenuss* made to pastors and teachers; these grants of rights of access to common lands and public fields were the subject of contention in the 1820s and 1830s as population growth in the villages made these lands more desirable and valuable, but they remained a central part of the teacher's income.[12]

Still, the whole tithe system that underlay teaching arrangements did succumb to the program of *Vormärz* reform. Gradually the whole structure of finance of schools was changed, as tithes were commuted along with the commutation of servile dues in the *Vormärz* decades.[13] Communities were authorized to buy out the claims of titheholders by paying them a sum equal to twenty times the annual income from the tithe. These payments were made through public debts contracted by communities and paid off over the course of fifteen or twenty years. Still, the long persistence of these older means of finance of schools allowed the reform of the schools to take place without imposing sudden new demands on communal finance.

The fiscal problems that plagued many communities in Vaucluse were thus avoided in Baden, but that is not the whole story of the relatively smooth schooling of the Badenese people. The nature of local political arrangements, and the persistence of the strong role of the religious community despite the secularization of the Napoleonic era, meant that the potential for political pressures to affect local schools was small. Church authorities supervised the schools; the political community was, to all intents and purposes, out of the picture. The system was not unchallenged. A continuous if sometimes subterranean movement among *Vormärz* liberals, many of whom were teachers, to make the schools into public institutions in the full sense persisted throughout the period.[14] But the schools remained insulated from the pressures that control by the political community would have entailed. Those who ran the churches—elders and professional church bureaucrats—also ran the schools. And those who remained outside of organized church life had no place in the cultural life of the Badenese community and no link to the schools.

The significance of this organizational feature becomes clear when contrasted with the situation in Vaucluse, where the schools were ultimately the responsibility of the local political community. Decisions about schools—not only about their establishment and financing, but also about their personnel, curricula, and clientele—were to a significant degree resolved through the political routines of communities. Sometimes that meant that grandiose state plans fizzled in the face of local opposition or local insolvency. Sometimes they were altered to suit the local notables or *coqs de village*, the wealthier peasants who often dominated local municipal councils. The social character of this opposition has to be taken into account in any assessment of the role of local government in school administration. There certainly are indications that local ruling cliques did not always share the enthusiasm for popular schooling exhibited by the central state authorities.

One Vauclusan schoolteacher, in writing to his superiors in 1831, claimed that the population of his region was without instruction "for want of principle." To clarify what he meant, he elaborated:

> *curés, seigneurs* and a few *bourgeois* . . . deprive the agricultural population of all instruction except that which leaves them in complete ignorance of all civilized principles, thus assuring themselves in their administration the means of containing opposition to their administrative acts, at which they are only too effective since in general it is impossible to elect councils capable of watching over the interests of all.[15]

He then suggested that the only way to get around opposition of this sort was to create communal endowments designated in perpetuity for educational purposes and immune from political machinations. (In other words, precisely the same system of school finance that prevailed in Baden.)

Obstinacy among local notables and hostility on their part to the educational program of the state was a constant problem for educational authorities. Not only were their reforms blocked, as they saw it, by local elites who saw in public education only its cost in terms of higher taxes, but they also had to cope with the systematic and principled opposition of the local groups opposed on religious and political grounds to the particular kind of education advocated by the Université.[16] Vaucluse was, after all, a center of legitimist and ultramontane opposition; Avignon was a capital of the Jesuit underground.[17] Hostile to any program issuing from Paris in the spirit of liberal reform, entrenched or restored local conservatives used their power to oppose the local takeover of the schools by the state. And none of the bureaucratic structures established by the various ministries of postrevolutionary France altered the dependence of Parisian planners on the cooperation of local communities both for funding and for administering their programs.

One method of subverting the reforms was to cause the public schools to fail. The more comfortable parents could choose to keep their children in private schools, while the *école communale* bore the brunt of the schooling of the poor. The results could be disastrous for the public school when the teacher was dependent on tuition payments. In Pertuis, for example, the inspector noted in 1835, the "least wealthy members of the artisanal classes and a minority of the *cultivateurs*" sent their children to the public school, while the children of "comfortable families" attended the free private school of the Brothers.[18] In this particular case, the Brothers' school, originally destined to be free schooling for the poor, was certainly serving as an ideologically preferable alternative to the public school for those who could have afforded to pay tuition. Behind the choice of the comfortable families of Pertuis to avoid the public school lay, no doubt, both a commitment to Catholicism and a suspicion about the modern, secular, and liberal education offered in the *école publique*.

The Catholic and legitimist cause had a natural agent in the local *curés*. They could be neither ignored nor trusted by Université officials, but they and their lay allies could be counted upon to disrupt secular education wherever they held power. The influence of *curés* in the villages, and their opposition to the *instituteurs*, is legendary. The political legacy of a revolution that had linked Jacobinism with anticlericalism on the one hand, and legitimism with Catholicism, on the other, could not help complicating reforms such as those proposed by the French educational ministry of the July Monarchy. This was especially obvious in regions like Vaucluse that were already so polarized along religious and political lines. The controversies produced by these interrelated religious and political antagonisms are best illustrated in the long battle between the *amis des frères* and the proponents of *enseignement mutuel*.

The Brothers of the Christian Schools had been restored to their teaching posts in many Vauclusan communities soon after the Concordat. When the Université made it official policy in 1816 to encourage *enseignement mutuel*, the scene was set for the confrontations that would occur and recur in towns in Vaucluse and elsewhere in France for the next two decades. At first, the Frères reportedly held sway. One supporter of the *école mutuelle* wrote from Avignon in 1821 that "the Brothers' schools [were] wholeheartedly favored by municipal councils, and the monitorial schools, on the contrary [were] totally discredited by fanaticism exacerbated by ignorance."[19] Despite the national policy encouraging the innovative monitorial schools, the power of local government in school administration was sufficient to thwart Parisian will. The *conseil général* of the département issued its own statement on educational policy in 1821, in which it gave priority to teaching by religious orders—this several years earlier than a similar policy switch in the national educational bureaucracy. The 1821 decision declared:

> in a monarchial and Christian state public instruction must in its essence be religious and monarchial, and if the monarchy is hereditary, political instruction must be based on the doctrine of legitimism. . . . Where can one find a sufficient guarantee of uniformity of principle, of belief and of religious and political doctrine? How can the danger be avoided that each individual employed in public instruction takes with him his individual spirit, his own thoughts and substitutes his personal opinion for unchangeable doctrine? Only teaching orders can avoid this danger. . . .[20]

In the wake of the *conseil*'s decision, and with the encouragement of generous grants from the département, towns began to replace *mutuelle* schools and other secular institutions with schools run by religious orders. The public subsidy of secular schools stagnated throughout the 1820s as more and more communities put their funds into religious schooling. Only in 1830, when the July Revolution brought a changeover in départemental and local, as well as national, government personnel, did the balance shift once again in favor of secular education. The *conseil général* began to encourage *mutuelle* schools and to bestow its grant money on them.

But the local supporters of clerical education were by no means silenced. If they lost their majority on many municipal councils in 1830, the regrouping of a new coalition favoring religious education was soon apparent in many communities. In Sorgues, for example, the municipal council continually debated the issue of support for the secular or religious school. The Brothers had remained in the commune with the support of private donations after their public subsidy was withdrawn in the early 1830s, but their cause was championed again later in the decade by some "new municipal councillors [who] along with a few older ones now make a majority who wants but one school—that of the Brothers."[21] By the end of the 1830s most of the *écoles mutuelles* of Vaucluse had been suppressed by what one member of their sponsoring organization, the Society for Elementary Instruction, termed "a permanent Carlist and sacerdotal conspiracy."[22] The dispute went beyond the walls of the municipal council chamber into the pulpits and the streets as well, where children from the rival schools engaged in name-calling and stone-throwing. The issue was a burning one, and the defeat by the end of the 1830s of the proponents of secular education was one of the earliest indications of the increasingly conservative character of the July Monarchy government.[23]

For if the issue of church domination over the schools was a burning one to many people in the South—to both the radicals who identified with the Jacobin past and the legitimists who opposed the July Monarchy government as too liberal—Université officials were not insistent on the point. Official policy recognized the importance of lay instruction, but the Ministry of Public Instruction was, in the late 1830s, no longer ardent in its defense of secularism. Many officials were inclined to see the inherent usefulness of the religious schools and were becoming short-tempered with the more radical proponents of lay education. State officials decried the perpetual squabbling over the issue that was so disruptive of public subsidy of schooling. Vauclusan inspectors of the later July Monarchy period, although clearly favoring *normaliens* in their reports, usually granted both religious and lay schools a place in the public educational scheme. Religious schools were best suited for the poorer of the urban popular classes; lay *instituteurs* could teach more advanced urban pupils and the rural communities. The prime concern was that some sort of state-approved schooling be made accessible to all, and that the educational laws of the state be obeyed. From the administrative perspective, local political battles, the persistence in seeing these issues in ideological terms, only made the task at hand more difficult. Inspector de Bayal summed up this emergent moderate position when he wrote in 1839:

> I am inclined to deplore simultaneously . . . both the intrigues of a few fanatics . . . and the calumnies of those who see a conspiracy against national ideas in the respect of any religious ideas. . . .[24]

The debate between proponents of lay and religious schools and the closely related political struggle that so complicated the history of education in France was far less significant in *Vormärz* Baden. A debate took place at the theoretical level, but the effective control over schooling held by the state-church bureaucracies, and the insulation of the schools from local political disputes, kept the debate largely theoretical.[25] The fact that the schools were administered separately by each religion did raise practical difficulties. The small Reformed community of Daisbach, for example, insisted on having its own teacher, even though church officials claimed that the expenditure for so few children was unwarranted. The same was true of the tiny Catholic community of only five families.[26] The Protestant Union of 1820, which combined the resources of the Lutheran and Reformed Churches, alleviated many of these sorts of difficulties in smaller communities of these two faiths.[27]

Jewish communities presented difficulties of their own. Most of them were too small and too poor to support separate schools, but as part of the assimilation campaign, all Jews were required either to send their children to Jewish schools or to Christian schools. By 1827, the private education of Jewish children was outlawed. Five years later only four of the ten sample communities having Jewish populations had actually opened Jewish public schools. In the rest, education in the Christian schools was the only option available to Jewish parents. Some Jewish families resisted the forced assimilation, even where a teacher of their own faith was provided. The Jewish teacher at Neidenstein, for example, complained that

> the community here is unspeakably opposed to accepting a public schoolteacher. The wish to interfere with me in my official capacity, arising from earlier habits of unfettered will and so injurious to the child's own welfare, is manifest among many members of the community.[28]

Only rare complaints like this have overtones of that religious opposition to state school plans so manifest in Vaucluse.

Competition among the diverse religious groups that shared the same political community also sometimes complicated local arrangements with teachers. Disputes over the allocation of the communal supply of firewood, the right to bell-ringing perquisites, and the like aggravated interconfessional relationships and annoyed administrators and teachers. These annoyances fed into the movement for secularization that persisted throughout the first half of the nineteenth century, a movement organized for the most part by teachers seeking emancipation from clerical supervision. By the late 1840s some communities were beginning to request the union of their separate schools into *Communalschulen* modeled on the French primary schools. The Evangelical majority of Neidenstein submitted such a proposal in 1845, since they claimed it was absurd for so small a community to have three schools. Many similar petitions appeared in 1848, although religious minorities, especially Catholics, were often opposed to the idea of *Communalschulen.*[29]

These problems originating in the religious administration of the schools and in the religious differences within communities in Baden remained unresolved as long as the churches retained their position in school administration—that is, until the reforms of the 1860s and later. Nonetheless, as much as the system violated the principles of its progressive critics, the contrast with Vaucluse makes it clear that the subsumption of school administration under the church bureaucracies effectively insulated the schools from the consequences of political conflict over them. By settling with the churches, the Badenese state had avoided creating a potential competitor in the field of education. By keeping the administration of the schools out of the hands of the political communities, the administrators of the state churches sidestepped local opposition or indifference to their plans for the schools.

The comparison of the connections between schooling and local political life points to some ironic conclusions. The relative stability and comprehensiveness of the Badenese school system seems to have depended upon the conservative character of fiscal and political arrangements in support of it. Because traditional forms of finance were not dramatically disrupted during the early industrial epoch, because local politics were not really allowed to intrude in the process of school provision, schools were permanent, secure, unchallenged. In Vaucluse, in contrast, not only did the dramatic upheavals in national politics affect local political institutions, administrative techniques, and sources of funding, but even local political conflicts could be translated into a threat to or interruption of public subsidies of schooling. This contrast certainly undermines any simple association between educational expansion and political development.

But from a different perspective, this apparent irony disappears only to be replaced by another, deeper irony. There is evidence to suggest that even if local politics had been more democratic in Vaucluse, it is by no means certain that indifference or opposition to the state school program would have disappeared. For this opposition was not simply the product of obstruction on the part of local notables; it was shared by many of the people toward whom the reforms were directed. Nor can we leap to the conclusion that the people of Baden were necessarily better off for being better "schooled." Certainly educational reformers and advocates assumed that the people were improved through schooling. But the people had their own perceptions about schooling, their own interests to pursue. And, as the next chapter will indicate, these did not always correspond with the agenda of the politically dominant classes, whether in their own communities or in the capitals of state.

CHAPTER 6

The People and the Schools
The Role of Schooling in the Popular Family Economy

THE HOSTILE RESPONSE TO SCHOOL REFORM ON the part of many local notables was perhaps predictable. But educational authorities may well have hoped that once good schools were available, the people would take to schooling with enthusiasm. That turned out not to be the case. Many parents, apparently more in Vaucluse than in Baden, seemed to be strangely indifferent to the potential blessings of education. The reports of inspectors and teachers record a litany of complaints on the topic and a persistent official effort to describe and account for this presumed obstinacy or irrationality. Certainly a number of possible explanations came to mind and appeared in educational communications: because the people were as yet unenlightened and unrefined, they were unable to appreciate the value of the improved schooling offered them; because they themselves were so poorly educated, they were unable to perceive the advantages for their children of the new institutions; precisely because of their long history of moral inferiority, the people were trapped in a vicious cycle of ignorance rooted in a popular culture for the most part indifferent to learning. The cycle needed to be interrupted through intervention on the part of the educated. In Vaucluse, where reformist educational officials encountered hostility, suspicion, or indifference at every turn, authorities were nonetheless constrained in their response to it by their own reluctance to coerce. Badenese school officials had more direct means at their disposal for circumventing or countering obstinacy in the populations they administered, but they, too, have left records that suggest that parents were sometimes recalcitrant, despite the penalties, when it came to sending their children to school.

These recurrent official complaints about parental attitudes toward schooling do offer some entry into popular interests. To be sure, the perspective is a distorted one and must be interpreted with due caution. Still, the evidence supplied by administrators suggests that many of the people must have held views about schooling that diverged from the official view. And, what is more, this divergence of opinion became increasingly troublesome to authorities as their commitment to universal schooling increased.

There was a certain irony in the popular response to the call to universal schooling. During the ancien régime, the campaign for improved popular education had been directed as an appeal to monarchs and aristocrats on behalf of the uneducated masses. It was the elite who needed convincing that they had nothing to fear from popular schooling. Now that the state was openly committed to the spread of schooling, the campaign had shifted ground. One inspector of the académie of Nîmes noted in 1837:

> for a long time now the poor and humble classes of society have asked to be permitted to enlighten and better themselves, to grow intellectually and morally; [those in power] always pretended not to understand needs of this sort, and refused to satisfy them. . . . [Now] the words Instruction, Popular Education are on all lips. The movement, the impulse, as they say, comes obviously *from above.* Is it the case that the classes who are the object of so lively and so general a solicitude understand the value of this benefit whose enjoyment we want to assure for them? Do they accept with enough rapidity and gratitude the sacrifices that are made for them in the name of a goal so elevated and so selfless? Now, does not the resistance come *from below*?[1]

As efforts to provide wider access to improved schooling began to have some impact, the resistance from below became more apparent and more troublesome. This inspector, like many other *universitaires* "could not help being profoundly affected by the coldness with which our own people still accepts that for which it has so pressing a need and which is so generously offered."[2] Early efforts to reform the schools and to bring all of the children into them produced a discouraging realization: the people could not be counted upon to be voluntary and enthusiastic partners in what school reformers regarded as their intellectual and moral improvement.

Popular indifference to schooling had troubled school administrators for as long as authorities had regarded schooling as a duty incumbent upon all.[3] Records of the drive toward universal attendance, already under way in the late eighteenth century in southwestern Germany, reflect the running disagreement between parents and school officials. An ordinance proclaimed in the Kürpfalz in 1751 berated Catholic parents who "out of pure stinginess, in order to save school fees and firewood, condemn their children to irreversible damage to body and soul" by keeping them out of school. The edict set stricter punishments for truancy.[4] As efforts to corral children into schools became more intense in the following decades, Reformed and Lutheran authorities issued similar ordinances condemning parental negligence of schooling. The pastor of Heddesbach reported that in 1807 parents were still abusing and exploiting their children by making them tend flocks during church and school hours.[5] The pastor of Daisbach complained several years later that truancy was inordinately high in his parish, and that the payment of truancy fines was not being properly enforced.[6] Still, despite the persistence of complaints of this sort into the nineteenth century, it is clear that most Badenese children were enrolled in school by the early nineteenth century and attended class for at least part of the year. (See Table 8.)

In Vaucluse, on the other hand, school administrators encountered a population singularly unresponsive to the attraction of primary schooling. One inspector lamented in 1837:

> one of the biggest obstacles to primary schooling is the lack of enthusiasm for sending their children to classes which the poorer classes of the villages and the rural population exhibit. . . . there are parents who, even though aware of the usefulness of instruction, still prefer to put their children to work for even a small profit rather than to send them to school. For these people, the present moment is everything; the future of their families is nothing because they don't see it or are afraid they won't profit from it.[7]

School inspectors in Vaucluse continued to complain throughout most of the nineteenth century about the apparent shortsightedness of peasant parents. Often, inspectors were convinced, parental indifference toward schooling was more the product of benightedness than of poverty. One inspector noted that *cultivateurs* from Pertuis refused out of sheer "insouciance" to see the need for schooling; very few parents could actually demonstrate the need for the pittance their

TABLE 8
Proportion of Estimated School-aged Population* Reportedly Enrolled in School during the Wintertime in the Sample Communities of Baden and Vaucluse, 1800–1840 (Weighted Means of the Communities in Each Size Category)

A. Vaucluse	*Proportion of school-aged children enrolled:*	
Size of community	*Around 1800*	*In 1836/37*
Less than 2,000	25%	41%
More than 2,000	24	47
B. Baden		
Less than 2,000	92	87
More than 2,000	72	96

*For a complete description of the method of estimation, see Appendix II.

children were capable of earning. In La Tour d'Aigues, the small *cultivateurs* who comprised the majority of the population "couldn't begin to understand" the importance of schooling.[8] Local supervisors in the community of Jonquerettes reported in 1834 that the reasons for absenteeism were the "negligence, ignorance, and greed" of parents.[9] Their findings were echoed in a départemental survey of the late 1840s, which found that the overwhelming cause of persistent absenteeism in Vaucluse (cited in the cases of 760 of the 1101 absentees in the arrondissement of Avignon and 371 of 778 in Apt) was "parental indifference."[10]

Negligence of the education of daughters was even more common than that of sons, even if the explanation for it was similar. The inspection reports of the 1830s claimed, for example, that in Cabrières "the inhabitants, believing that instruction [was] unnecessary for their daughters, put them to work at home from their early childhood on." In St. Saturnin, "the mothers, who all [belonged] to the agricultural classes and, having no education themselves, [didn't] know how to appreciate the advantages of knowing how to read their own language," were opposed to sending their daughters to school.[11]

These complaints, in an almost identical language, persist into the Second Empire. The Inspector Rouossi reported even as late as 1856 on the continuing struggle to get the children of Vaucluse into the schools. Among the difficulties he cited were:

> the poverty of the inhabitants; the too great avarice of some families who, without being constrained by need, want to make some profit

> from their young children; the indifference of some parents who do not want for their children a benefit whose advantages they cannot comprehend because they themselves are deprived of it.[12]

These comments suggest that the dilemma was that of convincing the uneducated of the value of education, since appreciation of it was purportedly beyond the capacity of the ignorant. Three years after the Abbé Rouossi wrote his report, the new Inspector Arnault was prepared to see this latter explanation of persistent evasion of the school as the major one. He wrote:

> the biggest obstacle, I could say the only obstacle which stands in the way of the progress of primary education, since poverty should not be considered a factor here, is the indifference of parents who don't want for their children an advantage the privation of which they themselves don't feel.[13]

Even where parents did send their children to school, they did not seem to understand the importance of regular attendance. They sent the children at their convenience, apparently unaware that such a pattern was considered to be subversive of the intellectual development of their children. Again, these sorts of complaints can be detected as early as the late eighteenth century in southwestern Germany. The Reformed Council of the Kürpfalz reported in 1765 that "Parents [were] not industrious enough in sending their children to school . . . [many children] spent hardly a quarter [of the year] in school."[14] A similar complaint the following year from the Lutheran Diocese of Heidelberg attributed to irregular and infrequent attendance the consequence that "children soon forgot what they had just learned during the short time in the classroom."[15] Officials in this region fought the common practice of summer truancy throughout the late eighteenth and early nineteenth centuries, but even as late as the 1830s there persisted complaints about communities like Bockschaft, where no one attended school during the summer semester.[16]

In Vaucluse inspectors saw "the desire, the need to make money [as] the cause of the fact that there [existed] not a single agricultural *commune* in which the majority of parents [consented] to deprive themselves of their children during the rural work season, or if a few [sent] their children to school during this time it [was] because they [were] too young to be of real use to them."[17] In one hamlet in the commune of Gordes, the teacher was reportedly annoyed by the practice of children "coming at different hours of the day, only to pass a few moments in school."[18]

The pattern of complaint suggests that many parents did not share the convictions of school authorities that regular school attendance was necessary for their children's well-being and did not see the role of schooling in their children's lives in the same light as the educational reformers. Parents themselves rarely left direct statements about their visions regarding schooling. Still, the shreds of evidence that do survive about what parents thought and how they behaved when it came to sending their children to school allow one to go a bit beyond the suggestive, if prejudiced, views of school authorities.

One useful approach is to reconstruct the "family economy" of the popular classes—that is, to examine the constraints within which families lived their lives and made choices about the allocation of collective resources.[19] The decision to send a child to school was ultimately a family decision. It was so more clearly in France, where there was no legal compulsion to send children to school before the end of the nineteenth century, but even in the German states, where such laws impinged upon family prerogatives earlier, parental compliance was by no means assured. The laws, and their enforcement agencies, as well as changing social and economic conditions, altered the context in which choices were made, but families were the final arbiters where the behavior of their children was concerned. And in this period of transition to industrial capitalism, accompanied as it was by economic dislocation and periodic crises that left many families on the margins of indigence, simple survival was the dominant goal influencing family strategies. In order to increase the number of family members able to contribute to the collective income, children, particularly older siblings, were usually set to work as soon as possible. The evidence suggests that in both Baden and Vaucluse patterns of family economy in the early nineteenth century left most families dependent to some extent on the labor of their children. For these families, work and schooling must have appeared as competitors for their children's time.

In Vaucluse nearly every rural family had a small plot of land for subsistence, but probably two-thirds of all peasant families had to supplement the living provided by their plots with income from work on more substantial farms or from cottage industry. Although the rural work force was not wholly dependent on wage labor, the prevailing low wage levels did depress living standards throughout the first half of the nineteenth century. The salaries of day laborers varied according to season, reaching a maximum at harvest time, when a man could earn 2 francs or more in a day and a woman or child could earn 50 centimes or even a franc. During the rest of the year, however, wages for agricultural labor were lower, plummeting during the wintertime, when work was unavailable. Yearly incomes were constrained by the rhythm and length of the agricultural work season, which varied in Vaucluse between 200 and 280 days in length. At these rates, a bachelor *journalier* could just about support himself through the whole year on his earnings from wage labor, and he would have had to spend a full four-fifths of his income on food.[20] Obviously, women and children workers could not be self-supporting, but were paid wages that presumed them to be contributors to a family wage. A smallholding *cultivateur* could manage somewhat better by raising food on his own plot, but at the sacrifice of time worked for wages or of longer workdays. Male *cultivateurs* often relied on family members for either the work on the family plot or the supplementary wage labor, and census returns attest to the universality of farmwork of some sort on the part of women in *cultivateur* families. Some rural families in Vaucluse still drew income in this period from domestic industrial work, especially in textiles, but returns were meager and diminishing as the rural industries confronted competition from goods produced in mechanized mills in northern France and abroad.[21]

In the towns of Vaucluse, in the mills where work was becoming available for rural migrants, wages were in the neighborhood of 50 centimes a day for women and children—that is, roughly the cost of a kilogram of bread. In the 1830s the wages of men in unskilled occupations ranged from 70 centimes to 1½ francs per day. Skilled artisanal workers usually earned more, between 2 and 3 francs a day.[22] Although a general, if slight, improvement in living conditions occurred gradually over the first half of the nineteenth century, most agricultural and industrial workers continued to live close to the margin of subsistence. The average diet was composed of grains, potatoes, and occasional vegetables and salt. With bread costing 30 or 40 centimes a kilogram, and meat more than 1 franc a kilogram throughout most of the period, the wage of a single male adult could not support a family. The bulk of the family income was spent on food, and the amount needed increased with family size. There was a built-in pressure on family members to work as soon as their need for food was significant. In fact, with the exception of the families of fully employed skilled artisans and the wealthiest peasants, families of the popular classes were dependent on the earnings of women or children simply to survive.[23]

Real wage levels seem to have been slightly higher in Baden, if scattered dietary reports are to be believed. Potatoes were the staple food of the poorer classes, but one contemporary observer reported

TABLE 9
Daily Wages in Baden, Early Nineteenth Century

Industrial sector	*Wage*	
	Male	*Female*
Agriculture		
Winter	24–36 kr.*	18–30 kr.
Summer	40–48 kr.	30–36 kr.
(With meals)	15–20 kr.	12–16 kr.
Cottage Industry		
Spinning		6–12 kr.
Weaving	to 1 gulden	
Artisanal crafts		
Journeymen	40 kr.–2 gulden	
(With meals)	18–30 kr.	

Industrial sector	*Wage*		
	Male	*Female*	*Child*
Factory Work			
Textiles	39 kr.–1 gulden	18–30 kr.	8–16 kr.
Tobacco		20–24 kr.	
Chemicals	20–24 kr.		

*Kr. = kreuzer. A gulden was worth 60 kreuzer. Fischer estimates that the minimum income needed to support a family of five was an average of one gulden per day.

Source: Wolfram Fischer, *Der Staat und die Anfange der Industrialisierung in Baden 1800–1850* (Berlin, 1962), pp. 362ff.

that meat eating was common among the better-off peasants and the families of skilled workers.[24] Evidence about agricultural and industrial salaries in early-nineteenth-century Baden suggests that wage workers in many industries had trouble subsisting even if all family members worked. Presumably families in these poorly paid domestic industries supplemented their industrial earnings with yields from family plots, but the low level of wages indicates the desperation workers in these industries must have felt. (See Table 9.) Wage rates suggest that only skilled artisans and the best-paid male factory workers could support families on one income; unskilled and semi-skilled workers, and even artisans in many industries, were dependent on supplemental incomes to raise a family.[25] As in Vaucluse, the largest part of the family income, probably around 70 percent or more, was spent on food. In periods of crisis that produced unemployment and inflation in food and fuel—crises like those of the 1790s, 1810s, 1830s, and 1840s—the threshold of subsistence was approached and crossed; poverty was transformed into indigence, which could affect a substantial proportion of families in areas like Baden, where the dense and growing population strained the agricultural productive system. In this context, it was natural to expect children to begin "earning their bread" quite early. Sending children to school when work was available was a costly, often unthinkable, decision. Even where parents valued schooling, economic constraints would have pressured them to choose the immediate earnings of their children over some future potential gain from schooling. And so the structure of work opportunities for children necessarily affected their patterns of school attendance.

Work was a natural part of a child's life in the early industrial epoch. Like their elders, children filled jobs specified and limited by their age and sex and their family's social position. Their work opportunities were shaped by the local economy. And daily and seasonal rhythms of work, and the timing of their entry into full-time employment, set the pace for schooling.

Agricultural families relegated a specific set of tasks to their children. In Vaucluse, children in communities like Murs and Puget, where herding was important, went out at an early age to guard the flocks. Young shepherds and shepherdesses were among the most irrepressible truants of the countryside. In Murs they attended school at most a few months of the year; of the schoolmaster's fifteen pupils in 1837, only four had begun to learn to write. Elsewhere, children simply ended their schooling entirely to attend flocks.[26] Children were crucial for the cultivation of mulberry leaves, the dyestuff *garance*, saffron—all major cash crops for the peasants of nineteenth-century Vaucluse as they adapted to the increasingly commercial agricultural economy. Children were also indispensable for the intense work of feeding silkworms, and the onset of this labor was the signal for "the desertion [of the classroom] which began in the month of May . . . and was prolonged until November on account of the harvest and the gleaning."[27] Gathering dung for the omnipresent *fumiers* was a children's occupation in regions like Vaucluse, where peasants relied heavily on fertilization. Agricole Perdiguier reported spending countless hours as a young boy in the area around Morières, collecting manure on the public road from Avignon to Apt.[28]

Rural children in Baden had work routines as well. Some children's poetry, written at the turn of the nineteenth century for inclusion in a primer, refers to their tasks: guiding the reins of horses and mules during plowing; gathering, tying, and stacking sheaves during harvest. The poems also allude to the industrial side of the rural economy. A poem entitled "The Evening" illustrates the complex economic roles played by various farm family members:

> The shutters are closed and the evening work brought out:
> The maid peels a turnip, the lad carves a wheel,
> Mother sews a seam in my coat, then teaches us spinning while she spins along,
> Father makes nails as though he were a smith.[29]

These poems are obviously idealized presentations, but more prosaic sources like the reports of *Industrieschule* inspectors verify the image of intense levels of economic activity of various kinds on the part of children. One inspector wrote in his report of 1808:

> the Odenwald communities are small, dispersed and usually poor. Woodworking serves as an occupation for boys while girls drive the spindle. In the regions of viniculture, carrying night soil into the vineyards keeps boys busy on good winter days while girls spin at home. Where the woods are interspersed with fields, the girls occupy themselves in winter with women's work [i.e., the needle trades] for which the growing of hemp and flax provide a natural opportunity, while boys make benches, baskets and pots during the time when they are not taking care of the cattle and the pigs.[30]

In Handschuhsheim, another inspector noted, children of seven and eight years of age were already finding employment in the regional putting-out industries, which produced scarves and handkerchiefs.

Still, despite the variety and large number of tasks that rural families needed to do, the rhythm of their labor was distinctly seasonal. As a result, a seasonal school attendance pattern prevailed in rural communities; parents felt more able to dispense with their children's labor during off-seasons. This seasonal attendance, and the obverse, seasonal truancy, had bothered school administrators in Baden at least since the mid-eighteenth century. The Reformed Council report of 1765 had explicitly acknowledged and criticized this custom:

> the old complaint about the children, or rather the parents, is still appropriate everywhere: the latter are not industrious enough in sending their children to school. For the most part they send them in winter, but in the countryside the youngsters are used to being employed from an early age in fieldwork and other kinds of work and . . . spend hardly a quarter [of the year] in school.[31]

Direct evidence of the persistence of this practice in the middle of the nineteenth century is provided by Vauclusan school-enrollment rec-

TABLE 10
Summer School Enrollment in Vauclusan Sample Communities according to the Size and Economic Character of the Community, Inspection Reports of 1837

Community size	*Summer school enrollment as a proportion of winter school enrollment*
Less than 500	72
500–2,000	64
2,000–10,000	79
10,000+	100
Economic Character of Community	
Exclusively agricultural	68
Small nonagrarian sector	68
Significant nonagrarian sector	72
Majority nonagrarian	96

Refer to Appendix II for a discussion of the sources and calculations behind the construction of this table.

ords, which by then distinguished between winter and summer sessions. As summarized in Table 10, the enrollment during the summer semester (April 1 through September 30) was related to the size and economic nature of activities in the community. School attendance followed a seasonal pattern in rural agricultural communities but not in urban communities. The same contrast distinguished the more industrialized arrondissement of Avignon, where summer school sessions enrolled 90 percent of the number of pupils enrolled in winter sessions, from the more agrarian arrondissement of Apt, where the corresponding percentage was 67. In their efforts to divide their children's time between work and schooling, parents in agricultural communities apparently resorted to a chronological division of the year into a season for work and a season for schooling.[32]

This pattern was both more necessary and more prevalent in Vaucluse than in Baden, since in Baden the summer sessions were quite short—often only an hour or two a day—and often the schools were closed during the busiest times. Records of a summer truancy case illustrate the logic of this compromise. In 1840, school authorities in Neidenstein fined a certain family named Maier 3½ gulden for the truancy of four children during the month of July. In the course of that month, two sons had missed thirteen days each, a daughter had missed eight days, and a third son, one day. In a letter asking for exemption from the fine, the father excused himself in the following manner:

> I am the father of eight young children, completely without wealth, yes, I'm even so poor that I've been excused from paying taxes. . . . My children missed school during the time when they had to earn their bread for themselves and their family, that is, during the harvest time when they were occupied with the gleaning.[33]

Normally the conflict would have been reduced. Maier, who was Jewish, was quick to point out that the Christian schools in the community were closed during the times of heavy agricultural labor to allow children to work. The fact that the Jewish school remained open appeared unfair to him, since it deprived him of the labor necessary to take advantage of his gleaning rights. His letter documents the rural dependence on child labor and its effects on school attendance; agricultural labor demands produced, in the face of institutional inflexibility, seasonal truancy.

Patterns of work for children, as for adults, were different in the towns and cities. The children of the urban populace had to find niches in the job structure wherever they could. Work for children does not seem to have been as readily available as it was in the countryside. Nor was the demand for child labor as markedly seasonal as it was in rural communities. Children did work at a variety of occupations. Boys were employable in the crafts as apprentices in their early adolescence. Younger boys found easy access to occasional labor as masons' assistants in construction work in the booming towns. Girls occasionally were apprenticed, but female apprenticeship had become rare. More frequently girls did home work in their own home or that of a domestic worker who had hired them as live-in help. When the so-called *Industrieschulen* were opened to teach needle crafts in communities in Baden around the turn of the nineteenth century, parents in many towns and cities were unusually responsive to the opportunity to send their daughters to them, since the skills they taught were the most lucrative available to the urban working woman.[34]

By the 1830s a new opportunity had appeared. In addition to working in the crafts and in domestic industry, urban children were beginning to find work in the new factories in both regions. A Vauclusan school inspector attributed the absenteeism of more than three hundred boys and girls of the community of L'Isle-sur-la-Sorgue "principally . . . to the fact that this *commune,* because of its waters, [held] a large number of factories. Children [managed] to find profitable work there and parents [preferred] sending their children to work to having them educated."[35] At the end of the 1830s, the *conseil de prud'hommes* of Avignon prepared a report on child labor in that city in anticipation of forthcoming governmental regulation. Their report noted that

> Girls, for the most part, are employed from their childhood on in the silk factories. They find work suited to their capacities and enter at the age of ten or twelve. Their salary is ordinarily forty or sixty centimes a day. The length of the workday is thirteen or fourteen hours, of which two to two-and-a-half hours are used for moments of rest and meals. The children employed in the factories generally belong to the workers who work there, to which others are added according to the needs of the different shops. Their education is generally quite neglected. They rarely go to school from the time they are capable of earning a small daily wage to help in their maintenance.[36]

Factory work had also begun to attract school-aged children in Baden. Industrial statistics collected by the state indicate that by the late 1830s there were already more than ten thousand factory workers in the state, of which some two thousand were children. Mechanized industry located in small shops employed an additional four thousand or so workers, most of whom were women and children.[37] In both regions factory children were a dilemma for school authorities. Their visibility and the inflexibility of their work routines made it especially difficult to combine their work with schooling. But most urban children who worked earned their pittances in ways that were less visible, less regular, and less lucrative. Street peddling of small items (matches and thread were common commodities sold), sweeping chimneys, pilfering were all methods of adding to the family purse. It should not be overlooked that older siblings, especially girls, were generally expected to watch over younger brothers and sisters to free their parents for other work. And in front of the churches in Vaucluse, at the taverns of Baden, the common presence of beggar children was a public reminder of the persistent poverty of many families.[38] Still, the evidence suggests that, despite all of these possibilities, and despite their ingenious efforts to find sources of income, it was the case that urban children, unlike their rural counterparts, were generally hard pressed to find employment, which no doubt lowered the opportunity cost of schooling in most urban communities.

Since the cost of sending an employable child to school was greater than that of sending one unable to work, patterns of child employment are reflected in a predictable manner in school-enrollment patterns. First, the sex typing of child labor made the work of girls less valuable than the work of boys. Some of the jobs boys commonly did—construction labor and field work, for example—were done outside the home and were relatively well paid. Among girls, except for those employed in the textile mills, most child workers worked at home at occupations with flexible hours and very low pay, or helped with household chores. In other words, from the simple perspective of their potential contribution to the family pool of labor or income, sending girls to school was generally less costly than sending boys. There was an opposite pressure operating as well, since it is clear that schooling was generally considered more valuable for boys, and the anecdotal evidence at least suggests that, where choices had to be made, applying resources for boys' schooling took priority over that of girls. This would certainly help to account for the consistently lower literacy among women in both of these regions, but most markedly in Vaucluse, prior to the school reform era. What is interesting to note is that once fines and other punishments for truancy were applied systematically and equally for the truancy of boys and girls—as they were in Baden around the turn of the nineteenth century—the old pattern was reversed. It became more costly for parents to keep their daughters home than to send them to school, since their earnings were not high enough to offset the truancy fine. The tendency for enrollments of girls to catch up with those of boys and in some communities even overtake them during this period is probably at least in part a result of the increasing application of truancy fines.[39] This is even clearer in the scattered truancy records (see below, Table 11), which suggest that girls were truant less often than boys.

In Vaucluse, where school attendance was voluntary, enrollment patterns continued to reflect the prevailing greater concern for the education of sons. This was especially marked in Vaucluse, which displayed a typically southern French pattern of extreme divergence between male and female literacy patterns. If anything, parents in rural communities perhaps relied more heavily on daughters than on sons for domestic labor, in order to make schooling possible for their sons. In any event, it was in the rural communities that sex ratios among enrolled pupils remained the most unbalanced.

The child's age was the second consideration in weighing the choice between work and schooling. Schooling was a welcome solution to the problem of supervision of children too young to work. A few rare testimonies in the form of parental petitions about schools make this clear. One of these petitions emerged from the controversy over the *Winkelschulen;* school authorities wanted to repress them, parents defended them. The city officials of Mannheim had fined the *Winkelschullehrer* Flees 10 thaler in 1741 for opening a school without authorization. In response to this official action, the parents of the children Flees taught addressed a petition to the Lutheran *Konsistorium*, asking for official recognition of Flees. In the petition, the parents claimed that they had hired him

> 1. . . . so that we could send to him particularly our very little children who cannot be accepted by the regular schoolteacher on account of their too tender years and because of the large crowds of growing children. . . .
> 2. because we would like to keep our little children out of the streets and safe until they are old enough to go to the regular schools; [and as an afterthought]
> 3. . . . because of his good method of teaching children. . . .[40]

The very popularity of these types of schools reflected the real need for care of young children, and controversies of this sort continued to occur in Mannheim and other towns into the early nineteenth century. A similar attitude is reflected in a petition by a group of Catholic parents who complained in 1750 about the poor quality of their schoolteacher. In the course of their complaint they remarked that

> of course, there are little children who are sent to the school but only with the idea of keeping their noise out of the house for a few hours a day; as for the older ones, no matter how unlearned they are, we are better off setting them to handicrafts rather than letting them waste their time going to school.[41]

Both of these petitions, then, suggest that schooling was a positive boon for families with very young children. It was only when a child reached an age when he or she could usefully be employed that schooling posed difficulties.

In the agrarian economy, children were put to work at a very young age during the times of intense demand for labor. Full-time work was taken up only after a child had had several years' experience with occasional labor. The most commonly cited age of entry into full-time agricultural employment is twelve or thirteen. In France the *première communion*, a religious rite of early adolescence, seems to have served as a rite of passage with regard to economic status and dress as well; its completion signaled the entry into adulthood.[42] In Baden the *Konfirmation* played a similar role, marking the end of schooling and the beginning of adulthood. The school system in

Baden was specifically oriented around this turning point; a decision had to be made at the time of the *Konfirmation* between work and advanced schooling of some sort for those "not required to devote themselves at this age to a practical occupation."[43] There was a lot of flexibility in practice, of course, especially in Vaucluse, but it was certainly customary in both regions permanently to withdraw most children from school by early adolescence and start them to work full time. The legal school-leaving ages in Baden were established with an eye toward practice: thirteen for girls and fourteen for boys. Early-nineteenth-century registers suggest that school leaving often occurred somewhat earlier.[44] In Vaucluse the employment of adolescents played a role in shrinking their schooling time, if inspection reports are accurate. The level of instruction in the village of Jonquerettes was low in 1802; the inspector attributed this to the practice of permanently withdrawing children from school at the age of ten or twelve. Half a century later, children in this farming community were still leaving primary school early to take jobs in the fields. The school inspector reported in 1843 that in another village the children of the upper two divisions had left school, while those in the third, who were seven or eight years old, "were probably destined to remain on the benches for another few years."[45] At the end of the 1850s it was still reportedly the case that "fathers were impatient to put their children to work, and those who [sent] their children to school rarely [left] them there after the first communion, the time at which they [were] employed in fieldwork."[46]

Entry into the urban labor force generally occurred at a later age. There certainly were some very young children employed in factories and mines; reports indicate that child employees of eight or nine years of age were not unknown in either region. But children in the industrial sector were typically employed later than those in agriculture. Jobs for children were more plentiful and diverse in farming. The only direct evidence about this, the French census returns of the early nineteenth century, suggests that children in agricultural jobs claimed to be employed (or, rather, their parents made the claim about them) younger than those working in other sectors.[47] Entry into industrial labor, especially the skilled crafts, seems rarely to have occurred before the mid-teens. Apprenticeship contracts dating from the late eighteenth and early nineteenth centuries substantiate census returns; a usual age of apprenticeship of around fourteen is indicated in them. Records about the apprentices who attended the Badenese *Gewerbeschulen* agree; there were some apprentices as young as eleven years old, but they were rare.[48] In sum, even though the more pronounced seasonality of work demands allowed protracted part-time schooling in rural areas, the ability of even the very young to find work in farming areas meant that schooling was more likely to be interrupted or ended early and that full-time schooling was a possibility only for the very young in rural areas.

The generally higher levels of school enrollment characteristic of the urban communities of Vaucluse, in comparison with rural areas, originate in part in the later age of entry into work in urban areas. (Comparative schooling trends in different types of communities are discussed more fully in Chapter 9.) But shreds of evidence from communities of all sorts do consistently support the claim that younger children were more likely to be enrolled in school and less likely to be truant than their older siblings. By and large, older boys were the most truant of all school-aged children, followed by older girls. Reports from a group of Lutheran parishes in north Baden for the year 1802 indicate that school enrollments amounted to about 90 percent of children between the ages of six and ten, but only about 75 percent of children from ten to fifteen.[49] The few surviving school registers that indicate the age and sex of truant pupils are summarized in Table 11. Unexcused absences, which were virtually always attributed to parental demands for work from their children, were gener-

TABLE 11
Truancy by Age and Sex in Several Communities

	Average number of days of unexcused absence	
Community	*Boys*	*Girls*
Waldangelloch, 1809/10		
Ages 6–9	31.4	27.2
Ages 10–14	49.1	42.6
(n = 145)		
Mannheim, 1811		
Ages 9–10	27.6	
Ages 11–14	36.4	
(n = 103)		
Sinsheim, 1812		
Grade 2		2.5
Grade 3		6.9
(n = 107)		
Mannheim, 1848–49		
Ages 6–9	7.1	17.1
Ages 10–14	15.0	7.9
(n = 108)		

Source: GLA, 213/2570, 229/109025, 235/22776, 377/966.

ally higher among boys than girls, and higher among older than younger children (with the single exception of the atypical Mannheim Poor School, with its curiously high level of truancy among its young girl pupils).[50]

In short, existing school attendance records support the contention that work and schooling were viewed as options between which the parents of employable children had to choose. The more likely a child was to find employment, and the needier his or her family, the more likely parents were to keep him or her out of school for work. Some schoolteachers and administrators were aware of the problem and understood the logic behind parental choices, even if they did not always sympathize with them. Schoolteachers from Wiesloch, in a petition complaining about the ineffectiveness of enforcement of school attendance maintained that fines and even jailing for truancy were not enough. "Parents who are fined," they claimed, "don't take it seriously enough and often say, 'I'll gladly pay six or eight Kreuzer for one day missed since I'll save the wages of a man for the day, which costs more' or 'my child gathers wood and that is worth a lot more.' "[51] French school officials occasionally offered a similar explanation for parental reluctance to send their children to school. An inspector of the académie of Nîmes, who worked in the département of Gard, adjacent to Vaucluse, wrote to his superiors in 1832:

> one cannot deny that in the populous industrial cities, as in rural communities, there exists a rather large number of families who can only survive by the product of the labor of all the members which make it up. Even the most modest salary that a weak child can earn, whether in the fields or in the workshops, becomes for them an indispensable necessity. . . . For these children, the school doors are opening in vain. . . .[52]

These latter observations state what the structural characteristics of the early industrial family economy can only suggest: in thinking about schooling, parents from the popular classes had to take into account the often critical contributions of their children to the family economy. The choice of work over school, even if it violated the vision of childhood and the new role of schooling in it promulgated by educational and social reformers, was often a rational and necessary one when the two occupations were in conflict.

In comparing the way in which parents in the two regions responded to the demands of the family economy, on the one hand, and the school authorities, on the other, one encounters something of a paradox. In both regions, all reports agree on family dependence on child labor. There is little reason to suspect that differences in school attendance patterns in the two areas can be attributed to essentially different economic roles of children. Nonetheless, it is clear that children in Baden were combining work and schooling more successfully than were children in Vaucluse, where the two occupations are generally presented as incompatible. Part of the difference, I have argued, can be attributed to the fear of truancy fines, but that is not the only factor involved. The Badenese school system also recognized the need for child labor and, to some extent, took it into account. This appears most clearly in a comparison of school hours in the two regions. During the ancien régime schools in Vaucluse generally met only in the wintertime and at hours set by agreement between the teacher and representatives of the community. Little evidence survives about the nature of typical arrangements, but a schoolday of three hours in the morning and three in the afternoon appears most frequently in the records. With the centralization of school supervision, the schoolday of six hours recommended by the education ministry became the norm, although each arrondissement was allowed discretion about the spacing of those six hours and the timing of vacations. In 1830 an act of the Royal Council of Public Instruction suggested class hours of eight to eleven in the morning and one to four in the afternoon. These same hours appeared in the regulations for the arrondissement of Apt a few years later in 1834. Even the *mutuelle* schools and the Brothers' schools designed to appeal to the poorer urban classes held to a six-hour schoolday. Schools were kept open all but one month a year. The only concession to the common reliance on child labor was the stipulation that the schools be closed for one week during the *vendanges.* Summer hours were as long as winter hours. In fact, the committee of the arrondissement of Apt actually increased the length of the summer sessions in 1847. According to the new regulation, classes would meet from April to August for four hours in the morning and four in the afternoon.[53] This may well have been convenient for parents with young children, but it must have made summer school attendance less likely for older children.

In Baden the early evidence suggests that a great variety of schedules were followed. In rural communities the school year traditionally lasted from St. Martin's Day to St. George's (November 11 to April 23). In urban areas like Mannheim and Schriesheim, schools were open year round for six hours a day.[54] By the early nineteenth century, schools met between three and five hours a day in winter and only one or two hours a day in summer.[55] The school in Daisbach, for example, met from eight to eleven in the morning and two to three in the afternoon in winter, and from noon to one for older children and one to two for younger children in the summer.[56] The state ordinance of 1803 in fact stipulated that, even though all communities were required to hold summer school sessions, the schoolday should be over early enough for the older children "so that a good day's time still remained for them to help their parents."[57] It is easy to see how this official recognition of the incompatibility of a long schoolday with familial demands for children's labor facilitated the combination of work with schooling.

But an additional obstacle to schooling, that of paying tuition fees, still confronted parents willing or able to dispense with their children's labor in order to send them to school. Because of the nature of support for schools in Baden, this obstacle was far less serious. Primary-school fees were relatively low in Baden. Late-eighteenth-century fees had been in the neighborhood of 1 gulden a year or less, or about a day's pay per child per year. Fees were especially low in rural areas, where parents had more difficulty raising cash payments. Around 1800, the Catholic schoolteacher in Handschuhsheim received only 6 kreuzer a quarter, or less than ½ gulden a year in tuition.[58] As late as 1813, the schoolteacher in Rohrbach was entitled to only ½ gulden per year for each child he taught. Some communities like Walldorf had even set up their schools as "free schools," where no tuition was charged. Fees in the towns and cities were significantly higher, but still moderate. Urban rates were typically 2 or 3 gulden a year. By 1836 a statewide minimum fee of 1 gulden per year per child was established, and there was a tendency for the community to take over the collection of fees, which made evasion more difficult. At all times tuition fees were supplemented by *Schulholz* or *Holzgeld* levies: children were expected to carry logs and kindling wood to school each day during the wintertime, or to pay a special fee for firewood.

In Vaucluse fees were assessed monthly and were high. Only during the early years of the revolution was free schooling generally available. Afterward, as before, only a specified number of the officially declared indigent were excused from paying tuition. At the turn of the nineteenth century, tuition fees ranged from 75 centimes to 2 or more francs a month; that is, parents had to pay around a day's pay each month for each child's schooling. Fees were generally rising during the first half of nineteenth century, but so was access to free schooling, at least in the towns. Many religious orders and some of the monitorial schools charged no tuition. In fact, by 1859 only about one-third of primary school pupils in Vaucluse, mostly in rural communities, continued to pay fees.[59] But until the proliferation of free schools in the 1830s and 1840s, the high fees were a serious drawback to poorer families.

Just how significant an obstacle they represented is difficult to determine. Contemporary observers did not always agree. One school inspector in Vaucluse deplored the high fees but felt that the need for child labor was so significant that even if the schools were made free in rural communities, many parents would continue to keep their children home.[60] Subscribing to the opposite theory, the mayor of St. Martin de la Brasque claimed that the declining school attendance in his community was the result of high fees. Before the revolution, he maintained, the commune had given a salary to the schoolteacher and required that he teach indigents free.[61] As late as 1834 there was still only one student in this community excused from paying fees, and this because of the goodwill of the teacher rather than by decision of the community. The roster of pupils in the village school included only the sons of property-owning peasants and minor notables. The poor were simply excluded from the school.[62] But even where arrangements had been made for subsidizing the fees of poor children, there were more poor than there were subsidies. In Lourmarin in 1834 only 75 of 127 children of school age were enrolled in school. Sixty-five school-aged children in the community were declared indigent by the municipal council, but no funds were made available for their schooling. In Lauris there were reportedly 128 children of school age, of whom fewer than half were attending school. Although 48 were judged indigent and an additional 12 deemed capable of paying only part of the fees, the municipal council authorized subsidies for only 20 children.[63] In commune after commune there were reports of the inadequacy or abuse of the subsidy system. Within the sample communities, a high negative correlation between the level of fees and the proportion of the reported school-aged population attending school suggests that fees were literally prohibitive in some communities. Obviously, the connection is complex; communities where fees were highest were also the smallest and poorest generally. It might be argued that the high fees were in some case as much a product as a cause of lack of interest in schooling. Still, the connection between high fees and low levels of attendance is strongly suggested by the cumulative evidence.

In Baden, where fees were appreciably lower, there is no detectable association between community-level attendance patterns and the amount of school fees. Still, even these minimal fees were a problem for the poor; the difference was that nonpayment of fees did not preclude enrollment and attendance. Indeed, children were required to attend, regardless of their ability to pay tuition. Even during crisis periods, when many families were thrown into the ranks of the indigent, most children continued to attend school but paid less regularly, producing predictable complaints from underpaid schoolteachers. In 1795 a schoolteacher from Heidelberg submitted to his superiors a list of forty-three pupils whose families owed him money for tuition and firewood. He remarked that even if everyone paid, there still would not be enough firewood to last the winter, because of inflated prices.[64] Around this same time, schoolteachers with small classes flooded the school administrators with requests to raise the tuition for those who could still pay, but those who could not comprised an ever increasing proportion of their pupils. Of the 161 pupils in the Catholic girls' school in Heidelberg in 1802, 85 were excused from tuition payments.[65] In the Mannheim Lutheran school in 1804, 20 of 90 pupils were officially classified as poor, and among the remaining 70, 14 could pay only a few months each year. The same pattern was repeated in other schools, and the situation seems to have worsened by the end of the first decade of the nineteenth century. By 1809, only 140 of the 290 Lutheran schoolchildren of Mannheim were judged capable of paying the 4-gulden yearly fee.[66] In a similar situation, the pastor of Heidelberg complained that things were getting so bad that he felt there were actual consequences for school attendance:

> among the parents in our community, there are many who find themselves reluctant to send their children to school because of the cost of the *Schulgeld,* which is admittedly a noticeable burden where there are several children [in one family]; these parents are not prosperous enough to pay the *Schulgeld,* but are not poor enough, or are too proud to inscribe their children on that list of those for whose schooling a fixed sum is paid each year from the poor relief fund.[67]

The decades at the end of the eighteenth century and the beginning of the nineteenth were particularly difficult, it is true. Series of bad harvests, economic dislocation caused by the French Revolution and the Napoleonic wars made subsistence problematic for many families. But although evidence about economic hardship interfering with the payment of tuition is especially plentiful during these years, the problem remained a chronic one throughout the early industrial period. Poverty severe enough to prohibit the payment of even small fees for schooling was the lot of a substantial segment of the popular classes. In Mannheim as late as 1838, about one-tenth of all Catholic parents were unable to afford school fees—these over and above the officially destitute, whose children attended the police poor school.[68] Records of requests for help in tuition payments demonstrate patterns of hardship: a widow with four children who was supporting herself and her family as a laundress found tuition payments beyond her means; Sophie Schwartz, another petitioner, was supporting herself and one son; a third woman complained that her husband had deserted her and their three children and was no longer sending any money; a ragpicker for the paper industry had five children under the age of eight. This set of records tells the stories of a number of families every year who requested and received special exemptions from school fees they were unable to pay.[69]

In sum, this evidence suggests that difficulties in raising even the minimal school fees requested in Baden plagued some families at all times. Those hardest hit were the female-headed households and households with many young children, who were always apparent among the urban poor of European cities. Periods of special crisis threw many more families into the category of those unable to pay. But the lower dependence of Badenese teachers on tuition fees meant that classes could continue even if many pupils did not pay. And pupils were not excluded from classrooms because of their poverty. This presents a marked contrast with Vaucluse, where payment for services rendered was the norm for all but a handful of officially declared indigents. For the rest of the poor, and the sometimes poor, schooling remained out of reach until well into the nineteenth century.

Both the decision to choose schooling over work and that to make the necessary expenditures for fees and other schooling needs would, of course, be influenced by the perceived likelihood that schooling investment would bring some future return. To the minds of the promoters of schooling, such benefits were beyond question. Resources invested during childhood would be amply rewarded, much as capital wisely invested brought future returns. Only the shortsightedness of the people prevented their appreciation of this possibility, observers felt and expressed in their records. The assumed benefits of schooling are implicit in the reform endeavors, but are often made explicit as well in statements by educational officials like the following inspector's report about Vaucluse:

> the most powerful motive encouraging parents to send their children to school is without a doubt the hope they have that their children will find in the instruction they receive the means to increase their well-being and

> even arrive at a certain condition of fortune; but these distant results are little appreciated by the poor because they don't concern themselves with the prospect of fortune, which is too remote for them, but simply with living from day to day. So they obstinately keep their children by their side no matter how small the wage they can earn.[70]

No doubt the inspector's comments reflect a growing tendency to regard schooling as an investment of sorts. Among the middle classes, and even for wealthy peasants, educating a son was one prerequisite to setting him up in a profession or in the church. Still, for people to accept the claim that schooling assured a more solid future to most children, they had to be convinced, first, that planning for the future of their children made sense at all, and second, that educational accomplishments could be converted into enhanced opportunities. This would have entailed a reorientation in the general population of attitudes about childhood similar to that which Philippe Ariès demonstrated among the upper classes beginning in the seventeenth century or so. The transformation of attitudes was related to simple demographic realities, for, as Charles Tilly has pointed out in his commentary on Ariès, it was difficult for parents to be calculating about the future of children whose survival was by no means secured. High infant and child mortality rates discouraged the adoption of Malthusian attitudes toward procreation; it seems likely that they would also have discouraged a calculating approach to schooling.[71]

A comparison of the demographic constraints within which families in Vaucluse and Baden developed their plans for their children's future suggests some difference that may well have mattered. In Vaucluse, as was generally the case in France, women began to limit their fertility around the turn of the nineteenth century. Declining levels of marital fertility are already in evidence during the first third of that century.[72] In Baden, crude birth rates remained quite high. Natural fertility patterns predominated throughout the first half of the nineteenth century, but genealogical records suggest that in scattered communities, at least, some families were beginning to limit births precociously by German standards.[73] The broad evidence suggests that the adoption of a more instrumental attitude about fertility was thus neither necessary nor sufficient for the establishment of general investment in schooling, but the evidence is far from being refined enough to explore the connection with precision.

The evidence about trends in mortality is fuller and more suggestive. Entries in the vital registers of sample communities in the two regions indicate that people in both areas witnessed a steady, if slight,

Figure 3
Estimated Infant Mortality, Deaths <1/Live Births
(Unweighted Mean of Sample Communities)

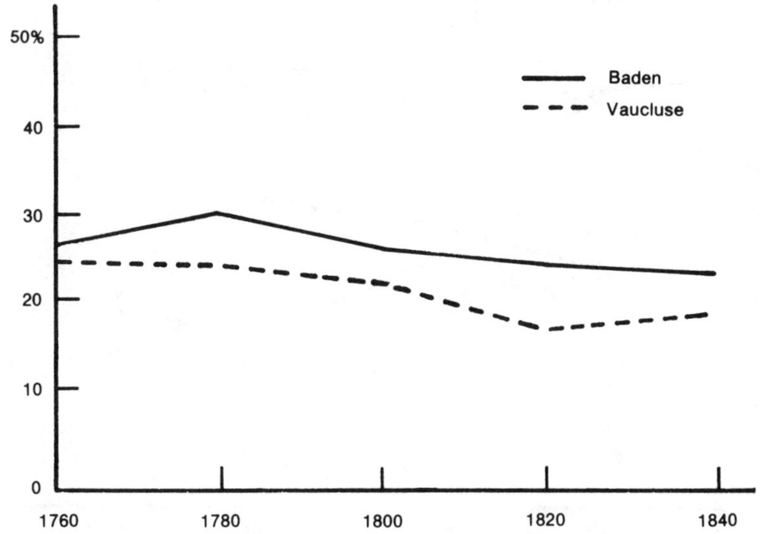

decline in the high levels of infant mortality during the century between 1750 and 1850. (See Figure 3.) Because of the slow rate of decline, it is likely that most people were not even aware of its occurrence. It is even less likely that a decline in infant mortality alone would have produced a general reorientation in attitudes toward childhood. But there also appear to have been some changes in child mortality that were perhaps more pertinent. Although more difficult to measure with accuracy from the registers, child mortality seems to have begun to drop fairly dramatically in Baden around the turn of the nineteenth century. It also began to drop in Vaucluse, but later and more slowly. (See Figure 4.)

The index of mortality among children (defined for demographic purposes as those between the ages of one and twenty) was much more volatile than that of infant mortality. Child deaths were connected with environmental factors; children, especially toddlers, were especially vulnerable to death in epidemic and subsistence crises. Years of crisis mortality were still common in the eighteenth century in both regions. They were still apparent in Vaucluse in the early nineteenth century, when freezing weather and crop failures or

Figure 4
Index of Mortality of 1 to 20 Year-Olds,
Deaths 1–20/Births Surviving to Age 1
(Unweighted Mean of Sample Communities)

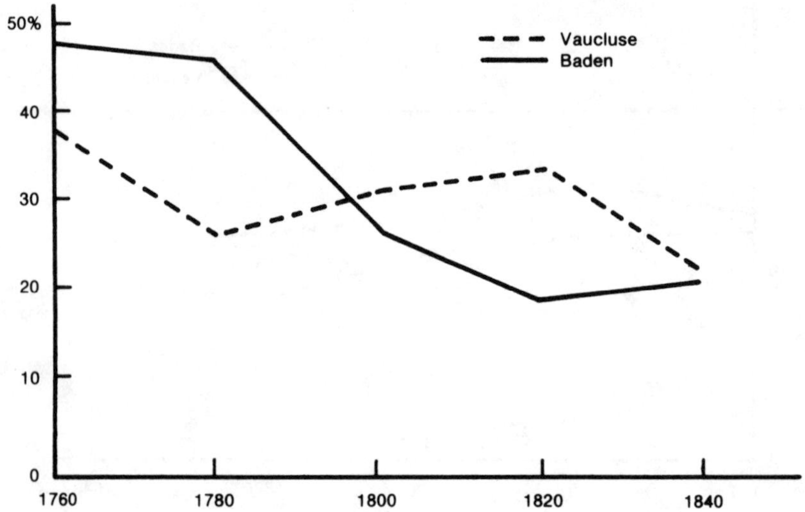

epidemics still could produce demographic catastrophes in some communities. Figures 5 and 6 illustrate the patterns of crisis mortality in the bourg of Cucuron and the village of La Bastide des Jourdans. During the crisis of the early 1820s, the surplus mortality was largely the result of increased mortality of young children. As is illustrated in Figure 4, there was no observable decline in child mortality in Vaucluse until after the 1820s.

The patterns of crisis mortality that punctuated the demographic history of Baden had altered somewhat by the early nineteenth century. The slightly better living conditions there no doubt meant better diet for children as well as for adults. There is also some suggestion that medical intervention was more frequent in Baden. The effects of medical intervention in this period are still a subject of considerable debate, but there is some evidence to suggest that one disease of particular importance for child health, smallpox, was in abeyance, possibly as the result of the practice of vaccination.[75] Whether or not the control of smallpox was the cause, child mortality was decreasing more dramatically in Baden than in Vaucluse, and the decline began quite a bit earlier. At the very end of the eighteenth century, both

Figures 5 and 6
Crisis Mortality Patterns in Cucuron and La Bastide des Jourdans, 1820–1824

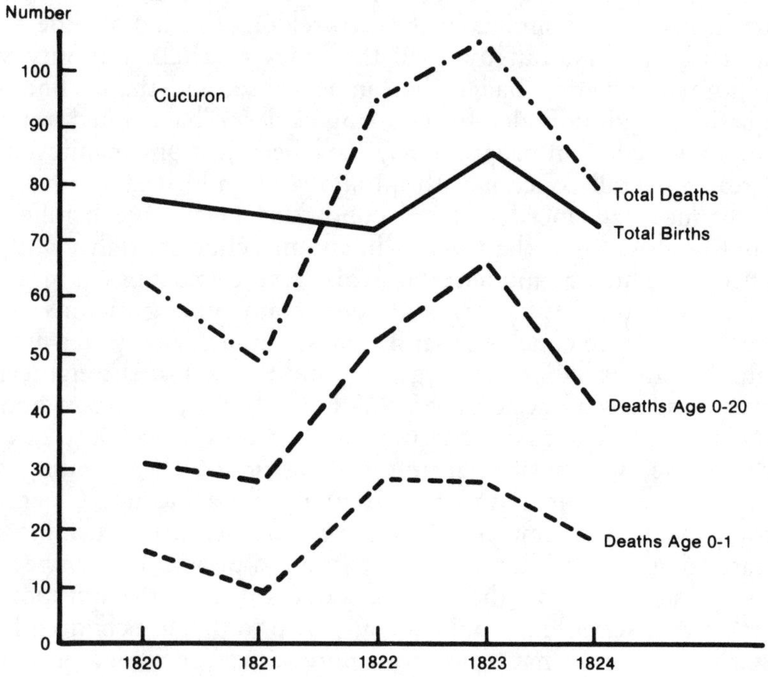

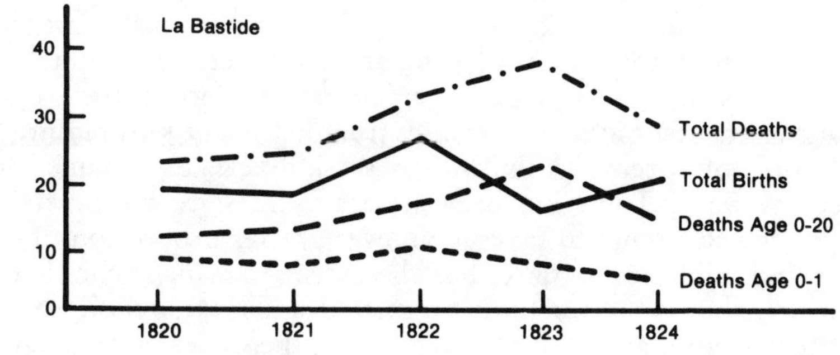

infant and child mortality had been higher in Baden, though the levels in the two areas were not significantly different. Levels of infant mortality remained similar in the two regions throughout the early nineteenth century, but by 1840 the index of child mortality was significantly lower in Baden than in Vaucluse, and the decline was dramatic enough in Baden for contemporaries to have noted it.[76] The smallpox vaccination program may have been just one manifestation of greater overall concern with questions of child welfare or of the slightly more advanced material conditions of average families. It should be noted that the level of infant and child mortality still remained quite high by modern standards. Severe epidemics of measles, scarlet fever, and dysentery still took many young victims. It is nonetheless fair to conclude that Badenese parents witnessed a decline in childhood mortality that began around the end of the eighteenth century, and saw a once dreaded childhood disease, smallpox, apparently succumb to medical intervention.[77] Parents in Vaucluse saw no such decline, at least not before the 1830s or so. These findings are compatible with the claim that declining child mortality, perhaps accompanied by a new belief in the possibility of controlling the diseases that made childhood so hazardous a period, encouraged interest in schooling on the part of parents.[78] Still, the question of whether that schooling would actually help to prepare children for a better future, once that future was more secure, remained questionable.

Even in the twentieth century, the link between schooling and career selection is tenuous at best. Critics of contemporary Western educational systems have made a strong case that the meritocratic arguments that originated in the era of school reform have served primarily to rationalize existing inequalities. Educational institutions reproduce from generation to generation the "cultural capital" required for access to prestigious careers preselected on the basis of social characteristics.[79] It is certainly true that many jobs require the acquisition of specific skills, but these skills can be obtained in a variety of ways. There has been a clear trend since the nineteenth century for schooling to take up an ever greater proportion of children's and adolescents' time, but the extent to which schools have taken over the task of teaching job-related skills is less clear.

Furthermore, access to schooling, even theoretical access, cannot be equated with access to careers. In the early industrial world (and even today, if these criticisms are valid) access to a particular career had very little to do with skills or certification acquired through schooling. A child's future was largely settled by his or her family on the basis of its needs, its aspirations, and its capacities to invest in expensive and time-consuming training that was a prerequisite for many futures but not a guarantee of entry into them. In general, schooling made sense as an investment only for those to whom the desired future was already open. For the rest, mere schooling was a downright waste of time if not an impossibility from the investment perspective.

For that majority of the early industrial population that still drew livelihood from the land, the path to the future was largely marked by the social and demographic situation of the family. Children who were in a position to inherit land from their parents could expect to follow the pursuit of agriculture; nonheirs could expect to change occupations. The children of the landless and land-poor were, of course, less motivated to follow in their parents' footsteps, but the dearth of resources in these families made any investment in alternative training unlikely. In either case, learning to farm entailed work alongside elders, which began early in life. This does not mean that peasants had no use for schooling, but only that they did not rely on it as the primary source of information about how to do their work, nor did they regard it as a prerequisite for the running of a farm.

There is some suggestion that peasants were becoming more interested in some aspects of schooling for reasons connected with the changing conditions of the agricultural economy. Inspectors' reports in Vaucluse note at times the apparent interest of peasants in skills that could help in the management of property and in the mastery of the increasingly intrusive market.[80] Peasants in Vaucluse were in general little concerned with the niceties of grammar—not too surprising in a population whose everyday tongue was different from that taught in the schools. On the other hand, they reportedly "held a great store in arithmetic because they made use of it more frequently . . . there [were] a lot of children interested in it."[81] One inspector was surprised to find during his 1836 rounds children who (despite their absenteeism for farm work during six months of the year) "could read passably [and], although little learned in grammar, the usefulness of which they couldn't appreciate, were applying themselves more diligently to arithmetic."[82] This same interest in arithmetic apparently even encouraged adults to return to school, as, for example, in Gadagne in 1838, where ciphering was the principal interest of the evening pupils, many of whom were "fathers of families who sense each day the need they have to know how to keep accounts."[83] These testimonies suggest that even if the agricultural classes of Vaucluse were as yet unwilling to cooperate with the government's program of full-time elementary education, it is apparent that certain sectors of that population, particularly peasants with property to manage and market dealings to master, were showing some interest in the acquisition of basic literacy and numeracy skills through occasional schooling.

It should be noted that this early evidence of peasant interest in schooling was largely limited to schooling for sons. Discriminatory behavior with regard to the schooling of boys and girls continued in Vaucluse, particularly in rural areas. This was in part the result of the old and new taboos against coeducation; where a separate girls' school was not available, girls were not sent as frequently as where there was one. But it does seem to have been the case that schooling was considered to be less valuable for girls.[84] The sexual division of labor within the peasant household allocated the tasks of management and marketing of major crops to the men. Comments suggest that the education of girls was usually the domain of mothers, and these usually, though not always, decided that schooling was unnecessary. In St. Saturnin d'Avignon, for example, there was a girls' school for teaching reading and writing, but no grammar was taught, since "mothers of families, all belonging to the agricultural classes, [were] opposed to having their children devote themselves to studies which they believed [served] no purpose but to make their children waste their time."[85] In Beaumont the female pupils were reportedly not making much progress because their attendance was too often interrupted by excessive parental demands on their time.[86] Families in Vauclusan rural communities continued to be less likely to send their daughters to school even after they began to send their sons. Still, the evidence is not unambiguous. According to the testimony of Agricole Perdiguier, who came from a family living from farming and industrial work, the picture was not so simple. He recalls his father deciding that schooling was a waste of time for girls. His mother, however, felt differently and she decided to send her daughters to school, paying the tuition money herself from her earnings from the sale of small amounts of farm produce and handicrafts.[87]

Although the evidence suggests that in the late eighteenth century girls in Baden were less likely to be in school than their brothers, the old pattern of higher enrollment of boys had largely disappeared by the early nineteenth century. Even if schooling was considered to be less important for girls from the point of view of their work expectations, the enforcement of fines for truancy, coupled with nonmaterial interests in schooling, was sufficient to encourage parents to send their girls to school even more frequently than their boys.

For those children of propertied peasant families who were not destined to remain on the family farm, as well as for the children of families in sectors other than the agrarian one, specialized occupational training was a routine part of childhood and adolescence. For those destined for artisanal careers or the management of small commercial enterprises, that training came through some form of formal or informal apprenticeship in the family business or another shop.

For entry into the skilled industrial classes, apprenticeship was still routine, although the legal status of the guilds, and their control over the transmission of industrial skills, was undermined earlier in France than in Germany. Apprenticeship contracts preserved in notarial archives record the outlines of the apprenticeship system of late eighteenth- and early nineteenth-century Vaucluse. First, apprenticing a child entailed forgoing the benefits of his or her labor for a period of between two and five years, although the typical length of apprenticeship was becoming shorter. Secondly, apprenticeship entailed the payment of a lump sum intended both as payment for initiation into the mysteries of the trade and as a contribution for the child's support during the early nonproductive years. Some contracts specified that the parents were to continue to supply a certain amount of money for the apprentice's maintenance. The fees paid to the master at the time of apprenticeship ranged from 18 to 200 livres in the late eighteenth century and from 30 to 400 francs in the early nineteenth. In other words, the cost of apprenticing a child was between a month's and a year's pay or more; it entailed substantial saving and sacrifice and was, of course, out of reach for most families.[88] It should be noted, however, that the apprenticeships these contracts record were the more formal ones, often to learn prestigious trades. It was certainly the case that many children learned trades at a lower cost from their own families or in less formal situations.[89]

Apprenticeship as a means of access to occupations is a form of training distinct from schooling, and its persistence in this period as a stage in the life cycle of many young people had implications for schooling patterns. Since apprenticeship could begin before school-leaving age, a potential conflict existed between school authorities, on the one hand, and parents and masters on the other, over control of the apprentice's time. Nonetheless, since apprentices were destined for careers that often entailed running a small shop, buying and selling, and keeping accounts, apprentices had a stake in the perfection of the skills the schools did teach. Despite the conflicting demands on their time, apprentices and journeymen in the towns and cities of both regions managed to combine their vocational training with classroom instruction. Many of the pupils in the industrial schools of Baden, the *Gewerbeschulen,*[90] were the young apprentices required by law to attend school until their fourteenth birthday, but a substantial number were older apprentices and even journeymen, who enrolled voluntarily in the classes teaching basic or advanced subjects.[91] In Vaucluse apprentices and journeymen filled the classes of the various evening schools and adult courses offered in the towns.[92] Artisanal families and artisans-in-training clearly valued schooling; but although schooling could help an artisan better manage a shop, or keep up with technical improvements in his field, or help an artisan's wife or daughter keep the family accounts, access to the profession was still in the hands of artisans themselves and would continue to be until the end of the nineteenth century. Schooling was a supplement to, rather than a substitute for, on-the-job training.

Children who were not in a position to inherit land or to invest in training of any sort, those under pressure to begin their work lives young, drifted without resource into whatever unskilled or semiskilled work was available, in the mills and mines, in construction and transportation, in service. The occupations of the popular classes were not taught in the schools. This was not true in the same way for the middle classes. For them, even if specific techniques for each profession were learned on the job, the certification required for entry into the careers they followed was indeed provided through the classical schools and the universities.[93] But by and large, these educational institutions were closed to the children of the people. Primary schools were their schools, and they were the most they could expect.

One cannot help concluding that the reform of the primary schools did little, in the short run at least, to improve the prospects of the children who attended them.[94] The somewhat enhanced access to basic skills was a boon to those subsectors of the population formerly cut off from them, even if that group was smaller than the school promoters' claims would suggest. But the direction of most of the early reforms—geared as they were toward making schooling a more engrossing experience and making its lessons more responsive to state than to parental concerns—actually had the effect of making schooling less compatible with the demands of the family economy of the more marginal families. The ways in which universal schooling clashed with the family economy became clearer only as authorities tried to fulfill universal attendance goals. Conflicting expectations about how children should employ their time caused reformers to rethink the practicality of establishing a single common elementary school. The following chapter will describe the variety of supplementary educational institutions that buttressed the basic primary school in its tasks.

CHAPTER 7

Schooling Society
The Expansion of the School System

FAMILIES IN VARYING CIRCUMSTANCES REACTED differently to the promise of schooling, however universalistic the claims about it. Moreover, the drive to bring the children of even the poorest and least respectable of the people into the classroom had the unanticipated consequence, as some school officials saw it, of corrupting the school environment and endangering the children presumed to be more righteous. Still, commitment to schooling as a necessary stage in the preparation of a citizen and functional human being was not abandoned. Instead, publicly supported educational institutions proliferated; more and more schools were created to serve the supposed needs of increasingly diverse and specific clienteles. Even as "the people" evolved under official scrutiny into a stratified group comprising comfortable shopowners and peasant landowners, artisans in hard times and workers in the new factories, as well as landless agricultural workers and casual urban laborers and their families, it gradually became clear that no single institution was capable of meeting the educational needs of so diverse a population. And so the reform of the simple primary school was accompanied by the eventual creation in many communities of an array of different institutions designed for those for whom the regular primary schools were inappropriate.

Again a contrasting style of approach to this problem of social diversity is notable. Badenese authorities, in order to make obligatory primary schooling possible, also had to create a system that was flexible enough to encompass even the very poor. French administrators shared the vision of schooling for all, but, consistent with their more universalistic and voluntaristic model of social relationships, shied away from the straightforward recognition of special interests of any sort. The assumptions pervading administrative thought in France required that facilities be available equally to all comers, at least theoretically, and that the mechanisms of parental choice be allowed to operate fairly freely. They were not troubled by the existence of unequal abilities to take advantage of these facilities, indeed relied on those inequalities to assure that the schools would not be disruptive of the social order. But the commitment to political egalitarianism, in the context of a society governed by the constraints of class, produced a situation in which there was no easy solution to the dilemma of parents who found it difficult to accommodate themselves to the demands of institutional uniformity. Badenese authorities, more willing and able to think in the old terms of the persistent *Ständestaat* model, were quite capable of creating institutions designed for the specific constraints of each situation. It was this archaic legal recognition of the realities of social stratification that built into the Badenese school system both its obviously undemocratic character and its realism.

The Badenese school ordinance of 1803 had made allowance for only two types of schools, the *Landschule* and the *Stadtschule*, which, it was assumed, would teach slightly different kinds of lessons to their peasant and urban clienteles respectively. It soon became clear to local authorities that the single primary-school model would not work, especially in the increasingly complex urban communities of the early industrial period. There was, of course, the problem of the growing number of urban poor. By law, all children were required to attend school, and smaller communities had usually financed the tuition for the poor from the local poor funds and sent them to the same schools as those who could afford to pay. As the poor grew more numerous in the epoch of social unrest around the turn of the nineteenth century, there was a tendency to try to make special arrangements for the schooling of the poor. One city official in Mannheim wrote in 1810:

> the growing number of poor children of all religions whose parents draw their sustenance from the city's poor fund demands the creation of some

> employment for these children which will keep them from begging and idleness, and through the income they get from their work, make them useful to their parents and help to lighten the burden of poor relief . . . the fact that the poor, whose children are most in need of instruction, are most negligent of their schooling [suggests the necessity of] founding a poor school . . . where the necessary instruction can alternate with useful or paid labor. . . .[1]

The Police Poor School, as the new institution was called, combined a workhouse with a school for children of families on public relief, as well as for a number of children who were sent there because they were neglected or delinquent.[2]

The official poor school took care of the children of certified indigents in Mannheim, and even gave them the opportunity to earn a pittance. But the much larger and less well-defined group of merely or occasionally poor presented authorities insisting on universal attendance with a different kind of problem. Catholic officials in Mannheim were particularly concerned with the nonindigent poor, since a disproportionately large number of the Catholic residents of the city fell into this category. The poor sometimes sent their children to school, but poverty interfered with regular school attendance. Furthermore, the poor children were regarded as a moral menace to the better off. In 1817 the Catholic School Conference for the city reported to the director of the Neckarkreis about a project to open what they called a *Mittelschule*—one between the regular elementary school and the police school for the indigent. In the proposed institution, lessons in industrial skills would be combined with the instruction in reading, writing, and arithmetic. The motives for the establishment of this new school were stated in the report:

> school age is the time when the tendency to acquire good or bad habits and manners as observed in the environment is most intense; the moral behavior of the family, the example of parents and older siblings usually works to advance the moral education of the children, but this example is lacking in the families of those of the people without property. It is often the very example of the parental household that guides the morality of the children from early on. The careful protection of children from evil and the observation of evil, all the domestic teachings of upright parents will be fruitless if the better children observe children who have taught themselves in accordance with the example of crude and immoral parents.[3]

The teachers and administrators on the council felt that many parents from the more comfortable strata of the popular classes were reluctant to send their children to the public schools precisely because reforms were bringing more of the poor into the classrooms. Instead, they were beginning to send them to the crowd of private schools competing with the public institutions. In this same year the Catholic deacon of Mannheim submitted a second report, calling for the establishment of a second separate primary school for "those children who in many regards corrupt the better ones like a creeping poison," namely, the children of

> 1. extremely poor, as well as extremely unfortunate parents;
> 2. those very needy parents who see the importance of education for their children but whose poverty forces them to neglect their schooling the whole summer and a large part of the winter in order to earn their bread. . . .[4]

The deacon believed that there were at least two hundred such children in the Catholic community of the city. If they were left in or brought into the regular primary school they would corrupt the better children, have trouble keeping up with the lessons, and have to give up their begging or working entirely because of the hours of school. Because of the considerations expressed in these reports, a Catholic free school was duly established, where class hours were shorter and there was no tuition charged. The free school thus solved a dual dilemma: poorer children could both attend school and work, and at the same time they were kept isolated from their social, and presumed moral, superiors. And officials were apparently satisfied with the results. In 1831 the inspector reported that the institution fulfilled its purpose:

> the poorer classes who formerly could in no way be constrained to uninterrupted school attendance now attend for the most part regularly, and not only receive instruction sufficient for their future occupations, but also an appropriate religious and moral training.[5]

There was no parallel creation of public schools destined specifically for the poor in Vaucluse, although the schools run by religious orders were sometimes expected to serve this function. Certainly during the ancien régime the schooling of the poor had been the main motive for the establishment of the schools run by orders like the Brothers of the Christian Schools and the Sisters of St. Charles. This central concern with the moral reform of the poor is apparent, for example, in the records of the deliberations of the municipal council of the city of Avignon about the opening of a Brothers' school in the Madeleine parish in 1756. The council explained its decision to subsidize the school in the following words:

> there are [in the Madeleine] a lot of river sailors and haulers who are nearly always traveling and cannot teach their children, cannot even teach themselves. . . . At the time of the last mission there were found in this parish some boys pretty well advanced in age who were not going to communion, several of whom did not even know how to confess. The establishment of a . . . school in this parish is the only means that can be employed to remedy this profound ignorance; inasmuch as the Brothers will teach the children about religion during the time they are teaching them how to read, these children, having been imbued in their youth with the first principles of religion, will be able to teach themselves in adulthood by reading pious books.[6]

Part of the explanation for the quick reestablishment of the Brothers after the Concordat was their history of teaching of the poor. But during the first few decades of the nineteenth century, their schools were not only teaching the poorest children. Recruitment was broadened and the content of the curriculum expanded slightly as well to appeal to the more ambitious sectors of the popular classes. It was this aspect of their new program that seemed most to distress officials of a more liberal bent. There were educational officials of the July Monarchy period who were willing to grant the usefulness of the Brothers' schools as long as they stuck to "following the goals behind the order's foundation . . . consecrating themselves to the instruction of the poor classes who needed to find for their children the basic moral and religious instruction which they were themselves lacking."[7] It was this same concern for the role of religious orders in the teaching of the poor that prompted some members of the municipal council of Apt to remonstrate against the council's decision to withdraw public subsidy from the Brothers there in 1831. "The people," the remonstrance claimed,

> who constitute the immense majority of the Nation, in whom resides a redoubtable superiority, who alone supports all the burdens of society and whose passions, so quick to be moved and afterward so difficult to damper, demand a bridle to keep them to the path of duty . . . only education, and a religious education, is capable of imposing this restraint.[8]

The anticlerical sectors of the administrative classes could not share this view, even though they appreciated the special problem of educating the poor. Many preferred to rest their hopes in *enseignement mutuel,* which, while not useful only for the poor, was certainly appropriate for them. Instruction was designed to proceed quickly through the basic subjects so that pupils could finish their elementary instruction at a younger age. The more optimistic expectations about the possible consequences of the new schools for the poor are expressed in a wall poster put up by the mayor of Bollème in 1831:

> It is necessary that children entering this era of equality and of industry and emulation are capable of gaining knowledge extensive enough to get out of the rut in which they find themselves trapped by the old methods of instruction. . . . The material improvement which will accrue to you as a result of these innovations is equally precious, above all for those who are without fortune. Your children will not have to supply books or papers or pens. We require of them only good conduct and the desire to learn and to become good citizens.[9]

In a society where the presence of poverty was tangible, institutions like the Brothers' schools and the *écoles mutuelles* did no doubt help to bring into the classroom a number of children who might not otherwise have entered. But neither of these was explicitly a "poor school." Both in theory allowed pupils from different social conditions to enter the same classes. The hope was that the appeal of low or free tuition, and even the offer of free supplies, along with the promise of a better future, would attract the children of the poor into the classroom and keep them there long enough to usher them into the era of equality (or social order).

In both Baden and Vaucluse, the drive to bring the children of the poor into the classrooms also led parents and educators to search for educational alternatives for the better-off children. But the search for public instruction appropriate for the more comfortable and ambitious of the people took divergent paths in the two regions. In the towns of Vaucluse, parents who wanted more for their children than a simple elementary education in an overcrowded primary school could send their sons to the increasingly popular elementary or preparatory classes attached to the communal collèges, the Latin schools. In Apt, for example, about half of the pupils in the collège during the 1840s and 1850s were enrolled in the primary classes of the institution. In the collège of Pertuis, primary pupils actually outnumbered those in secondary classes.[10] For the daughters of ambitious families, the publicly subsidized female teaching orders in the larger towns often held special classes in elementary and advanced subjects. Their special classes charged several francs' tuition a month, a device that effectively barred the poor from them. Even though it did not explicitly recognize social distinctions in its structuring, the French educational system still effectively allowed communities publicly subsidized educational facilities for those more comfortable families who desired a separate and superior education for their children.

In Baden the early-nineteenth-century reorganization of the

school system did produce separate schools for separate social groups. The plan for the better-off followed the outline of that for the poor: a school whose hours and curriculum were tailored to the needs of the more ambitious. In Heidelberg and Mannheim, parents have available to them, beyond the poor school and the free school, the so-called *Einfach-* and *Erweiterte-Volksschulen.* The simple elementary school offered the three Rs and not much more, in relatively crowded classrooms. The advanced school taught additional subjects like French and drawing to smaller classes of children. In 1840 in Mannheim, for example, there were 109 children enrolled in the single class of the Catholic free school, 323 children enrolled in the three classes of the ordinary *Volksschule* (which charged 2 florins' tuition), and 468 children in the ten classes of the *Erweiterte Volksschule* (charging 8 florins per year). In the somewhat wealthier Evangelical community of the city, nearly 600 children attended the more expensive *Erweiterte Volksschule,* whereas just over 300 attended the simple *Volksschule.*[11]

By the middle of the nineteenth century, the elementary school system in cities like Mannheim had evolved into a highly stratified set of institutions, which provided a variety of alternative primary educations, each geared to the presumed needs of a different sector of the populace. Built into the system was the assumption that families in different social situations had not only different ambitions for their children, but also different amounts of resources, including their children's time, to invest. It was imperative to school administrators that every child be schooled, but there was no apparent commitment to the principle of equal schooling. This is best reflected in the hours of instruction children in each type of institution received. The poor school of Mannheim kept the longest hours, since supervised work was combined with instruction, but actual instructional time was brief. Children were kept from 8:00 a.m. to nightfall in winter and from 7:00 a.m. to 6:00 or 7:00 p.m. in summer. Elementary instruction hours were from noon to 1:00 p.m. and from 4:00 to 5:00 p.m. The free school taught boys from 8:00 to 10:00 a.m. and 1:00 to 2:00 p.m. in winter and only two hours a day in summer. Girls attended classes from 10:00 a.m. to noon and from 2:00 to 3:00 p.m. in winter and also had their instructional hours reduced to two a day in summer. These hours reportedly were established because "boys usually worked in the construction industry [and] these were their free hours."[12] Table 12 charts the number of instructional hours offered in the different Mannheim primary schools in 1849. The explicit recognition of the constraints under which families in different social cir-

TABLE 12
Time Schedules for the Different Primary Schools of Mannheim, 1849

School	*Number of instructional hours weekly*	
	Boys	*Girls*
Police Poor School	10	
Free School		
Grade 1	15	
Grade 2	15	
Grade 3	17	
Einfache Volksschule		
Grade 1	30	
Grade 2	20	19
Grade 3	25	22
Erweiterte Volksschule		
Grade 1	20	20
Grade 2	23	20
Grade 3	24	20
Grade 4	26	22
Grade 5	30	26

cumstances lived, reflected in these schedules, allowed the institutional flexibility to bring about universal enrollment in an increasingly stratified society. The more universalistic French system, based as it was on an ideology placing more emphasis on theoretical equality of access, was less successful in incorporating all of the children of the people.

But even as school authorities grappled with the special problems of educating "the poor" or "the comfortable" among the people, the very categorization was under challenge as a result of the social and economic changes occurring during the early nineteenth century. Simply to think in terms of "the people," even as nuanced by references that distinguished among them, seemed no longer appropriate to some observers. Particularly palpable in the thinking and planning of authorities was the threat to the social and moral order that the growing numbers of seemingly wild, unsettled, and unskilled proletarians represented. They were not the same as the old poor. And the unease many observers were feeling emerges most clearly in the debate over the factories and the education of factory children.

Long before the factory was the place of employment of a large number of workers, the proletarian image of the future that it evoked led concerned administrators to anticipate and attempt to preempt its presumed evil consequences. The factory was a special concern to educational authorities, since it attracted child laborers, competed with the schools, and affected the lives and moral futures of working children. It is interesting to note that factory children were the one special-interest group for whom special educational provision was made in both France and Baden.

The debate over child labor in the factories was colored by the conflicting evaluations of the meaning of the changes that were occurring, and the role the factory would play in human evolution. One Badenese deputy, in testimony before the lower chamber on the issue of wayward children, gave voice to an unease many were feeling:

> a class is growing among us which is truly indifferent to all which we here stand for . . . it is not simply the growth of poverty we are witnessing, but the complete de-civilizing [*Verwilderung*] of the poor. Contemporary conditions bring that in their wake. . . .[13]

Such apprehensions about the *Verwilderung* of the masses surface in parliamentary debates on many issues, in church inspectors' reports, in the writings of school proponents, and in particular in the debate over the schooling of factory children. If the adult proletariat were beyond salvation, the *Verwilderung* of their children could perhaps be avoided through timely schooling.

The problem of combining factory work with schooling was especially tricky. The factory schedule was more rigid than any work routine formerly known. Factories could not bend their routines in order to allow attendance of their child workers at any existing schools. The implication was that if children were to be allowed to work in factories, either they would have to remain unschooled or else special provisions would have to be made for them. There were heated debates in both France and Baden over the moral condition of the factory child, beginning in the 1830s. And the terms of the debate reflected the disagreement over the moral value of the economic changes represented by the factory. In Baden the eventual ordinance passed to begin the regulation of factory employment of children stated in its preamble that measures had to be taken "to prevent the flourishing of the factory at the cost of the moral and physical degradation of the people" and to avoid "the storms . . . which in other states have broken out in the factories."[14] In France the commission investigating factory conditions in the late 1840s applauded modern industry as "the triumph of enlightened thinking applied to the material needs of an advanced society" but pointed out that the factory workers remained in a state of ignorance because

> the industrial system [with its] division of labor pushed to the extreme, [left] nothing more to the immense majority of workers than the automatic repetition of a single identical movement, than the unchanging attention to a single detail of manufacture.

The commission claimed that the first remedy to combat the ensuing spiritual degeneration was "to reserve in childhood a sufficient time for education."[15]

Authorities in both regions began to express the need to oversee child labor in the factories and to push both factory owners and parents, who were continually blamed for their shortsightedness and greed, to do what they (the authorities) believed to be in the best interests of the children.[16] The blame, especially in Vaucluse, was laid most often at the feet of parents. In the mill town of L'Isle-sur-la-Sorgue parents "preferred to employ their children [in the factories] rather than having them taught."[17] The prefect of the département reported in 1846 that there were some under-age children working in the factories there, but "if there were some who weren't receiving any education, the fault must be attributed uniquely to parental negligence."[18] Most commentators agreed that the unregulated labor of young children in factories was an affront to the moral order and a denial of the state's responsibilities, but only a minority felt during the early nineteenth century that this labor could or should be prevented entirely. The spectrum of opinion on the question was similar in Baden and France, but, in legislative terms at least, the proponents of a greater degree of voluntarism and parental discretion in the employment of children again held greater sway in France.

In Baden opposition to child labor in the factories was largely rural and conservative in character. One Badenese pastor, for example, claimed that in his parish "children of ten years and even younger were already working in the factories"; factory schools were no solution to the moral problems such labor presented, since "they were not attended with the same regularity [as regular schools] and the children were too exhausted from their day's work to profit from two hours a day of schooling." Furthermore, since factory children "belonged, for the most part, to poor parents, it was important for them to have somewhat more schooling since the public school had to take the place of domestic learning for them."[19] Echoing these sentiments, a deputy in the lower chamber of the Badenese legislature decried the whole practice of child labor in the factories and the implied legitimation that state regulation of it would provide:

> I am against factory schools, all the more so because I am against any facilitation of [child] employment in the factories, to which I will never

> acquiesce. I'll never grant that children under fourteen years be sent into the factories.[20]

Another opponent to child labor in the factories pointed out an inconsistency he saw in the insistence on the part of liberal advocates of factory schools that peasants send their children to the *Volksschulen.* Peasants, too,

> [found] their children most necessary for various kinds of work; it is simply that [the deputies in question] do not take any notice of that although the work these children do is just as necessary for their parents as the wages of the others from the factories. . . . The factory owner can just as well regulate his hours [according to school hours] as the farmer must his.[21]

The more realistic and ultimately triumphant camp had little patience with statements of this sort. As they saw it, the plain facts were that children were working in factories and owners were not about to adjust their schedules to accommodate the schooling of factory workers. To evade the issue with assertions that children should not be allowed to work in the factories was to deny the state's responsibility for their education.

Indeed, behind the advocacy of factory schools was the active approval of child labor that many observers were willing to express. If the official administrative position in Baden in the 1830s and 1840s suggested that the abuses of the practice had to be curbed, it was nonetheless recognized that the employment of children had its advantages as well. An ordinance passed in 1838 maintained that

> it is a great boon for inhabitants of poorer areas when even the children can already bring in some income. Just as great is the advantage to factory owners, since the wage of a child, even in relationship to what he does, is always less than that of an adult and because there are many jobs a child can do just as well and just as quickly as an adult.[22]

Proponents of the government perspective were quick to point out that child labor was only to be permitted where it would not be harmful to the interests of the child. The effects of factory labor were different in various industries, but they claimed that

> there [were] many branches of industry where a child [could] be used with profit without causing any disadvantage to his moral or physical development. . . . [In many factory jobs] children have very easy work to do, where they can develop much better than they would if they were sent to gather or steal wood by their parents, or used for hard labor like [the children] of peasants.[23]

This was also the conclusion of the Dupin commission in the late 1840s in France, which structured the debate over factory legislation there. The report of the commission maintained that

> the admission of children into the factories from the age of eight years is a means of surveillance for their parents, a beginning of apprenticeship for the children, a resource for the family; the habits of order, discipline and work must be acquired early. . . . To those who propose to delay . . . the age of admission of children into the factories, we ask who will guarantee that these . . . years left to the child outside the surveillance of his parents will profit his elementary and religious instruction? Who, on the contrary, sees not the occasion for demoralization and vagabondage or apprenticeship in vice: the school of the streets is the worst school of all. It teaches idleness and disorder. It is not there that good workers are produced. The child who enters the workshop at eight years, accustomed to work, habituated to obedience and possessing the first elements of instruction arrives at the age of ten more capable of resisting fatigue, more agile and more educated than the child of the same age reared in idleness.[24]

The laws that were passed to curb abusive child labor practices and to guarantee that child laborers received some instruction were earlier and more restrictive in Baden than in France. The state of Baden limited the employment of children under twelve years of age to nine hours a day in 1833. The law requiring all children to attend school was not waived for factory children, and factory owners were made responsible for providing access to some sort of schooling to their youthful employees. Later laws added restrictions to the hiring of older children and altered the conditions of the earlier laws regarding child employment. The major law of 1839 outlawed factory work for children below the age of eleven and limited the workday of those between eleven and sixteen to ten hours, including the time for lunch, breaks, and schooling. The first regulatory law was passed in France in 1841, and its provisions were more tolerant of child employment than the Badenese law of two years' precedence. The French law set the lower age limit for factory employment at eight years; children between the ages of eight and twelve could work for eight hours a day; children between twelve and sixteen could work for twelve hours a day. The law also stipulated that child factory employees under the age of twelve had to attend school—thus making them the first population subject to obligatory schooling in France—but no provision was made for schooling for these children.[25] Conditions of child labor in factories continued to be the subject of debate and regulation in both states until the era of abolition of child labor. But enforcement in this early period was difficult; neither parents nor factory owners cooperated with the regulations. In some localities in Baden there is evidence of the fining of parents and owners who evaded the laws, but local officials were often slow to act and were generally unwilling to take steps against entrepreneurs.[26] The evidence from Vaucluse suggests that the French laws were little enforced even as late as the 1850s and 1860s. Still, the passage of the laws assuaged the consciences of progressives, who saw in the factories their potential for expansion of human productive capacities, but who were often the very same people who were ardent proponents of progress through education as well. If the plight of the child laborer was something of a paradox, the fiction that factory work and schooling could be combined covered it up.

Making special provisions for the schooling of the working children so hard to lure into the regular elementary schools was one kind of response to the conflict between universal schooling and the demands of the family economy. In theory, at least, elementary schooling was thus made available to all. The devotion to universal schooling was continued even in the face of the evidence that there were many families who did not want and could not afford the luxury of full-time schooling for their children. In fact, the compass of the school was actually expanded in the first half of the nineteenth century to include not only those children within some increasingly well-defined "school age,"[27] but even many of those outside the bounds of this categorization. And for one age group in particular—pre-schoolers—early schooling began to appear to be absolutely critical.

The theories of human psychology developed during the Enlightenment and so appealing to educators in the nineteenth century stressed the openness to influence, the almost infinite malleability that was characteristic of the human personality.[28] One implication of this theory was that exposing children to the proper environment in their early years could not help improving their subsequent character development. The reform of the elementary classroom was colored by this belief, but teachers in some of the classes now pulling in more and more of the children of the people began to feel that their influence came too late.

School officials and educational theorists agreed: the problem was that many children were entering primary school with their moral potential already corrupted by the home environment to which they were exposed in their early years. Contemporary writings on the character of early childhood emphasized the extreme importance for future development of the toddler's experiences. The echo of new scientific findings sounds even in the words of the Vauclusan Inspector Arnault describing the département's first efforts to found infant schools:

> the age from two to six is perhaps the most important for the development of the intelligence because it is at this age that the child shows himself to be the most eager to learn, so that, according to Lord Brougham, the destiny of the whole life depends on how these years are occupied.[29]

Unfortunately, according to educators, it was precisely during these years that the children of the working poor were most likely to be neglected. And the administrative response to this dilemma came—not surprisingly—in the form of a new kind of school, the *salle d'asile,* as it was known in France, or the German *Kleinkinderschule.*

These infant schools were created as substitutes for mothering, presumed to be deficient in poor families. In both Baden and Vaucluse, proponents of infant schools hoped the institutions would rectify the moral disorders that stemmed from the neglect of children in their early years. A recommendation by the Badenese Studies and School Commission of 1833 that the state begin to subsidize such schools claimed that *Kleinkinderschulen* would care for children who would otherwise "be left alone in their ignorance, thoughtlessness and weakness, so that the hearts of these young children, so open at this age to external influences, respond to all vices and moral dissolution."[30] Advocates of these schools often were sympathetic to the plight of the poor and tried to refrain from condemnation, but it was nonetheless taken for granted that the conditions under which working-class families lived were not conducive to the reproduction of morally responsible and intelligent human beings. A middle-class women's organization in the town of Schriesheim, which was attempting to organize a *Kleinkinderschule* in that town in the early 1850s, reported that

> many children, before they are even of school age, must do without bodily and spiritual care, in part through the fault of loveless and irresponsible parents, in part because their swarming households and the work outside the home which keeps many mothers, through no fault of their own, from devoting the necessary time to their little children.[31]

The school commission had argued earlier that the consequences of such neglect could be of long duration:

> a large number of children, before they even start school, are so neglected and corrupted in the most basic foundations which affect the

> body, soul and mind for their whole lifetime, that even the best instruction in the elementary school must remain without fruit.[32]

The Inspector Arnault in Vaucluse advocated *salles d'asile* in precisely the same language and for the same reasons:

> [children] neglected by working-class parents who don't know how to give [them] the appropriate care [need some alternative]. In this class [of people] in effect, one cannot dream of developing the intelligence of the child and causing to blossom in his heart those sentiments which it is crucial to cultivate. The children enter the school with their minds dulled and even corrupted by the vices of their early education.

In the *salles d'asile,* these children could contract early on "the habits of order, obedience and work."[33]

Institutions designed to care for children too young to enter the primary schools proliferated in the 1830s and 1840s. These were sometimes established by private women's organizations of a charitable sort, but state authorities were enthusiastic supporters of the movement and even contributed subsidies to the cause. The Badenese school commission of 1833 even regularized the state subsidy there to aid neglected children, who now could be "instructed under supervision in order and cleanliness and accustomed to moral ideas."[34] The stated goals of local authorities in the establishment of a *Kleinkinderschule* in Mannheim, opened in 1836 with the help of the state, included:

> 1. Good supervision of young children.
> 2. The encouragement of schooling for their older siblings usually charged with the care and raising of the younger ones.
> 3. The encouragement of the children's free development and physical strength; the turning of their feelings in a moral, religious direction; guidance toward order, cleanliness, obedience, and industriousness; a preparation for elementary school.[35]

The infant school founded in Avignon in the same year had similar purposes. Because of its establishment,

> little children, so often and so dangerously left alone by the poorer classes . . . [could] contract from their entrance into life the habits of order, discipline and steady occupation which are the beginnings of morality, and at the same time receive their first lessons, some elementary notions which prepare them to follow more fruitfully the instruction which other institutions will offer later on.[36]

The apparent enthusiasm with which many families responded to the creation of infant schools suggests that they filled a real need. If older children found family demands running counter to the official push toward the classroom, this was not the case with the little ones. Children too young to work were a liability, insofar as their supervision prevented parents and older siblings from working. Ironically, the reforms of the elementary schools tended to evict many younger children from those schools and left parents in a more difficult position that they had been before. Awareness of this problem occasionally surfaces in the discussions of school officials. Officials in Heidelberg, for example, noted in 1815 that the schools were particularly overcrowded. They considered instituting split shifts but decided against that since it would cause difficulties for parents who relied on the schools for supervision of their children.[37] The same consideration prompted parents in Apt to petition for the continued support of the *école des Frères* in 1830.[38] Still, the general trend was clear: pedagogic reform dictated that the toddlers be evicted from the elementary-school classroom. The Brothers of the Christian Schools set a minimum age of seven in order to prevent a flood of toddlers from entering their free classes. In some towns like Cavaillon, they even raised the minimum age to eight. French public schools were closed to children below the age of five. In Mannheim and Heidelberg, the minimum age of entrance was set at six years.[39]

As these children were excluded from the public schools, their care became a more serious problem for working parents, a problem only exacerbated, of course, by the movement of industrial production out of the home. To a certain extent, the need for care for little children was filled by the unofficial "dame schools" or *Winkelschulen*, which persisted but were subject to increasing official discouragement.[40] These schools shared a characteristic nonchalance concerning the age of their "pupils," and most had the additional virtue of charging a minimal tuition. These existed in most of the major towns of both regions. Inspectors in Vaucluse even visited them on occasion and reported, for example, on one of three such schools in Cavaillon, where all of the pupils were below the age of six and the atmosphere in the classroom was "*fort turbulent.*"[41] In this context, the free or very inexpensive infant schools founded with state aid must have come as a relief to many of the working poor, who now had access to supervised care for their toddlers. When the Sisters of St. Charles of the town of L'Isle-sur-la-Sorgue proposed opening such a school in 1843, the major applauded the idea, which would be appropriate in a "*commune* where so many factories [and presumably, so many mothers working outside the home] [were] to be found."[42] Even the largely agricultural community of Lourmarin opened one in 1837. Predictably, the seasonal enrollment pattern there was the reverse of that in the urban communities: the *salle d'asile* enrolled forty toddlers in the summertime and none in the winter, and mothers in the community were reportedly "extremely pleased over the establishment of the school which allowed them to be absent from their homes, without anxiety, for work in the fields."[43]

By 1848, nine communities in Vaucluse had opened successful *salles d'asile.* The enrollment in the largest, that in Avignon, had reached 360 by this time. In north Baden, *Kleinkinderschulen* were opened in Mannheim, Heidelberg, and Sinsheim by midcentury. Shortly after its opening, the school in Mannheim enrolled two hundred toddlers.[44] If parents responded positively to the creation of these schools because of the inexpensive or free and dependable supervision they offered to their young children, authorities valued them as well for the opportunity they offered to teachers to mold the young before it was too late. Inspectors in Vaucluse who visited the schools found the children "submissive, silent and very well cared for," or "docile, and attentive [and] . . . cared for with affection."[45] In general, the children in the *asiles* presented to inspectors a sharp contrast to those "abandoned to themselves" and subject to "that multitude of accidents that come so easily to plunge into mourning peaceable and happy households" and to "those habits of laziness and libertinism which will be impossible to extirpate later on."[46] Even if school authorities and parents would have defined the usefulness of the infant schools in different terms, the schools' creation nonetheless marked the first clear meeting ground of state policy and family plans.

Infant schools addressed the problem of those too young to enter the primary schools, but those beyond the school-leaving age, particularly adolescents, were also the focus of administrative concern. The unruliness of the decades ending the eighteenth century and beginning the nineteenth seemed to originate at least partly in a breakdown of familial authority that was reflected in the vagrancy, criminality, and illegitimate sexual activities of the young.[47] As discussed earlier, school and church reports and even statistical observations of these decades reflect the general concern of the educated with the problems of youth. There were "single young lads missing religious services."[48] Servants, journeymen, and soldiers were frequently cited offenders when they lived away from home in the dangerous cities. But even rural young people were not innocent, as the popularity of village dances and the rising incidence of illegitimacy seemed to attest.[49]

Since the youth in question were beyond the school-leaving age, the primary schools were of no use. In Baden a series of ordinances was passed that created supplemental institutions for the schooling of those beyond the age of elementary instruction. The earliest ordinances required the attendance of all unmarried people below the age of twenty at Sunday school. Evening schools were also established in these late-eighteenth-century ordinances, in which boys who were not attending other educational institutions were supposed to enroll.[50] During the early nineteenth century efforts were made to increase attendance at these *Fortbildungsschulen* and to make evasion of them more difficult. An 1815 law required "all unmarried soldiers and national guardsmen, no matter what their religion . . . to attend Sunday school until their twentieth year."[51] In order to keep track of wandering domestic servants, Badenese state authorities required as of 1824 that all young people leaving their place of birth for service "give, under penalty of law, a certificate to the pastor of their new place of residence" and that "not simply reaching the age of twenty, but rather passing a test of basic knowledge of the most important religious truths . . . was necessary for exemption from attendance at religious lessons."[52] The Sunday schools were regarded not simply as places of moral instruction, but also as part of the system whereby some measure of supervision over footloose youth could be asserted.[53]

Although they too expressed disapproval of youthful dissipation, French authorities made no effort to force adolescents into institutions that would help to keep them in the right track. As was the case with primary schools, attendance at the various evening classes in France was left voluntary. *Instituteurs* were encouraged to offer evening courses for those too old for the primary school. Towns often established courses to make available instruction in more advanced subjects. According to a Vauclusan inspector writing in 1838:

> adult classes are multiplying these days now that each farmer is becoming involved in industry as well in this region. Young people reaching the age of eighteen or twenty regret not knowing how to read and write and do arithmetic because they feel that they are missing these abilities for the conduct of their affairs. Those among them who have not yet contracted the bad habits of gaming and café life fill their winter evenings by educating themselves.[54]

By the late 1840s teachers in at least half of the Vauclusan sample communities were holding evening classes during the wintertime. In the villages, these schools enrolled a handful of adults and adolescents. In the cities, the numbers of pupils could be huge, as in Avignon, where evening courses enrolled nearly seven hundred pupils, according to the reports of the 1830s.[55] Enrollment lists for evening courses in the town of Carpentras indicated that about three-quarters of the pupils there were between the ages of fifteen and twenty-four, suggesting that these urban evening schools enrolled a substantial proportion (perhaps 15 percent) of the young men of the towns.[56]

By the middle of the nineteenth century, then, there had evolved in both regions a number of supplementary institutions that provided supervision of and instruction for those school-aged children not reached by the regular schools, as well as many young children, adolescents, and adults beyond the reach of these elementary institutions. The network of peripheral institutions was predictably more comprehensive and coercive in Baden than in Vaucluse. The difference was indicative of that pattern of paternalistic compulsory legislation that seemed to mark all government policy in Baden. But the contrast also reflected official willingness in Baden to recognize existing social differences explicitly and to build them into institutions. Social distinctions certainly played a role in the formulation of educational policy in France as well, but state authorities there typically recognized them only implicitly and allowed the operation of parental choice, which of course remained subject to the more subtle influence of market factors, to play a freer role. The persistence of voluntarism as a central characteristic of the French educational system allowed the process of social reproduction to operate more subtly, but with important consequences. Indeed, the blatant inequalities in educational accomplishment were more dramatic in France than in Baden. In France, poverty was sometimes translated into illiteracy in the middle of the nineteenth century, whereas in Baden, despite the persistence of poverty, illiteracy had been virtually eliminated.

Still, we need to be cautious in drawing conclusions from this comparison of general literacy levels. The question of whether, or to what extent, deprivation of primary education represented a handicap independent of the poverty with which it was closely associated, remains open. Evidence presented here and in other historical studies suggests that simply knowing how to read and write did not make new options available for the vast majority of early industrial working people.[57] Improved prospects for completing a primary-school education were not necessarily connected with more open access to the advanced schooling that was a prerequisite for respectable careers. On the contrary, during precisely the same period when reforms of elementary education began to draw more and more children into the primary schools, other reforms were enacted to secure elite secondary schools against invasion from below. The antidemocratic aspects of the school reform process become more explicit as one leaves the realm of primary schooling—the schooling for the people—and enters the realm of classical secondary education, from which the people were deliberately and effectively cut off.

CHAPTER 8

Beyond the Basics

The Role of Secondary Education in State and Family Plans

EVEN AS THEY INTENSIFIED THEIR EFFORTS TO INcrease enrollments in primary schools, state authorities sought to restrict access to higher education. Although they rejected the obscurantist fears of universal primary schooling, school administrators were nonetheless wary of overeducation or inappropriate education at the postprimary level. Misplaced ambition rooted in mere schooling had to be avoided even as the possibility for self-improvement through appropriate education was held open. The problem of maintaining this delicate balance was a tricky one, especially in France, where the claim was more often made that schooling was the route to careers befitting abilities. The reforms of the secondary schools reflected this contradictory situation, but the general thrust of changes in the secondary schools during the first half of the nineteenth century pushed them to become more highly stratified and more finely tuned to the task of launching pupils into careers deemed appropriate according to their social origins. The channeling mechanisms were more subtle in France than in Baden, but in both regions they worked to insure that educational expansion at the primary-school level would not bring reverberations that would shake the social order.[1]

State officials had long been concerned about the connections between schooling and career. In both regions state interest in vocational education predated the revolution, and even preceded the onset of the industrial revolution, originating rather in mercantilist aims to increase popular productivity. The *Industrieschulen* opened in many German states in the later decades of the eighteenth century reflected an essentially mercantilist policy. As explained in the first article of a Badenese provincial ordinance of 1807, their purpose was straightforward: "the goal of the industry schools is to habituate children to work, [to] support poor parents, and [to] advance industriousness."[2] These schools, intended primarily for girls, met during hours taken out of elementary instruction, especially during that time of the year when the children were most likely to be idle. The schools were designed primarily to teach the various needle skills to rural girls. Boys were normally excused where they could be usefully employed; but the ordinance stipulated that

> where agriculture does not provide employment for the whole year, which is the case in many mountainous regions, or where herding is still practiced so that the children who are cattleherds pass their time in idleness and are subjected to provocations which can easily endanger their morality, boys should be required to learn knitting.[3]

Teachers for these schools were to be selected from among the most skilled women of the village and were to be reimbursed from fees or communal subsidy. Reports indicate that such schools were in existence in many north Badenese communities in the early nineteenth century. In Heddesbach, for example, ten girls produced six shirts, three pairs of gloves, and four pairs of stockings during one month at the *Näh- und Strickschule.* The seventy-six boys and girls in the school in Schriesheim produced seventy-three pairs of stockings, sixteen pairs of gloves, and an assortment of other articles.[4] Although not vocational schools in the usual sense of the term, the industry schools nonetheless functioned to increase the skills and productivity of children who would later be employed in the domestic industries of the region. In addition, they were designed to accustom children to work, and their establishment reflected state officials' beliefs that education could be a factor in economic planning.[5]

But Badenese authorities, like their counterparts in other German states, soon saw a need to establish schools to supplement the training of artisans as well. *Gewerbeschulen,* schools for apprentices in the industrial trades, had existed in some German towns as early as the end of the eighteenth century, but they were created in large numbers in the 1830s, apparently in response to the crisis affecting some artisanal trades in the wake of early industrialization. The Badenese *Gewerbeschule* Commissioner Buhl reported in 1831 that "in the last century, education has suffered a setback as a result of the decay and degeneration of the guilds. . . . Since the invention of the spinning machine and the steam engine . . . a great revolution in industry has been occurring . . . industry has become a science."[6] *Gewerbeschulen* could teach the science of industry to future industrial workers. Teaching subjects like design, arithmetic, chemistry, geometry, and accounting, these schools were designed to accompany the practical instruction in a single craft that the apprentice was receiving from his master. With the exception of those in a few trades for which such supplementary training was deemed unnecessary, all apprentices were required to attend *Gewerbeschule* classes if the town in which they were apprenticed had them. School hours were set to accommodate the apprentices' work schedule: one hour on weekday evenings and on Sundays and afternoons off. Because attendance was mandatory, teachers kept a record of the attendance of each pupil, and also of his comportment and capacity.[7]

The institution of *Gewerbeschulen* and the enforcement of attendance at them became wedges with which state officials could force themselves into the processes of training artisanal workers and regulating access to the trades. This potential became more obvious with each successive regulation concerning these schools. In 1839, after *Gewerbeschule* inspectors complained that apprentices were entering the school without sufficient elementary skills, state authorities reminded local guild officials that they were forbidden to accept as apprentices boys who did not have an *Entlassungsschein* certifying the completion of elementary school. When they learned that apprentices and journeymen at the apprentice school in Mannheim were disorderly and inattentive in class, the police of the city established a rule that lack of attention and misbehavior in the schools would incur the same penalty as truancy.[8] Since truancy from a *Gewerbeschule* in theory could delay the time of *Ledigsprechung,* or advancement from apprentice to journeyman status, and also entailed fines, evasion brought the risk of considerable punishment and gave state officials a lot of room to intervene in the apprenticeship process.

Of course, the government could enforce these controls over apprenticeship only with at least some cooperation from guild officials. The *Gewerbeschulen* were, in fact, in part subsidized through contributions from guilds, and guild members sat on their governing boards. But it is also clear that masters in many crafts were unwilling to grant to state authorities the degree of control over apprenticeship implied by the *Gewerbeschule* regulations. During the 1830s and 1840s, continued resistance of masters to the claims of these schools attests to this unwillingness. The resistance also placed limits on the degree of control over access to industrial trades and industrial training the state could take over, but the *Gewerbeschulen* nonetheless created an important state inroad into the regulation of vocational channeling.[9] And the impact of the institution was apparently increasing toward the middle of the nineteenth century. Attendance at the *Gewerbeschule* of Heidelberg climbed from 84 in 1833 to over 250 by the end of the decade. In the mid 1830s, authorities in Mannheim complained that although over one hundred apprentices were enrolled in their school, many more were truant. By the mid-1840s, the enrollment had risen to nearly 250 apprentices, and 78 journeymen attended voluntarily.[10] The rising attendance, and especially the presence of journeymen in these schools, suggests that they taught skills valued by the artisanal classes. Still, authorities' attempts to force all apprentices to attend produced continual clashes with both apprentices and their masters.[11]

In France vocational training was available in the state-supported *Écoles des Arts et Métiers* in Paris and a few provincial centers during the late ancien régime. But then and later, supplementary training for artisanal apprentices was largely the responsibility of the municipality. In the early 1830s most cities sponsored some such courses; Avignon, for example, subsidized free public courses in design and painting, linear design, chemistry, and mathematics. These were evening courses, and their pupils were mostly apprentices and journeymen. In 1834 classes of design and painting enrolled over 250 pupils; 64, mostly "in mechanical trades," were enrolled in the class in linear design; the chemistry course attracted 50 pupils "from the artisanal and manufacturing classes"; finally, in the mathematics class there were over 40 pupils, and its alumni included "gifted mechanics, joiners and masons able to direct large enterprises."[12]

In addition to the classes run by the city, there were others made available through the workers' own organizations. Agricol Perdiguier recalled that at the *mère* of the *Devoir de la Liberté* in Avignon, one of the *compagnons* taught courses in linear design during the early 1820s. The laws outlawing guilds in France certainly inhibited organizational activities and self-education of this sort. But it seems also to have been the case that the subterranean character of organizations like the *compagnonnages* made them and their educational efforts more impermeable to government interference. But even the city courses for artisans were not functioning as regulatory agencies in the manner of the Badenese *Gewerbeschulen.* For all intents and purposes, the French state still remained aloof from involvement in industrial training in the middle of the nineteenth century.

But it was not so reticent when it came to the training of those who would find their way into elite occupations. This training, which in both France and Baden still took place in classical schools, was the prime concern of educators and school officials interested in secondary education. And the institutional focus of most secondary-school attention and support was the Latin school created in the Renaissance period and passed down essentially unaltered in its curriculum to the era of political and industrial revolution.

To be sure, there had been some changes. The moral reform era of the seventeenth century and the later Enlightenment brought challenges to traditional pedagogy, which eventually affected these schools. In France orders like the Brothers of the Christian Schools opened *collèges,* where the curricular emphasis was more modern and allocated more time to the study of French and mathematics than did the dominant Jesuit *collèges.* Some newer institutions designed to meet the advanced educational needs of specific groups were opened under state and private sponsorship.[13] State governments were particularly active in creating educational institutions for those professions deemed essential to the running of the state itself—administrative, military, and technical personnel. In the German trade centers there were a large number of commercially oriented secondary schools opened in the later decades of the eighteenth century. But education in the classics still dominated the curricula of most secondary institutions. And despite the spate of criticisms of Latin learning that had been appearing since the seventeenth century, despite the decline in enrollments that many *collèges* and *Gymnasia* experienced during the eighteenth century, classical schools continued to dominate the field of secondary education. State efforts to bring educational institutions into a rationalized system under state direction necessarily involved a reexamination of the functioning of these schools; in the process, classical learning took on a new meaning and was preserved and even revitalized. If pedagogues of the eighteenth century by and large dismissed Latin learning as so much noise, those of the early nineteenth generally considered it crucial to the formation of an intellectually complete human being.

Classical training found many supporters in the early nineteenth century. In their defense of it, educators usually claimed that the study of the classics produced the capacity for thinking clearly and behaving well in any profession.[14] This abstract quality, the capacity to train the pure intellect, was emphasized and valued precisely because it seemed divorced from the merely practical and distant from the mundane concerns of career. Thus the *recteur* of the *académie* of Nîmes wrote to Paris in 1817 that the role of the royal *collèges* was "less a matter of teaching such and such a thing than of making [the pupils] capable of teaching themselves on leaving the *collège.* The study of the classical languages and the familiarity, contracted early in life, with the classical authors is the surest means of succeeding at the development of all the moral faculties."[15] The precise balance between the classics and the sciences in a secondary curriculum remained a subject of heated debate in France, but few educators denied that both were necessary for the education of the upper classes. If the number of hours devoted to classical studies in the *collèges* rose and fell with political fortunes and changes in administrative personnel, they were always a substantial part of the curriculum.

The same was true of the *Gelehrtenschulen* in Baden. Latin and Greek studies always comprised about half of the class hours in the *Lyzeum* or *Gymnasium.* This training, according to the description of one early-nineteenth-century educator, was designed to

> lay claim to the noblest capabilities of the elected youth . . . who will with the blessing of a rich education apply them directly or indirectly in life's various callings, so that as judges or lawyers, as teachers or preachers of the Word, as higher state officials or, what is more, as noble educated human beings even without public function, they will invest within the narrow or broad spheres of their activity the capital of knowledge, wisdom and professional loyalty to the profit of all those around them.[16]

The possession of classical knowledge marked its possessor as morally and intellectually superior to those with mere practical knowledge. Even as it became imperative for the people to be schooled, one might say because of the rising level of primary schooling, it became imperative for the social and political elite to distinguish itself through its superior education from the merely schooled. The classical schools, which turned out men capable of quoting in Latin or Greek the noble words of favorite authors, served this purpose admirably. And the proof of educational superiority served as a more viable justification for elite status in the postrevolutionary world than did inherited wealth or position. And so, despite the far-reaching changes in secondary educational institutions in the reform era, the central place of classical instruction in its curriculum remained.

One thing that did change was the nature of access to classical learning. This kind of learning was, by plan and in fact, becoming the prerogative of a shrinking elite. During the epoch of their foundation and throughout much of the seventeenth century, Latin schools often attracted many pupils from the popular classes. In many towns they enrolled substantial proportions of the boys from artisanal families. Already in the late eighteenth century, however, state and local authorities began to express unease with this situation and talk about the problem of overeducation. The Jesuits' policy of offering free instruction to the sons of town residents in places where they held classes became suspect, and apparently contributed to the attack on the Jesuit order and its schools that came to a head in the expulsion movement of the 1760s. In Avignon the municipal council took action to replace the town's Jesuit *collège* in 1768, and some of the applicants for the position of supervision of the *collège* found it politic to set themselves apart from the policy of their predecessors regarding admission to the school. The order eventually selected to replace the Jesuits, the Benedictines, had stated clearly in the proposal that they differed from other congregations in their policy of "admitting into their institutions only children from good families who have prior instruction; an unlettered child, or the son of an artisan, would present himself in vain; we would never admit him."[17]

The sentiments persisted into the nineteenth century, even if their expression were more muted. M. Pazzis remarked in his statistical observations that the number of *collèges* and *pensions* in Vaucluse was too great, and pupils in them generally abandoned their studies after only two or three years anyway. The *recteur* of the *académie* of Nîmes agreed, noting in 1817 that the number of *collèges* in the département was too great for the real need. The director of the *Lyzeum* of Mannheim revealed a similar concern when he complained in the early 1820s that there were too many poor pupils attending his school and requesting dispensation from tuition.[18]

One response to the fear of overenrollment in institutions of classical secondary education was the creation of alternative institutions for those classes who could afford secondary schooling but whose social position and career potential made classical training inappropriate. The experimental institutions that had existed since the latter part of the eighteenth century became the models for a new set of public institutions—the *höhere Bürgerschulen* in Baden, and the *écoles primaires supérieures* in France—that were designed to channel the wrong sorts of pupils away from the classical schools. The director of the *höhere Bürgerschule* in Heidelberg summarized the goals behind his institution's foundation in his annual report of 1856:

> the former Third Estate has split itself into three further groups: the educated and official classes, the upper industrial and commercial classes, and the working and serving class. For the education of the first there are the institutions of higher education which have been established for the most part for centuries—*Gymnasia, Lyzeum* and university; for the lower popular classes, who used in the old days to be deprived of all education, the state in alliance with the church has made provision through the foundation of the *Volksschulen;* but for the middle orders, these offer either too much or too little. . . .[19]

The *höhere Bürgerschule* met the presumed needs of the middle sector.

The *höhere Bürgerschulen* of north Baden taught religion, German, and French, and offered a selection of optional classes in Latin, arithmetic, geometry, geography, natural science, technology, mechanics, history, and drawing. The emphasis was on the applied knowledge useful for a variety of industrial and commercial occupations. Some pupils entered the schools on leaving the primary school at age fourteen, "those boys who were not compelled to take up a practical occupation already at this age, but rather [had] the good fortune to devote themselves to the accumulation of useful knowledge for a longer time, to the age of sixteen or twenty years."[20] Boys could enter much younger, however, since all that was required for entrance was the ability to read and write. The lower grades of the *höhere Bürgerschule* occasionally even prepared a boy for entrance into a *Gelehrtenschule,* but their main goal was clearly the extended education of boys who were not destined for classical studies. Still, the institution was distinguished from simple vocational training and from elementary training. In contrast with the *Volksschule,* which taught "only what no adult should be without and what was sufficient for the great majority of future state citizens," but "left dissatisfied the needs of those who would choose a middle-class occupation demanding a high level of spiritual development and a more encompassing knowledge," the *höhere Bürgerschule* satisfied the demand for a more refined education even while it deflected ambitious pupils from the costly and inappropriate classical alternative.[21]

That French educators created analogous institutions as an alternative to misguided classical schooling is no coincidence. The French were familiar with the *höhere Bürgerschulen* because of the well-publicized mission of Victor Cousin to Germany and his subsequent report to the French minister of education about schools there.[22] Furthermore, the Badenese mistrust of inappropriate higher education was shared by French educators. One founder of vocational schools in France wrote that

> the education given to a child is often irrelevant to his destined career and . . . the family, unable to have him apply it other than to its own occupation finds itself deluged with filial scorn. . . . Don't put the child destined for industrial work next to young men destined for letters, academies, law, administration, medicine and so forth, under penalty of creating, instead of an intelligent successor, a censor who will smile with pity at your language, who will disdain your occupation, your surroundings. . . . The higher education which the young master has received, the education side-by-side with the son of a dignitary, by giving him the mad hope of becoming an orator, lawyer or doctor, sidetracks him from the true path he was supposed to follow."[23]

It was to prevent such inappropriate mingling of young men of great and moderate expectations that the *écoles primaires supérieures* were founded. In presenting the motives for their establishment to the French chamber of deputies in 1833, Guizot appealed to these concerns:

> it is necessary to make it possible for a large number of our compatriots to arrive at a certain level of intellectual development without imposing on them the necessity of resorting to secondary education which is so expensive and, I do not fear to say it because I am speaking before statesmen who understand my meaning, so expensive and at the same time so dangerous. Indeed, for [the sake of] the few fortunate talents which scientific and classical training develops and usefully transplants from their prior condition, how many mediocrities contract [through education] tastes and habits which are incompatible with the modest condition to which they must return . . . and emerge ungrateful, unhappy and discontented beings?"[24]

The implication, of course, was that the encouragement of a few talents was not worth the cost to the mediocre and to society. Instead, the new schools, which were to be founded in every community of over two thousand people, would provide a more limited postprimary schooling to the ambitious.

Local governments proved unwilling for the most part to finance the *écoles,* even if state administrators greeted their creation with enthusiasm.[25] The prefect of Vaucluse commented on the occasion of the opening of the *école primaire supérieure* of Avignon that "those aspects of positive knowledge so commonplace, so practical and profitable at every instant of life and in all careers are finally made available to those who could not achieve this education before." The mathematics and elementary notions of the physical sciences that the school would teach would "explain to many minds still too inclined to the marvelous the principal phenomena of nature; education, descending from the elite of the working population into the whole class, will destroy dangerous practices and be of great utility to those who possess it."[26] The *recteur* of the *académie* of Nîmes shared the prefect's enthusiasm and wrote to Paris in 1843 that

> many fathers of families in this area, without aspiring to push their children toward the liberal professions, are wealthy enough to maintain them above the level of the working class and to bequeath to them a small commercial or industrial enterprise which involves extensive commercial dealings. They are thus not looking for a classical education for their children, but only some positive knowledge of both general applicability and immediate use for their material interests.[27]

While there is a suggestion here that administrators were perhaps not in complete agreement about the true clientele for these schools, it was clear that neither the *höhere Bürgerschulen* nor the *écoles primaires supérieures* were intended for all of the people. The instruction they imparted was limited, and probably of use to all, but the assumption was that only the upper sectors of the emergent commercial and industrial petit bourgeoisie would patronize them. This assumption was reflected in the levels of tuition charged. *Schulgeld* in the *höhere Bürgerschulen* of Mannheim and Heidelberg was at first set at a prohibitive 30 florins a year. In the late 1830s, *Schulgeld* was lowered to 16 florins, since so few boys were attracted to these schools. In 1849, in a gesture with political significance in an era of political revolution, tuition in Heidelberg was again lowered, to 10 florins.[28] But at the time of their foundation these schools were not attempting to attract pupils through low fees. The same was true in France. Guizot wrote in 1833 that "since the *école primaire supérieure* is destined for a rather comfortable class, it is unnecessary for it ever to be free of charge."[29] Indeed, free tuition was discouraged, since the goal of these schools was to channel pupils away from classical education rather than to encourage extended education for the poor.

The assumption behind these policies—that schooling was a consequence rather than a determinant of career choice—was also reflected in the official neglect of advanced schooling for girls. Private schooling was the only option for parents who desired more for their daughters than elementary schooling. In Baden and Vaucluse there were a number of private secondary institutions for girls, suggesting at least some parental interest. In Avignon, for example, at the pension of Mlles Dusseriez and Rovin, girls were taught by "the best professors in the city." In many bourgs the subsidized female religious orders who taught the poor free also held classes for the daughters of better-off citizens, in which tuition was charged and more advanced skills were taught. In Le Thor, for example, poor girls were taught reading and needlework during a few months of the year, and the wealthy paid for lessons in reading, writing, arithmetic, history, geography, and fancy needlework.[30] In Baden both Mannheim and Heidelberg had private *Tochterschulen* for the postprimary education of the daughters of the comfortable classes. But no public subsidy for advanced female education appeared before the third quarter of the nineteenth century. Girls, it was presumed, even girls from the bourgeois classes, could best be prepared for their domestic futures at home or through small private classes, an assumption that would only be shaken later when the demands of middle-class housekeeping also required specialized training, and when the intellectual distance between men and women of the middle classes threatened the unity of the couple. And from another direction entirely, middle-class women began to insist upon advanced schooling to enable them to provide for themselves upon necessity; but in the early decades of school reform state authorities showed no commitment at all to the provision of advanced training for girls.[31]

Maintenance of the existing sexual division of labor, regardless of innate intellectual capacities, was as much an assumption behind educational legislation as was maintenance of the social status quo. Because of the constraints on their options, assumed to be innate in their sex, women were simply left out of most state vocational and career training plans taking form through the schools. The emergent school system, with its multiplicity of increasingly specialized institutions, channeled children into the social and sexual niches they were naturally expected to occupy as adults. And, for most school officials, that was as it should be; educational institutions were designed to preserve and reproduce the social order, not challenge it. Changes in the schools were supposed to make people better able to fill their destined roles but not to lead them into questioning how those roles were allocated.

Official concern with the potential hazards of overeducation seems not to have been generated by a real upsurge in enrollments in publicly subsidized classical secondary schools. As Figures 7 and 8 illustrate, enrollments in the *collèges* and lyceums of north Baden and Vaucluse fluctuated around a steady level throughout most of the early nineteenth century. Scattered enrollment records for classical

Figures 7 and 8
Enrollment in Public Classical Secondary Schools in the Arrondissements of Avignon and Apt and in the Lyceums of Mannheim and Heidelberg, 1800-1850

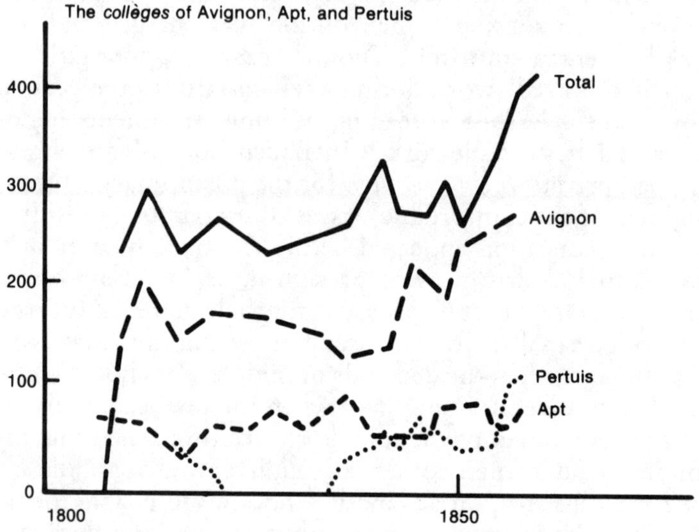

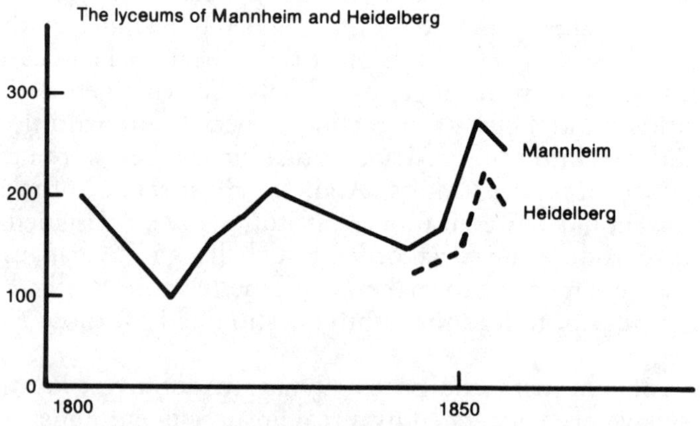

Source: ADV: T, Collèges; A. M. Bastit, "Personnel et élèves . . .";
MStA: KFG, 40/1971; HStA: 274/1.

For an indication of general population trends in this period, refer back to Tables 1 and 2 in Chapter I.

institutions in these regions suggest that they all had substantially higher enrollments in the early modern period than they did in the nineteenth century.[32] In the middle of the nineteenth century, only about 3 percent or less of the Vauclusan male population between the ages of ten and sixteen was enrolled in public secondary institutions. In Baden, the proportion was slightly higher, but per capita enrollment in these schools was stagnating or declining in both regions during the first half of the nineteenth century.[33] Even these enrollments are somewhat larger than the actual proportion receiving classical instruction, since many pupils in classical schools were enrolled in preparatory and elementary classes. The report of 1843 about secondary education in France indicated that among the thirty thousand or so pupils attending *collèges*, more than fifteen thousand were enrolled in primary, preparatory, or elementary classes. Of the remainder, close to ten thousand were still in the early grades of Latin grammar. These national trends were also apparent in Vaucluse: in the *collège* of Apt, forty-one pupils were taking Latin courses, while forty-seven were in the elementary classes; in Pertuis elementary pupils also outnumbered those in Latin classes. As Figure 9 suggests, even the rising enrollments detectable in these institutions toward the middle of the nineteenth century can be attributed to the practice of sending boys to the *collèges* for their elementary schooling.[34]

Although the concerns of educators about overeducation were

Figure 9
Enrollment in Secondary Courses and Total Enrollments at the *Collèges* of Apt and Pertuis, 1800-1860

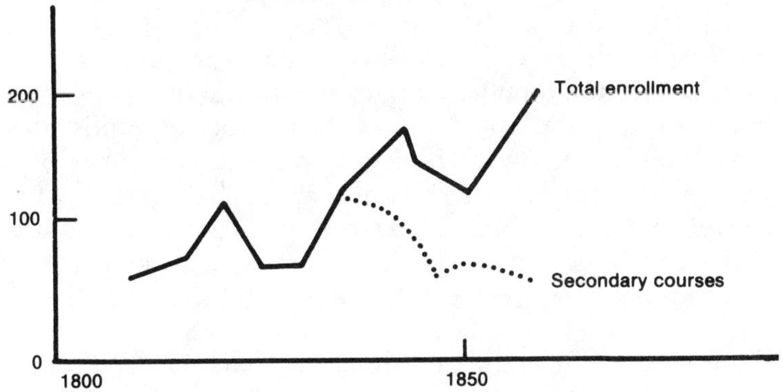

Source: ADV: T, Collèges.

TABLE 13
Enrollment by Grade in Secondary Institutions, Baden and Vaucluse, 1800–1860 (All Ordered from Least to Most Advanced Grade)

Lyceum of Mannheim, 1818	*Lyceum of Avignon, 1820*
Grade 1—27	Grade 8—17
2—27	7—18
3—24	6—38
4—21	5—24
5—10	4—14
6—14	3—16
	2—16
	Rhetoric —16
	Philosophy — 5

Communal Collèges, 1843	*Apt*	*Pertuis*
Primary and Preparatory	33	32
Elementary (8–7)	14	6
Grammar (6–4)	21	15
Superior (3–1)	20	6

Sources: ADV; T, Collèges; MStA: KFG, 40/1971; GLA: 356/696, 362/1616.

not strictly limited to fears for those who completed secondary studies, the fact that so few did so would tend to mitigate the potential problem somewhat as well. It was common for pupils to attend secondary school for only a few years, and most did not complete their studies.[35] Table 13 illustrates the pattern of diminution from the more elementary to the more advanced grades within the classical curriculum. The relative rarity of completion of studies is also apparent in scattered records about the pupils' taking school-leaving examinations, which were in fact also products of this era of official efforts to reduce the number of claimants to the title of educated. In the middle of the nineteenth century the number of pupils who took the *baccalaureat* exam was about a tenth of the number of pupils enrolled in *collèges;* of these, only about half passed. Lists of *Abiturierende* from the Mannheim lyceum suggest that about a third of all pupils who began their classical school actually ended up receiving the school-leaving degree.[36] Those who finished were an elite of an elite.

The low levels of enrollment in classical schools and of completion of secondary studies are in part the result of official discouragement and in part the results of contraints that prohibited the vast majority of families from even considering a classical education for their sons. Furthermore, investment in schooling could not really pay for most parents; state restrictions superimposed themselves on limits inherent in class structure. Certainly some of the skills and contacts useful for careers in the professions and commerce could be acquired through schooling, but recruitment into those careers operated in such a manner as to reduce the independent value of schooling. The costs of the required training in school and afterward, as well as those involved in setting up a career, made simple scholastic preparation useless to all except those who stood the chance to inherit or afford the necessary shop, notarial study, capital stock, or clientele. The only types of careers open to the merely educated were careers in the lower echelons of the state or church or business bureaucracies. Educational credentials, and these alone, occasionally qualified the talented younger son of a prosperous peasant, or occasionally even a poor boy, to enter careers of this sort. However, such "sponsored mobility" through schooling was open to very few.[37] Church-controlled patronage in the form of support for education and employment had certainly declined by the early nineteenth century. In France the revolutionary seizure of church properties destroyed the material basis of this patronage. In Baden the secularization transferred many of these resources more directly into the hands of the government. The military patronage already apparent during the ancien régime persisted in France, especially during the Napoleonic period, but its impact on the sponsorship of education and careers diminished thereafter. The growing civil bureaucracies of the state were certainly recruiters of the educationally qualified, as were those of large commercial and industrial enterprises. But the impact of these on the structure of the labor force were as yet minimal in the mid-nineteenth century; the total of all persons employed in teaching, civil service, clergy, the professions, and "white-collar" occupations in industry and commerce totaled only about 3 percent of the adult male labor force in Vaucluse and about 4 percent in Baden.[38] The limited recruitment into these sectors could not yet produce an upsurge in enrollments in the educational institutions that would feed into them, although it is likely that a barely perceptible rise in the number of pupils in secondary institutions toward the middle of the century may have resulted from the awareness of new possibilities. Research on French secondary education during the Second Empire suggests that the municipal *collèges,* if not the more elite *lycées,* began to provide access to a modest degree of social mobility for the sons of the more prosperous peasants and artisans.[39] But this concrete, if limited, embodiment of meritocratic principles contrasts with the aims of official policy during the early decades of school reform.

Furthermore, even if some parents eventually became aware of changes in career possibilities associated with the growth of the tertiary sector, extended schooling remained out of reach for the vast majority of children throughout the era of increasing attendance in primary schools. The family's need for the labor of adolescent children was more pressing than for that of the younger siblings; their potential earnings were greater; the costs secondary education entailed were substantially higher, including not only the high tuition fees, but also the costs of room and board for all but the residents of towns where the schools were located.

Tuition had been free in some of the institutions of classical education during the early modern period, but most forms of free schooling had disappeared by the end of the eighteenth century. Tuition fees ranged widely, depending on the type of institution and the proportion of the school's expenses that were subsidized. But for all of the institutions of classical learning—the *collèges* and *lycées* in France and the Lyzeum and Gymnasia in Baden—a substantial part of the cost of education was borne by the pupils' parents. In Vaucluse in the middle of the nineteenth century, between a third and a half of the educational budgets of secondary schools was derived from tuition payments. The situation was similar in north Baden; the Gymnasium drew support from state, church, and city contributions, but parental payments contributed between a third and a half of the budget. Even the more heavily subsidized *Lyzeum* relied on tuition fees for between a quarter and a third of its income.[40]

In this situation, tuition fees were necessarily high. In Vaucluse, fees in the early nineteenth century ranged from around 2 francs a month for elementary subjects to 12 for the advanced grades of the collège.[41] In some towns of Vaucluse during the Napoleonic era, sons of town residents were apparently admitted to municipal schools without charge, but this practice disappeared during the restoration. More typically, the municipal council stipulated the number of town residents who were to be admitted free as part of the contract between the town and the *collège.* The fees charged in the *collèges* were rising during the first half of the nineteenth century; in the 1820s, classes often cost around 5 francs a month, but by the 1840s, only the elementary classes charged so little. Pupils paid around 10 francs a month for advanced classes both in the state-subsidized *collège royal* in Avignon and in the communal *collèges* of the smaller towns.[42] These fees, amounting in a year to about two months' income for a skilled artisan, put secondary schools out of reach for all but the well-off and scholarship pupils.

The vast disparity in the cost of primary schooling that distinguished Baden from Vaucluse largely disappeared at the level of secondary schooling. Larger state and religious subsidies did lower the cost of higher education to families, but the difference was not important. In the middle of the nineteenth century lyceum fees were between 20 and 30 florins per year, an amount that had risen slightly since the beginning of the century.[43] This yearly tuition amounted to a month's income for an artisan. The *höhere Bürgerschulen* were less expensive, but even their lower cost was prohibitive for many families.

In neither place was poverty an absolute barrier to higher education. A few poor scholars were able to make their way through the system with the help of scholarship aid. But one product of the concern with overeducation was a reduction in the availability of such aid in the early nineteenth century. At the end of the eighteenth century there had existed a large number of endowments supporting advanced studies; often these led to positions in the churches. In the city of Avignon, for example, there had been 150 such endowments during the ancien régime, and the families who sponsored them named the beneficiaries on a yearly basis.[44] Similar scholarship aid, in generally somewhat smaller amounts, was also available for pupils in the *Lyzeum* of Mannheim and the Heidelberg Gymnasium. Endowments of this sort were losing value over time as a result of inflation; in France most were lost entirely as a result of the revolutionary seizure of church property. By the early decades of the nineteenth century, the aid that was available in both regions was diminished in value and more closely controlled by educational administrators. In the French lyceums a set number of scholarships were established during the epoch of reorganization under Napoleon. At first the sons of military officers received most of these. The exceptions, those free places sponsored by local governments, went to the sons of local notables.[45] Furthermore, the number of scholarships available in the *lycée* (later *collège royal*) of Avignon diminished steadily over the first half of the nineteenth century. (See Figure 10.) Some fees were also occasionally canceled in cases of need, but such dispensations again favored members of the administrative and professional classes in financial straits. The few exceptions from the working classes were clients in the patronage networks around the school itself, in particular the sons of the artisans employed by the school.[46]

Scholarship aid was also being reduced in Baden. Dispensations

Figure 10
Total Enrollment and Number of Scholarship Students, *Lycée* of Avignon, 1810–1843

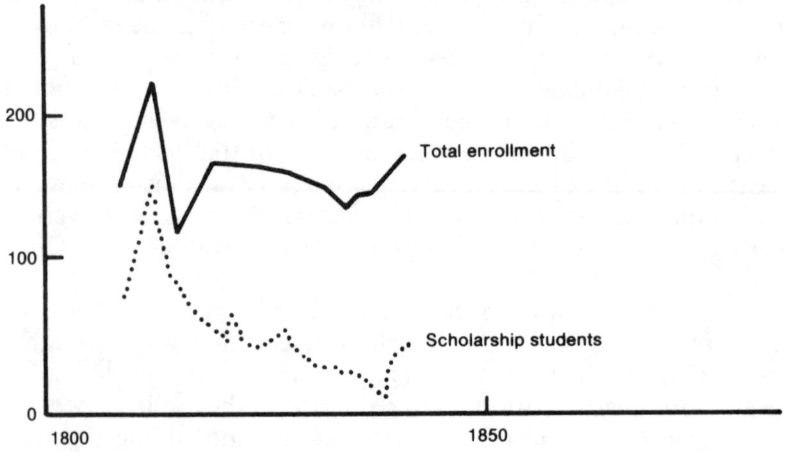

Source: ADV: Série T, Fonds de l'Inspection Académique, 37.

of *Schulgeld,* the most common form of aid, were becoming rarer. In 1820, 35 of the 120 pupils at the lyceum in Mannheim were dispensed from fee-paying. By 1824, the number of dispensations had risen to 48, and the director began to worry. Claiming that the institution was "certainly not a free school," he ordered that henceforward such dispensations would be granted only after one year of attendance, during which the candidate paid fees and showed signs of "industry, capacity and progress."[47] Eventually, following the lead of the directors of the Heidelberg school, he placed a ceiling on the number of fee dispensations—10 percent of paid enrollments. During the next twenty years, the dispensations that were granted went primarily to the sons of deceased, retired, or otherwise inactive or insolvent professionals and officials. These changes in theory and in practice restricted access to classical education.

The high costs and declining availability of scholarship aid meant that classical education became more than ever the prerogative of a social elite. The backgrounds of the pupils in the various kinds of secondary schools illustrate the extent to which channeling of pupils according to social origin and presumed destiny took place before secondary-school age. During the Napoleonic period, when the impact of state scholarship aid was still tangible, and *lycée* of Avignon drew about a third of its pupils from the artisanal and commercial classes. About a quarter of the pupils came from agricultural families. The remainder were drawn from professional, military, and official classes. By the middle of the nineteenth century, however, agricultural representation had virtually disappeared, and only about 15 percent of the pupils in the *lycée* came from the petit bourgeoisie; the school had become the training ground for the sons of professionals, military officers, higher officials, and the financial and commercial and industrial elite.[48] The communal *collèges* were typically more democratic in their recruitment, since their policies were subject to the approval of municipal councils more responsive to local political pressures. Thus in Pertuis, where the curriculum was more than usually geared toward commercial subjects, about half of the students in the collège were drawn from artisanal and commercial classes.[49] In 1852 the principal of the *collège* reported that "of thirty pupils who attend the *collège*, twenty-five are destined for commercial and industrial professions; only five are going into the liberal professions."[50] The local political influence of the petit bourgeoisie in many of the southern French bourgs seems to account at least in part for this phenomenon. In this milieu, a more democratic and meritocratic culture held sway. To be sure, recruitment even into these institutions was limited to the more prosperous and economically independent sectors of the popular classes, but at least the mix of classical and commercial subjects opened the possibility of access to the dominant culture and the professions to the talented offspring of the small bourgeoisie. The possibility of advanced schooling in a *collège communal* also made the alternative offered by the state—the *école primaire supérieure*—decidedly less appealing, and helps to account for the failure of these latter institutions in many bourgs.

In Baden restrictive recruitment into the classical schools was even more marked. There was no equivalent to the *collège communal*, whose administration was so much in the hands of the local government and whose classes mixed pupils in Latin and commercial subjects. Courses that were taught for the benefit of the commercial and artisanal petit bourgeoisie were taught either in the *höhere Bürgerschulen* or in the *Gewerbeschulen*. Thus, while a larger number of boys had access to secondary education in Baden, that access was structured so as to discourage contact and mobility between *Stände*. Furthermore, an incidental consequence of the creation of the *höhere Bürgerschulen* was to erect more solid social barriers around younger children as well, in the towns that had the new schools. One school inspector noted the trend and decried it for the deterioration it produced in the regular elementary schools:

> because of the establishment of our *Höhere Bürgerschule*, most of the children whose parents are concerned about the education of their chil-

> dren have been withdrawn from the ordinary elementary schools, especially those in the upper grades; for the most part, those who remain are those whose parents are poor or lacking in interest in their children's education.[51]

Those who attended the *höhere Bürgerschulen* were drawn from well-defined social classes; one historian of the institution estimated that between 80 and 90 percent of the pupils were destined for *bürgerliche* business careers—in this context referring to careers in commercial and artisanal shops.[52] Although an occasional student did transfer from the *höhere Bürgerschule* to a classical school, this was rare. Students chose the *höhere Bürgerschule* on the basis of their family occupation and presumed destiny; four-fifths of the pupils came from the same petit bourgeois backgrounds toward which they were destined.[53] The lyceums, on the other hand, recruited primarily for and from the class of professionals and government officials. Those achieving the *Abitur,* and even those excused from fees because of their poverty, were from these classes.[54] Badenese secondary schools, even more than those of Vaucluse, were institutions to channel and contain ambition and to preserve the correspondence between social status and educational accomplishment.

The narrowing of recruitment into the secondary schools was no doubt connected to the democratization of access to primary education. Even as enrollments in the elementary schools boomed, families from the more comfortable sectors of the popular classes, as well as from the professional and administrative bourgeoisie, began to send their children to more specialized and selective institutions for their primary and secondary schooling. The greater availability of schooling in no way eradicated cultural boundaries, even if it changed their nature. And in the absence of significant change in methods of recruitment into occupations, the expansion of primary education represented at best a very limited channel of mobility for the poor.[55]

The elite character of secondary schooling, which was apparent to everyone, coupled with the deliberate policy of restricting access to it, naturally created a potential for political conflict over its public subsidy. Again, the political struggle over the establishment and maintenance of secondary schools was more openly expressed and more significant in Vaucluse, where local government played a crucial role in the administration of some institutions of secondary education, than in Baden, where the administration of most secondary schools was handled bureaucratically. The problem of maintaining a network of secondary schools at the expense of the communes involved was especially complicated in Vaucluse, where the pattern of urban development had resulted in a large number of bourgs whose competing notables vied with one another for the retention of facilities in their towns. State officials were interested in preserving a minimal number of viable *collèges* in the region, and they felt that too many town governments were attempting to build complete programs of classical secondary education. The number of programs was too large for regional needs. State intervention in the establishment and certification of classical programs usually made them more expensive to maintain and intensified the competition for pupils among them. In this situation, where communal *collèges* experienced perpetual financial difficulties, political opposition to them flourished, and campaigns to close various of the *collèges* surfaced at several points in the early nineteenth century. The municipal council of Pertuis observed in 1824 that

> since the opening of the *collège* of Pertuis, two large establishments of public instruction have been opened at Forcalquier (B. Alpes) and at Aix (Bouches-du-Rhône). There are also *collèges* in the cities of Apt and Manosque (Basses Alpes) . . . that of Pertuis has [thus] been abandoned by the foreign boarding pupils, and today the school is attended by only about twenty day pupils from this locality.[56]

Without income from boarding pupils, the institution was almost entirely dependent on subsidies from the municipal council, and a faction in the municipal government doubted its worth. The problem of Pertuis was symptomatic of the difficulties many of the established older bourgs were facing. The urban growth of the early nineteenth century had left them behind.[57] These bourgs, or rather factions among their notables, strove to retain services, including that of secondary education, but stagnating economies and competition from more prosperous neighboring towns made the continued support for local institutions difficult. At midcentury the future of these institutions remained precarious, and the revolutionary upheavals of 1848 brought into the open the usually submerged conflicts that public subsidy of secondary education entailed.

On the occasion of his visit to the *collège* of Apt in 1849, the inspector warned his superiors that "the current municipal council, comprised for the most part of men who either cannot or do not want to send their children to the *collège*, takes no interest in it."[58] His warning was a timely one. The council soon decided to suppress the tax that had been voted by a previous council to finance the purchase by the town of a building to house the *collège*. The motives for the action are suggested by the inspector's warning: the revolution had brought to power a local government that was responsive to social interests, for whom the *collège* was an alien institution. This analysis is made explicit in a letter to the académie of Nîmes from the embittered owner of the house in question, who had spent ten years negotiating with the town over its transfer: "in 1848, a new theory relative to the *collège* sprang up in Apt: *the Collège of Apt was an Aristocratic institution; the local aristocracy should pay for it themselves. . . .*" In the election of 1850, in which the fate of the *collège* played an important role, a second council was elected, which was reportedly "democratic and anti-collegiate."[59]

Educational authorities had also been warned that in Pertuis "the existence of the *collège* [was] compromised. The communal authority [was, in August of 1848] in its entirety opposed to this establishment."[60] Municipal council debate records suggest that discussion centered not so much on the existence of the *collège* as on its democratization. The council eventually declared its support for the institution, but maintained that

> without wishing to establish distinctions between positions of more or less wealth other than those of merit or virtue, it is nonetheless just to give the latter more facilities for their education by according the poorest free places in the communal *collège*. . . . It is also reasonable . . . to make its instruction appropriate, no longer for the few exceptions, but for the vast majority of a commercial and agricultural population . . . without excluding the teaching of Latin and the dead languages for those who are called to them by a marked vocation or by the desires of their family.[61]

The council then established twelve free places at the *collège* and twenty more at reduced tuition, and called for a redesign of the curriculum to meet local needs. The suggestion to tailor the curriculum to the needs of broader segments of the local population was not new in 1848. Local day pupils had long been the mainstay of the *collège* of Pertuis, and many of their families belonged to the commercial and artisanal petit bourgeoisie, who dominated the town's economy. This history helps to account for the relatively benign attitude of the revolutionary government of the town, drawn from these same classes. In contrast, the *collège* at Apt, while hardly "aristocratic," had nonetheless catered to a different clientele. The town had a larger notable class, including more professionals, officials, and rentiers, whose sons attended the *collège.* The larger number of wealthy pupils drawn from the surrounding region, and the greater emphasis on Latin subjects, lent the institution a more elitist atmosphere. The social conflict that was brought into the open on the occasion of the revolution had slightly different consequences for public subsidy of secondary instruction in these two towns, but in both cases the elitist character of public secondary education became a matter of public debate.

In a move that was less dramatic, the council of the city of Heidelberg in 1848 used its more limited discretionary powers to lower the tuition at the *höhere Bürgerschule* so that it might serve "not only the propertied but the propertyless as well."[62] The events of 1848 barely touched the lyceums in Mannheim and Heidelberg (and, for that matter, in Avignon). Some students and professors in these institutions were involved in revolutionary activities, but the administrative machinery that ran them from state capitals ran largely uninterrupted. Calm was restored to the lyceum in Avignon at the cost of a few student expulsions. Officials in Heidelberg were happy to report that the unrest of June 1849 had resulted in no losses among the students and only three days of lost classes. It was noted without comment in the report that "several changes in teaching personnel occurred."[63] The lyceums, the most elite of all the public secondary schools, were, by virtue of their isolation from public opinion and public control, preserved from challenges even during a period of massive social and political unrest; but they were the only schools to escape notice.

The Revolution of 1848 raised questions about public education at all levels, not merely secondary schooling. In France the national debate over the merits of free and obligatory primary schooling was reopened, to remain an issue until the beginning of the Third Republic. In Baden as well, where primary schoolteachers had long been activists in the support of progressive political causes, demands for the secularization of public education and the establishment of free schools held a prominent place in the political programs produced by the revolutionary movement. The program for free, secular, and obligatory schooling became official policy in both countries by the end of the nineteenth century, but the more fundamental issues raised during the revolution remained, and still have not been resolved. The question of whose interests are served by the public subsidy of advanced forms of education to which only a minority of the population has access persists to trouble us even today. The battle for public subsidy and control of education was so entangled with the simultaneous political struggle for the limited extension of political rights and civil protections that the two have often been confounded as earmarks of democratic development. That government subsidy could in practice be undemocratic, that state-controlled schooling could be a form of class domination—observations that seem valid on the basis of the historical evolution of school systems—shock us precisely because of our acceptance of the equation between political progress and public schooling. Hard questioning of the form and impact of public subsidy of education, then as now, often seems like a return to the days when the people were kept ignorant as a matter of policy. The specific attack on the subsidy of elite secondary schools also continues to produce unease, for it points to a dilemma as yet unresolved. We have come to defend schooling as an institutional means for countering the transmission of inequality from one generation to the next, a belief that affects educational planning not only in France and Germany, but in much of the industrial world. But the examination of the historical origins of modern school systems suggests that they were initially designed to reproduce rather than to alter class positions, a function that, several contemporary studies suggest, they perform to a surprising extent even in the twentieth century.[64]

It would not be valid to conclude, of course, that public education is to blame for the persistence of inequality. But the evidence does suggest that our expectations about schooling are unrealistic, and that the prevalence of meritocratic beliefs only masks basic social and economic inequalities that shape educational patterns more than they are shaped by them.

CHAPTER 9

The Impact of School Reform

THE PROCESS OF SCHOOL REFORM WAS BY NO means complete in the middle of the nineteenth century, nor were the problems it was intended to address solved. The contradictory character of the expectations surrounding schooling in the evolving industrial capitalist societies of Western Europe made it unlikely that the schools would ever be able to satisfy demands made upon them. Continual reform—whether to adjust for perceptions that the schools were producing too many or two few skilled people, or to rectify deficiencies in the popular character, or to meet often conflicting expectations about how large a role schooling should play in career determination—has become a perpetual process.

Nevertheless, the basic features of the school systems of the modern epoch—the commitment to universal childhood education, the ultimate control of the state over the realm of education, the careful effort to link schooling with both civic preparation and occupational training, and the assumption that schooling is a prerequisite for political and economic adulthood—all are products of the era of school reform here described. And it is fair to say that even in the late twentieth century the school systems of Europe bear the mark of patterns established in the late eighteenth and early nineteenth centuries.

I have described how schools evolved in two specific local contexts. The regions examined were similar in many regards, most notably in terms of their level of economic development, but they exhibited many differences in the character of historically evolved political and social institutions, differences that had important consequences for the history of schooling and caused that history to diverge further even as the two regions confronted similar social and economic transformations.

As this study has illustrated, the incorporation of the people into schools took place earlier, more smoothly, and more completely in Baden than in Vaucluse. But the more successful schooling process in Baden was not a consequence of a higher level of economic development. It had even less to do with the development of democratic political institutions.

The relative slowness of the French state to accomplish its educational goals in Vaucluse was only in part the result of an inherited scarcity of material resources. The character of political domination, the nature of the political struggle in France during the reform era seem to have played a major role in the highly politicized issue of school reform. The commitment to voluntarism in education that was so compatible with the ascendant liberalism of the increasingly bourgeois national government of France had the ironic consequence of allowing local governments to obstruct school reform plans, and of allowing parents to keep their children home. The somewhat contradictory emerging meritocratic ideal of open access to uniform schooling, accompanied by a principled refusal to take into account the very real economic constraints under which families made decisions about their children's futures, already presaged the central and persistent dilemma of liberal educational policy in industrial capitalist societies.

The success of the Badenese system in integrating children in the schools was, in some respects, a product of its very conservatism. The persistent recognition of the connection between social status and political status, a holdover from *Ständestaat* society, allowed for the multiplication of specialized educational institutions planned for and then imposed upon a specific clientele by a paternalistic state and its coercive apparatuses. The supposed educational needs of each child were thus linked more directly than in France with his or her social origin and destiny; each child had a niche in the social and political universe and in the school system. In practice, of course, things were not quite so smooth or simple, and educational officials found themselves continually scurrying to patch up the latest challenge to the system. Nevertheless, the institutional variety and flexibility that resulted from the Badenese assumptions did accommodate a wider spectrum of familial circumstances.

These broad differences in the political philosophy and political institutions that helped to structure the school system were reflected in the different pace and timing of the success of the new sort of school as a pervasive institution of socialization. Access to publicly supported schools had become universal in both regions by the middle of the nineteenth century. But in Baden all communities had assumed the responsibility for supporting schools by the turn of the nineteenth century; in Vaucluse, only at the end of its fourth decade. In both regions a growing proportion of the "school-aged population" (the concept itself a creation of this epoch)[1] was brought into the school system. Enrollment figures need to be handled with caution, since their precision in this period is dubious, but the trends are stark enough to be more than the artifact of problematic statistics: enrollments were always significantly higher in Baden, but were rising in both regions in the early nineteenth century. By the middle of the nineteenth century, virtually all Badenese children, in communities of all sizes, spent some time in school. In Vaucluse there was more systematic variation in enrollments according to the size of the community, and the schools even at midcentury drew in fewer than half of the school-aged children; but the rise in enrollments, particularly between 1820 or so and 1840, was marked. It took only another two decades for the schooling of the children of Vaucluse to be completed.

Not only were more children enrolling in school in this period, but school attendance was also becoming more regular, and the duration of schooling was increasing. The early-eighteenth-century Badenese school register cited earlier suggested that few of the oldest pupils in this particular class had been enrolled more than four years. Not a single one had been enrolled as long as six years, despite the theoretical seven- or eight-year legal minimum. Closer enforcement of obligation laws seems to have pushed enrollments closer to the stipulated duration, even if it is clear that many pupils were still leaving before the age of thirteen or fourteen.[2] Furthermore, by the middle of the nineteenth century, schools in Baden were opened year round, and if summer sessions were short, attendance at them was well enforced. Scattered records of truancy suggest that, even if truancy remained significant until the second half of the nineteenth

TABLE 14
Ratio of Summer to Winter School Enrollment in Primary Schools by Size and Location of Community, Arrondissements of Avignon and Apt, 1822–1837

Size of Community	*1822–1823*		*1836–1837*	
	Boys	*Girls*	*Boys*	*Girls*
<500	.41	.27	.66	.51
500–2,000	.49	.30	.70	.64
2,000–10,000	.54	.51	.85	.79
10,000 +	.79	.76	1.00	1.00

Community	*1822–1823*		*1836–1837*	
	Boys	*Girls*	*Boys*	*Girls*
Arrondissement of Avignon	.66	.69	.89	.92
Arrondissement of Apt	.47	.32	.79	.72

century, levels were certainly not exorbitant in the early decades of the century.[3]

In Vaucluse the duration of schooling was certainly shorter. Again, the evidence is poor but consistent. Where they could, pupils apparently started school very young; teachers in the sample communities reported in 1833 that five was the most common starting age. In the same survey, more than half of the teachers stated that pupils generally enrolled for five years or less.[4] In other words, if children spent fewer years in school in Vaucluse than they did in Baden, the proportion that spent at least some time in school was on the rise, and the actual proportion of the population that had had some schooling was higher than what is indicated by the number of children in school at any one time. Furthermore, if school enrollments continued to follow a seasonal pattern in Vaucluse, the seasonality was already less marked in the 1830s than it had been in the 1820s. (See Table 14.) In both regions, enrollment and attendance patterns clearly suggested that the trend toward universal schooling was set in motion.

The basic skills the schools taught were also becoming more common, although the precise connection between schooling and literacy remains elusive. In Baden, where promotion to upper grades was supposed to be contingent upon the demonstration of a measured level of accomplishment rather than the attainment of a certain age, it is likely that the children in the advanced grades of the primary schools had already acquired at least minimal literacy skills. Of course, not all schoolchildren reached the upper grades. In fact, in nearly all of the communities in Baden for which there is evidence on the subject, enrollments dropped off sharply in the upper grades; pupils enrolled in those grades in which the ability to read and write was assumed were always a small minority of enrolled pupils.[5]

In Vaucluse, where the elementary schools were often ungraded, it is even more difficult to say anything about the level of accomplishment of the average pupil. The monitorial schools were the only ones to report about their pupils' accomplishments; their reports indicate that between one-half and one-third of enrolled pupils could read fluently and write on paper. However, the number of enrolled pupils who possessed these skills changed little in the two years during which records were kept, suggesting that either pupils entered with these skills or left soon after learning them. Indeed, the turnover rate was high; in any one quarter, about 10 to 20 percent of the pupils left the school.[6]

The different levels of school enrollment in the two regions were reflected in levels of adult literacy as well, although here too there was a notable increase in both areas during the early nineteenth century. The ability to read and write was apparently almost taken for granted by the beginning of the nineteenth century in Baden. In the year 1817 the Catholic deacon of the city of Mannheim reported to the minister of the interior that he had "made the sad discovery of sixteen-to-eighteen-year-old young people of both sexes who had never in their lives attended school and couldn't even read and write." As far as the deacon was concerned, their ignorance placed them "on the lowest level of Humanity, only a little removed from the [African savage]."[7] That the deacon saw fit to make this comparison of course betrays the biases inherent in his own social and ethnic position; nonetheless, his shock at the illiteracy of the urban youth is instructive and reflects the strong commitment to the written word pervasive in Badenese officialdom. He assumed that literacy was a precondition for civilization. His opinion may well have been distinct from that of many of the Badenese people, but there are indications that literacy was indeed broadly enough diffused by the early nineteenth century that it was regarded as a normal accomplishment for the average man, and increasingly, for the average woman as well.

What indications there are of levels of popular skill, mainly in the form of records indicating people's ability to sign their names, suggest that they were rising during the early nineteenth century; basic literacy was a virtually universal phenomenon in north Baden by the third quarter of the nineteenth century.[8] The *Bürgerlist* for the town of Schriesheim in the year 1780 indicated that only thirty-seven of the town's male citizens were incapable of signing their names. A literacy rate among this somewhat select population on the order of 80 percent is suggested, although a later commentator claimed that the majority of wives were probably illiterate.[9] This latter claim is borne out in a special series of marriage contracts from the village of Daisbach in the late eighteenth century. Nearly nine out of ten bridegrooms were capable of affixing their signatures, while fewer than half of the brides could.[10] Acts of paternity acknowledgment, numerous in the early decades of the nineteenth century, when illegitimacy was so common, provide some evidence that literacy among the generally poor fathers of illegitimate children was also on the rise. In the Mannheim suburb of Sandhofen there were thirty-one baptisms of illegitimate children in the Evangelical church between 1821 and 1824. Twenty-seven of the children were recognized by their fathers, of whom twenty-three were capable of signing the act of *Vaterschafterkenntnis.* By the early 1840s, very few illegitimate children were recognized by their fathers at the time of the baptism ceremony, but the fathers of those who were could all sign.[11] These high rates of literacy indicated for the fathers of recognized illegitimate children are important because they suggest that even for the very poor (much of the illegitimacy in Badenese communities resulted from the inability of poor couples to meet the minimum income requirements for marriage), the ability to sign was becoming common. And despite the common association between illiteracy and immorality, surveys of the prisons of Baden suggested that even the criminal class there was surprisingly literate. A mid-nineteenth-century report indicated that between 1830 and 1847 about 85 percent of the inmates in the state's prisons were capable of reading and writing. By 1853, 91 percent of male inmates were deemed fully literate, as were 98 percent of female inmates, the first evidence that points to the truly remarkable rise in female literacy that occurred in the first half of the nineteenth century.[12] These reports are confirmed by signatures in the civil registers, which were kept beginning in the early 1870s. By this time, literacy, as indicated by the ability to sign, had reached virtually 100 percent among the adult population of the city of Mannheim of marriageable age.[13]

In contrast, the school inspectors who visited Vaucluse during this same time period may well have regretted the extent of illiteracy they found, but they could not equate it, at least not openly, with savagery. This would hardly have been acceptable in a region where literate people were still, even in the 1830s, in the minority. After his tour of 1834, the inspector applauded the efforts of the *curé* of Lagarde d'Apt to open a school in his village, "which counted only three citizens who could read and write." He also noted that in the village of Lioux, still without a school, "only two of the municipal councillors know how to sign their name."[14] Nonetheless, by the time of his observations, change was already underway. The proportion of bridegrooms who were capable of signing their marriage acts had begun to rise in the late eighteenth century, that of brides by the 1820s. (See Figures 11a and 11b.) Following a typical regional pattern,[15] the ability to sign in the Vauclusan sample communities was low, particularly for women, but among both men and women, literacy was on the rise.[16]

In their broadest outlines, then, literacy patterns apparently mirrored school attendance patterns. Although the connections between the two are by no means straightforward, it does appear that by the mid-nineteenth century schools were beginning to take over the function of teaching literacy skills formerly taught and learned in a variety of contexts. Prior to the early nineteenth century, people who learned to read did so in a number of settings. School was one, but people often learned from family members, neighbors, and friends, in the family home or at evening gatherings like the *veillées* so popular in southern French villages. Bible-reading cultures in particular produced numerous individuals who learned or practiced reading in nonscholastic situations, like, for example, the Badenese peasant-turned-prophet J. A. Muller, who reported in his memoirs that "already by the age of thirteen [he] had read the Bible completely . . . on winter evenings and Sundays, we read two chapters aloud in the family, taking turns."[17] The assumption that learning to read and write takes place primarily during childhood and in the classroom simply was not yet valid. Still, it seems likely that it was during the early nineteenth century that the school began to monopolize the transfer of literacy skills. In the same communities of Vaucluse, trends in literacy and school attendance, especially for women and especially in the smaller communities, were beginning to merge. The correlation between community-level literacy measures and school-enrollment levels also rose dramatically between 1800 and 1840.[18] By the middle of the nineteenth century, schooling was becoming the normal path to follow, even as literacy was becoming a common, indeed expected accomplishment.

Figures 11a and 11b
Proportion of Brides and Grooms Able to Sign Their Marriage Acts, Vaucluse Sample Communities, 1760–1860, According to Community Size

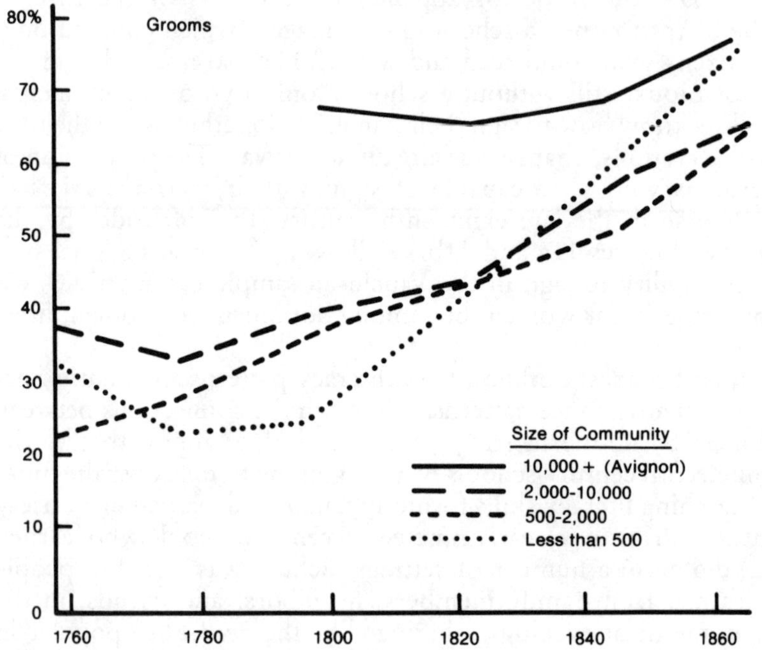

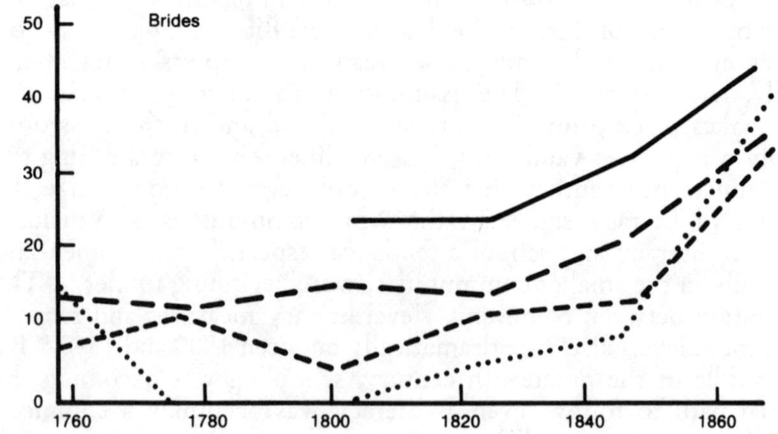

The rise in literacy was accompanied by linguistic shifts as well. Local dialects began to succumb to the power of the national tongue. Heunsich noted of Baden in 1857:

> What affects the habits of speech in our cities increasingly shows up in the dialects of the surrounding countryside as well. The educated classes, schooling, and foreign commerce obliterate the old habits more and more, and people who speak a true Mannheimerisch, Karlsruherisch or Freiburgerisch are quite rare.[19]

The author of a French grammar for Provençal speakers made a similar claim about his region in 1836:

> Provençal is disappearing . . . everything has changed in the last half-century; reading is more generally taught, military service although obligatory for everyone especially calls the young men of the lower classes and forces them to learn French; the huge number of commercial agents and foreign peddlars who roam through the countryside, this deluge of employees of all sorts who are sent down from Paris in exchange for the men of talent absorbed there, all this must inevitably bring the downfall of Provençal.[20]

These observations neatly summarize the sorts of transformations that encouraged the adoption of the national tongue. Even in Vaucluse, where the question of language was a sensitive political issue, French was quietly replacing Provençal. By the early nineteenth century, the ordinary people of Vaucluse were learning French. Evidence on linguistic habits is difficult to interpret, but any picture of the early-nineteenth-century Vauclusan countryside as a stagnant cultural backwater is belied by the records of educational and linguistic change that was occurring there.[21] In the very complaints of the school inspectors there are hints of that change; their own records suggest that claims about the local ignorance of French were exaggerated.

If French was not the mother tongue in Vaucluse and indeed represented to many Southerners the culture of the alien and often oppressive state of Paris, it was becoming a common second language. For most people it was rarely used but not unfamiliar. It was the language of the school, of the notary, the *état civil,* tax collector, often of the landlord and even the church, despite the familiarity of local administrators with the patois. An inspector's report of the 1850s suggests the special character of French speech, maintaining that "Provençal alone [was] used in the countryside except within the walls of the classroom," and predicted that "it [would] take centuries more for the French language to become that of their thoughts." But despite the fact that French was rarely used except where it had to be, the same report did admit that "the French language is understood, and spoken when needed [with more or less difficulty] all over."[22] Comments like these, added to the testimony of the civil registers and the linguistic evidence, all suggest that cultural change was ongoing. It is quite likely that the people of the Midi were in this epoch becoming functionally bilingual; many could read and write French, even if their spoken French did not satisfy the listeners from Paris. And if for political and cultural reasons they preferred their own patois, many also knew the value of learning French, if only better to manage in a world increasingly dominated by speakers of that tongue.

It is important to note in this context that the sorts of changes alluded to here—changes in linguistic habits, in the proportion of people learning to write, and so forth—began *before* the intensified involvement of the French state in schooling. They date back at least to the third quarter of the eighteenth century. It is certainly not coincidental that the proportion among young men in Vaucluse and elsewhere in France who could write began its slow and steady climb between 1760 and 1780 or so, that is, around the time cited by French historians as an era of qualitative change in the process of commercialization of the agrarian economy and a boom period for agricultural prices. The precise local dynamics that connected the growth of a national market to the involvement of local peasants with commercial dealings have yet to be traced. Still, it is tempting to ascribe to commercialization a role in the rising peasant interest in learning to read, write, and cipher.[23]

Not all of these changes brought profit to the peasantry as a whole, of course. Only those with substantial property, a small proportion of the peasants in regions like Vaucluse, actually had a surplus to market, and for these, high literacy skills had reinforced other barriers between them and the rural poor since at least the late decades of the ancien régime. (See Figures 12a and 12b.) For many, the economic structural changes that accompanied early industrialization brought only disruption and hardship. The erosion of industrial opportunities in the countryside, the overpopulation, and the crises that drove many out of agriculture altogether often forced the outmigration of sons and daughters who could no longer be supported at home. Indeed, the evidence from the Vauclusan sample communities suggests that it was precisely among the poorer agricultural classes that the early-nineteenth-century rise in literacy was most obvious.

Figure 12a
Male Literacy Patterns by Occupation, Vaucluse, 1800–1844: Signatures on Marriage Acts

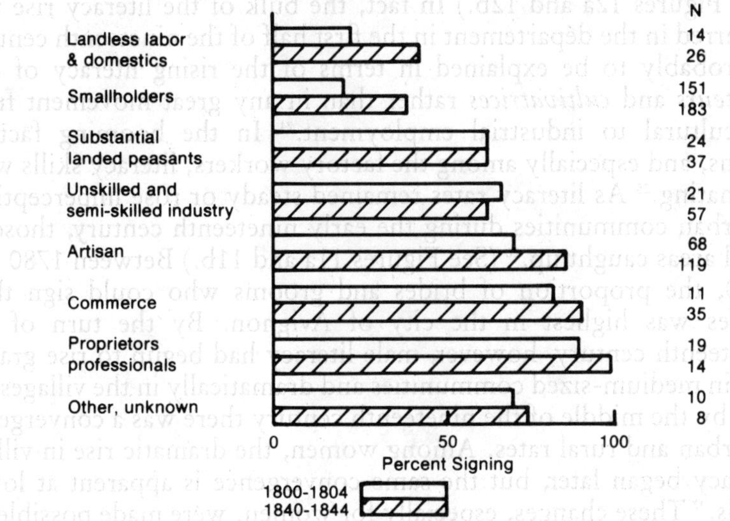

Figure 12b
Female Literacy Patterns by Occupation, Vaucluse, 1800–1844: Signatures on Marriage Acts

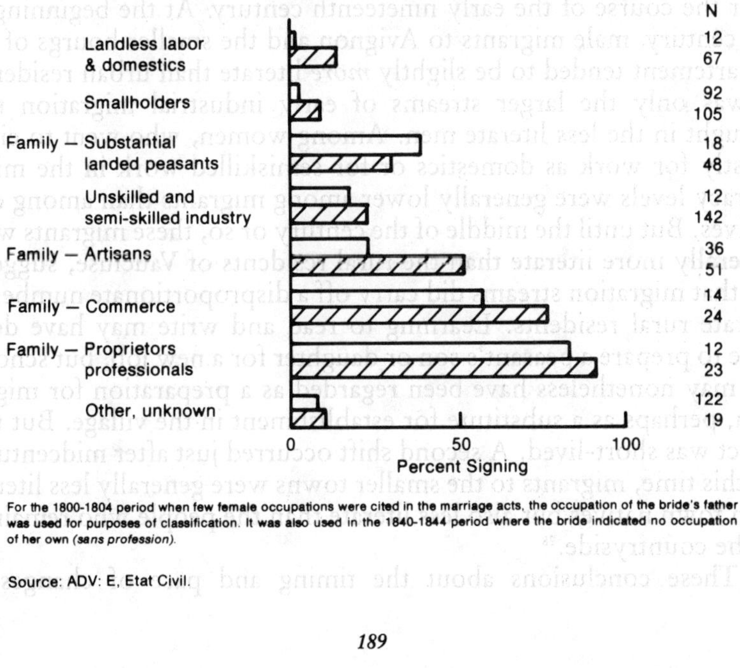

For the 1800-1804 period when few female occupations were cited in the marriage acts, the occupation of the bride's father was used for purposes of classification. It was also used in the 1840-1844 period where the bride indicated no occupation of her own (*sans profession*).

Source: ADV: E, Etat Civil.

(See Figures 12a and 12b.) In fact, the bulk of the literacy rise that occurred in the département in the first half of the nineteenth century is probably to be explained in terms of the rising literacy of *cultivateurs* and *cultivatrices* rather than in any great movement from agricultural to industrial employment.[24] In the booming factory towns, and especially among the factory workers, literacy skills were stagnating.[25] As literacy rates remained steady or rose imperceptibly in urban communities during the early nineteenth century, those of rural areas caught up.[26] (See Figures 11a and 11b.) Between 1780 and 1840, the proportion of brides and grooms who could sign their names was highest in the city of Avignon. By the turn of the nineteenth century, however, male literacy had begun to rise gradually in medium-sized communities and dramatically in the villages, so that by the middle of the nineteenth century there was a convergence of urban and rural rates. Among women, the dramatic rise in village literacy began later, but the same convergence is apparent at lower levels.[27] These changes, especially for women, were made possible by the better provision of schools in rural areas, but it should again be noted that, for men at least, the rise in rural literacy had begun before the epoch of state intervention in schooling.

Part of the explanation for the stagnation of urban rates lies no doubt in the migration patterns that brought less-educated migrants from the rural areas into the towns. However, this pattern also shifted over the course of the early nineteenth century. At the beginning of the century, male migrants to Avignon and the smaller bourgs of the département tended to be slightly *more* literate than urban residents. It was only the larger streams of early industrial migration that brought in the less literate men. Among women, who went to cities mostly for work as domestics or for semiskilled work in the mills, literacy levels were generally lower among migrants than among city natives. But until the middle of the century or so, these migrants were generally more literate than the rural residents of Vaucluse, suggesting that migration streams did carry off a disproportionate number of literate rural residents. Learning to read and write may have done little to prepare a peasant's son or daughter for a new job, but schooling may nonetheless have been regarded as a preparation for migration, perhaps as a substitute for establishment in the village. But this effect was short-lived. A second shift occurred just after midcentury; by this time, migrants to the smaller towns were generally less literate than town natives but also less literate than the people who remained in the countryside.[28]

These conclusions about the timing and pace of changes in

schooling and literacy patterns in different communities in Vaucluse call into question some common assumptions about the connection between economic change and education. The revisionist studies of the early industrial transition elsewhere in Europe and North America have already suggested that the jobs created during early industrialization were often unskilled or semiskilled and were thus unlikely to have produced a rising demand for the literacy skills taught in schools.[29] This claim is borne out here. It is clear that the peasantry in Vaucluse was traditionally less literate than other classes, and migration to the towns did for a time select out the more literate rural residents. But even if this evidence can be construed as support for the claim that early industrial changes did induce some people to seek schooling, the effect was indirect and short-lived. The really significant change of the early nineteenth century, in Vaucluse at least, was the rising literacy among the classes who remained in agriculture, especially among the children of the poorer agrarian classes. An increasing proportion of parents from these classes were choosing to send their children to school despite the difficulties that entailed. And any analysis of the meaning of school reform must take this into account.

The broad comparative findings also suggest that common associations between access to primary schooling and economic and political modernization need to be reexamined. The early attainment of universal schooling in Baden was possible because the reform of the schools system permitted the institutional flexibility necessary to bring into the school system children from very different circumstances; children of peasants and rural laborers, of the comfortable *Mittelstände* and the urban poor all found in the array of institutions for popular education one that was more or less attuned to their particular needs and constraints. This flexibility made universal schooling possible despite the economic marginality of many families. But if it was this institutional variety that allowed all children to be schooled, the role of the coercive laws in actually getting the children into the classes cannot be overlooked. All the evidence suggests that if schooling were a matter of free choice, the levels of school enrollment and school attendance would have been much lower. And in Vaucluse, conversely, part of the explanation for the slower accomplishment of state schooling goals lay in material obstacles to schooling that the state itself created or failed to combat: inflexible hours, high tuition fees, burdensome fiscal outlays only in part countered by state subsidy. But in Vaucluse, the fact that parents were free to choose whether or not to send their children to school meant that the perception that schooling was not that useful for the children of the people could be translated into simple avoidance of the schools.

But things were changing in the early nineteenth century, and it seems likely that parental attitudes about schooling were changing as well. If coercion worked quickly and effectively in Baden to bring about universal school enrollment, voluntarism was working too. In Vaucluse more and more children were attending school every year. More significant, sectors of the population previously uneducated—notably the sons of poor peasants and rural laborers and the daughters of both the urban and the rural poor—were being lured into the classroom. And unlike the situation in Baden, the schooling of these marginal children was not the result of coercion, or of the creation of work schools and the like. Apparently parents from these classes were deciding that schooling was a good idea, and they were increasingly willing to spare their children's time for it.

Just what these parents expected from schooling, and what their children got out of it, is difficult to establish. Certainly they learned some basic skills, skills that, for some people at least, were previously out of reach. Still, the simple attainment of these skills did little to open a brighter economic future for them, brought little in the way of enhanced occupational opportunities. The extent to which literates fared better than illiterates is impossible to determine with precision on the basis of existing evidence, but there is little reason to think that the opportunities opened by literacy alone in this era were numerous. Harvey Graff, in a recent study of the history of literacy in several North American cities in the mid-nineteenth century, concludes that in that context there were few differences in the material well-being or life trajectories of literates and illiterates that could be attributed to their educational qualifications alone.[30] It seems unlikely that in a more rural context, even in the context of an increasingly commercialized agrarian economy, literacy would have been any more determinant of economic success. It is certainly possible that parents were coming to see schooling as a means of achieving less tangible rewards, and the relative insignificance of schooling in this epoch as a determinant of economic success does suggest the need to look elsewhere for an explanation of its dramatic triumph. Graff argues that the surge in school enrollments and the rise in literacy in the early industrial era in urban Canada were the products of the evolution in class relations, were both part of the process of and evidence of establishment of hegemonic domination, which was necessary for the success of industrial capitalist social relations.

The study presented here offers some evidence to support such a claim, but some qualifications as well. Certainly the proponents of schooling in Baden and Vaucluse shared with educational reformers elsewhere class fears and class antagonisms vis-à-vis "the people" about whom they agonized and whose nature they hoped to tame. Implicit and explicit in the program of school reform was the desire to create a governable citizenry and a productive labor force. But in the social-historical context of early-nineteenth-century Europe, the two were not necessarily compatible; the new expectations about the functions of the schools had political and economic aspects that sometimes ran counter to one another. Furthermore, states apparently had more than one kind of option available in their decisions about how to use the schools. The comparison between France and Baden illustrates this well. In both states there were government officials sympathetic to the needs of industrial entrepreneurs. This was especially clear in France after the accession of the July Monarchy government, but there had long been strong advocates of industrial interests in the Badenese government as well. But in neither state was the increasing domination of industrial capitalists over the economy translated directly into political influence. The political realm remained, to a certain extent, independent of the economic, however constrained by it. And in the final analysis it was the state more than the economically dominant classes that translated the need for schooling into institutional practices. (Indeed, the conflict in short-term interests that could divide the leadership of the two spheres over schooling policy is nowhere better illustrated than in the debate over the schooling of factory children.) And the subsumption of schooling under the activities of the state made them open to political pressures to which the economically powerful were immune.

The character of the school reform was thus contradictory. This was especially true in France, where the political control of the local community allowed for more open debate about the schools' function and about the interests served by the public subsidy of education. The susceptibility of the French schools to local political control meant that they generally served the interests of the local, if not national, power groups, but in moments of political revolt (and there were many between 1789 and 1851), the schools were even touched by the expression of popular interests that undermined the more usual tendency simply to reproduce rather than to challenge the laws inherent in the social status quo. All of this does not deny the claim that the schools served a hegemonic function. They no doubt did and would increasingly, especially in France, as the idea of meritocracy became the official guiding principle of government during the Third Republic. But the character of the schools as state institutions made them subject to the same contradictory expectations and claims to which the state itself was subject. Consequently, their effectiveness as institutions in service of an emergent capitalist hegemony was weakened to the extent that the capitalist classes themselves failed to control the state because of opposition from older elites and from popular contenders. Furthermore, there was even a sense in which the schools were doomed to fail precisely because of the contradictions inherent in the liberal program they came to embody; the French case at least suggests that tensions between liberal notions of freedom and equality came closer to the surface as the hold of liberals on state institutions, including the schools, tightened. Furthermore, the comparison also suggests that the French drift toward hegemonic means of social control was palpably less effective in the short run at "taming" the people, even if it might still be argued that in the long run it did effect a more stable domination by the capitalist order.

I would add one further qualification, on the basis of this study, to the general argument that the school reform of the early industrial capitalist era is to be understood as the imposition of a new kind of class domination. The qualification is simple. Whatever the intentions of school reformers, teachers and pupils took their own experiences and intentions into the classroom. The actual impact of the classroom experience on the child may not necessarily have been what was intended. Some of the ways in which actual classroom life diverged from the plans has been suggested by the institutional records presented here. Much of that history has yet to be written.

This study does suggest how the evolution in the organization of schools, in their purported functions, and in the way people used them transformed the character of socialization and created a huge potential impact for the school. The findings presented here challenge both traditional interpretations of schooling history and some aspects of the recent revision of that history. They suggest the need to examine more closely the local implementation and effect of school reform measures as well as the programs of school promoters, even as they add further substance to the argument that the demand for schooling for the people came distinctly "from above" and as a result of class fears and antagonisms. And, even if the message that the children of the people took from the schools was not necessarily the one intended for them, it is nonetheless critical to recognize the interests that fed into the movement for schooling for the people, the very real differences that affected the course and impact of this movement in different localities, and the character of the social-historical moment in which the movement triumphed. For their effects are still visible in the classrooms of today, which, with all their problems and promises, are the institutional legacy of that creative epoch.

APPENDIX I

List of Sample Communities

A. VAUCLUSE

Community	Population in 1836	Elementary school in		Secondary school in		Type of economy* in 1836
		1806	1836	1806	1836	
Apt	5,958	Yes	Yes	Yes	Yes	4
Auribeau	127	No	No	No	No	1
Avignon	31,786	Yes	Yes	Yes	Yes	4
La Bastide-des Jourdans	855	Yes	Yes	No	No	1
Cabrières d'Aigues	585	Yes	Yes	No	No	1
Cabrières d'Avignon	802	No	Yes	No	No	1
Cadenet	2,598	Yes	Yes	No	No	3
Cucuron	2,187	Yes	Yes	No	No	3
Gargas	865	Yes	Yes	No	No	1
Gignac	195	No	Yes	No	No	1
Jonquerettes	255	No	Yes	No	No	1
Lacoste	614	Yes	Yes	No	No	2
La Motte d'Aigues	451	Yes	Yes	No	No	1
La Tour d'Aigues	2,312	Yes	Yes	No	Pr	2
L'Isle-sur-la-Sorgue	6,277	Yes	Yes	Pr	Pr	3
Lourmarin	1,660	Yes	Yes	Pr	No	3
Merindol	762	Yes	Yes	No	No	2
Puyvert	213	No	No	No	No	1
Saumanes	588	No	Yes	No	No	2
Sorgues	2,797	Yes	Yes	Pr	Pr	3

*KEY 1 = Predominantly agricultural population (ca. 80 percent or more)
2 = Small nonagricultural population (ca. 30 percent or less)
3 = Significant nonagricultural population (ca. 30–50 percent)
4 = Predominantly nonagricultural population (50 percent or more)
Pr = Private school only

Sources: ADV: Série T. Diverse; Série M. Rencensement de 1836.

B. BADEN

Community	*Population in 1836*	*Elementary school in*		*Secondary school in*		*Type of economy in 1836**
		1806	*1836*	*1806*	*1836*	
Bockschaft	108	Yes	Yes	No	No	1
Brombach	357	Yes	Yes	No	No	1
Daisbach	701	Yes	Yes	No	No	1
Ehrstadt	590	Yes	Yes	No	No	1
Handschuhsheim	1,843	Yes	Yes	No	No	3
Heddesbach	357	Yes	Yes	No	No	1
Heidelberg	12,548	Yes	Yes	Yes	Yes	4
Horrenburg	436	Yes	Yes	No	No	1
Käferthal	1,542	Yes	Yes	No	No	3
Lampenhain	370	Yes	Yes	No	No	1
Mannheim	22,811	Yes	Yes	Yes	Yes	4
Mühlhausen	930	Yes	Yes	No	No	2
Neidenstein	846	Yes	Yes	No	No	4
Nussloch	2,051	Yes	Yes	No	No	3
Rohrbach	1,448	Yes	Yes	No	No	2
Sandhofen	1,105	Yes	Yes	No	No	1
Schriesheim	2,849	Yes	Yes	No	No	4
Waldangelloch	987	Yes	Yes	No	No	2
Walldorf	2,102	Yes	Yes	No	No	1
Wieblingen	1,261	Yes	Yes	No	No	2

*See preceding chart for key.

Sources: GLA: Diverse; A.J.V. Heunisch, *Das Grossherzogthum Baden* (Heidelberg, 1857); E. Keyser, *Das Badische Städtebuch* (Stuttgart, 1959).

APPENDIX II

ANY ATTEMPT TO EXPLORE SOCIAL HISTORY IN PEriods prior to those for which the systematic statistical evidence is available is complicated by the dearth of evidence and by the gaps in what does exist. The field of educational history is no exception. Historians of education have often avoided the problem by concentrating their efforts on the more accessible aspects of schooling history—central policy making, national trends, etc.—or by writing anecdotal accounts that describe the educational scene as it appears from the rather randomly gathered tidbits of information to be found in local sources. While any attempt to do local social history entails hunting around in a variety of sources, the search can be made more systematic. It was with a view toward systematization of data collection and analysis that the research design for this study was formulated. The bulk of the analysis rests upon a fairly exhaustive exploitation of the sources about schooling available for a preselected set of sample communities; research centered around a predetermined set of questions. The communities were selected randomly from among all communities within given size categories in each region and should thus be typical of all communities of their size within the regions. Before beginning research, I had a fairly clear idea of the kind of questions for which I needed answers. Actually finding the requisite information meant culling a variety of sources, and the search was not always fruitful. Gaps in the existing data had, on occasion, to be filled by interpolation from or manipulation of series data. The problem of interpretation of contemporary statistics proved to be a difficult one. While I often found direct information in the archives concerning, for example, school-aged population, it sometimes became clear that such information was unreliable. In this Appendix, I will discuss in more detail the types of sources used to compile the data set for the sample communities, and also outline the procedures used to estimate values for missing or unreliable information.

SOURCES OF INFORMATION ABOUT SCHOOLING

The earliest evidence about schooling in north Badenese communities comes from records of ecclesiastical administration. For the sample communities, these records were kept until the turn of the nineteenth century under the auspices of the Kurpfälzisch state churches, the Catholic bishopric of Speyer, the diocese of Mainz, and other small territorial authorities; many of these records have been collected in the *Generallandesarchiv* in Karlsruhe, where they are catalogued in special collections. These early records usually concern the hiring and payment of schoolteachers, and much valuable information about other aspects of schooling can often be gleaned from them as well. The most systematic of these are the *Kompetenzenbücher*, which list, parish by parish, the total income each teacher was receiving and the various conditions of his appointment. These reports often indicate the amount of tuition fees and the number of pupils enrolled as well. Church visitation records are also useful, although irregularly available. After the incorporation of the region studied into the Badenese state, school records were collected at various levels of administration: *Kreisregierung, Bezirksamt, Ministerium.* The Bibliography gives a complete list of the various archival sections consulted. The most complete account of community-level schooling conditions for the early nineteenth century is the set of reports submitted by each community in 1836, at the time of legislative reform. Collected in the *Generallandesarchiv* in the various communal and *Bezirksamt* sections, these reports indicate enrollments, fees, salaries, and so forth. Records about educational institutions other than elementary schools are also scattered through various levels of administrative archives; many are still preserved in local archives. For compiling the data set on Badenese primary schools, the most useful *Abteilungen* for the period before consolidation (i.e., prior to 1802) were *Abteilungen* 63/1, 63/74, 63/77, 63/131, 63/138, and 77/6087, all of which contain documents taken over by the Badenese government at the time of consolidation. For later periods, most information was found in the communal archives gathered in Karlsruhe (*Abteilungen* 204, 213, 229) and in the *Bezirksamt* records (*Abteilungen* 356, 362, 377, and 388).

For Vaucluse, information about schooling during the ancien régime is found mainly in Church records and municipal council minutes. There was no central agency of any sort responsible for the collection of such information, and except for an occasional mention by interested *intendants,* little word on schooling went back to Paris. It was only during the revolution that a centralized state schooling bureaucracy was established. From this time on, however, data collection was more highly centralized in France than in Baden. Evidence about schooling during the revolution is contained in Series L of the Departmental Archives in Avignon. Thereafter, Series T is the source of most information about schooling at all levels. Numerous surveys of the state of primary instruction were conducted by the national government, beginning in the first decade of the nineteenth century. The results of these surveys are kept in Series F^{17} of the National Archives in Paris. Gaps in reporting, discussed in more detail below, and local misunderstanding or misreporting often detract from the usefulness of these national statistics. Only in the 1830s, when state inspectors began actually visiting community schools and reporting their findings to Paris, do the national reports become more reliable.

From the above sources the following information was collected for the sample communities, concentrating on three periods, the late ancien régime, the turn of the nineteenth century, and 1836; the latter date was chosen largely because there were systematic surveys of schools undertaken in both France and Baden in this year.

School enrollment
Tuition fees
Communal subsidy of the school
Contemporary estimates of school-aged population (not always available)
Teachers' income

This evidence from schooling records was then supplemented with a variety of other types of information.

ESTIMATES OF SCHOOL-AGED POPULATION

Because contemporary estimates of school-aged population are often either unavailable or unreliable, a means of estimating this population for the sample communities from their vital registers was employed. Vital registers for the Vauclusan communities were used in the Departmental Archives, where copies have been collected; in Baden, use of vital registers entailed trips to various municipal and church archives, since registers are not all collected at central depositories. For the school-aged population, birth or baptismal and death or burial registers were used. The number of births, and the number of deaths by age (<1, 1–9, 10–19, 20+) in five-year periods at twenty-year intervals were gathered for all the sample communities, for the period between 1760 and 1844. To simplify the estimation of school-aged population (ages 6–13, for the sake of comparability), I assumed that mortality between ages 6 and 9 was equal to that between 10 and 13 (although it is, of course, slightly higher). Thus the size of a school-aged population in a given year was estimated by assuming that an average birth cohort of 10 years earlier, experiencing the mortality to age 10 characteristic of the community and time period, would be one-eighth of the surviving population between 6 and 13. While the method of estimation should in general produce fairly reliable results, there are two potential sources of error. In a situation where mortality rates could fluctuate dramatically from year to year, estimations based on average mortality over a five-year period may not be accurate enough to gauge the mortality experience of a cohort over thirteen years. This fluctuation could be particularly marked in small communities. In an attempt to minimize the error due to fluctuation in small communities, several communities were usually grouped together for purposes of analysis. The problem would persist, of course, if mortality fluctuated in a similar manner in all communities as a result of epidemics or other environmental factors. The second potential source of error in these calculations is the migration of families with school-aged children. Actually, the impact of migration was relatively small, since typical migrants were single young adults. Nonetheless, some children were involved. In the cities of Sorgues, L'Isle-sur-la-Sorgue, and Avignon, for example, which were communes with highly mobile populations, children born outside the commune represented the following proportion of child deaths:

Age group	*% foreign-born*
1	2
1–9	9
10–19	14

Since outmigration of children born in the communes probably compensated only in part for this increase due to inmigration of children, school-aged population estimates for communes that were growing as a result of migration may be too small by a factor of up to 10 percent or so; in areas of outmigration, of course, the error would be in the opposite direction. The following table indicates the amount of discrepancy between estimates from vital registers and contemporary reports for two years for which such reports were available for the Vauclusan communities:

	1836		*1848*	
Size of Community	*Estimates from Vital Records*	*Contemporary Estimates*	*Estimates from Vital Records*	*Contemporary Estimates*
<500	173	210	178	183
500–2,000	950	893	878	702
2,000–10,000	2,854	3,627	2,760	2,716
Avignon	6,014	3,980	6,100	3,173

The greatest discrepancy is obviously that in the city of Avignon. While projections from vital registers are bound to be less reliable for large cities with mobile populations than for more stable areas, I suspect that officials in cities also had more trouble estimating school-aged populations than did those in smaller towns. In a town like Avignon, the error in the vital register estimate should actually be in the direction of underestimation, not overestimation, which leads me to suspect that the true figure is closer to the larger one. The drop in school-aged population reported between 1836 and 1848, when the overall population of the city was rising, is also suspicious and further suggests underreporting in contemporary figures. The other major discrepancy, that in towns of 2,000 to 10,000 in 1836, is also puzzling, but seems to be a result of misreporting rather than dramatic population change. The estimate from registers for 1848 is actually quite close to the lower contemporary report of that year, which suggests either an improbable decline or substantial inflation of the earlier figures. In the absence of concrete information about the generation of contemporary figures on school-aged populations, I am inclined to accept the vital register estimates as the more reliable of the two. But without more concrete information about migration patterns in the sample communities, even these estimates must be interpreted with caution.

INFANT AND CHILD MORTALITY

Vital registers were also used to calculate infant and child mortality indexes. The index of infant mortality is the number of deaths of children below the age of one year in a given five-year period, divided by the number of live births in that same period. In the earliest periods, stillbirths were not always clearly identified as such in Vaucluse; therefore the denominator is slightly inflated, and actual mortality would thus be a bit lower. (Births and deaths in institutions for unwed mothers were kept separately, since mortality levels there were considerably higher than average.) Child mortality indexes were calculated by dividing the number of deaths to persons aged one to nine and ten to nineteen by the number of survivors to age one during five-year periods. These are rough estimates, whose precision is diminished by the fact that the births at risk have actually been occurring over a period of twenty years, and by the factor of child migration, which was discussed above.

LITERACY

As was discussed in the text (Chapter 5), inferences about literacy were drawn from variations in the ability to sign series of documents, generally marriage registers. Beginning with the establishment of civil registration in 1792, registers for all the sample communities in Vaucluse were available in the Departmental Archives. Prior to that, signed registers were available only for those communities in the arrondissement of Apt, since the Papal State did not require signatures on marriage acts. Most of these early registers are also available in the Departmental Archives, since they were made in duplicate, but for Protestant communities the only existing registers are usually in communal archives. Data on the ability to sign were gathered for three- to five-year periods (depending on the size of the community) at twenty-year intervals. In addition, some information about occupation of groom and bride (or, lacking that, bride's father) was collected for a subgroup of the sample communities. Badenese marriage registers were unsigned until the beginning of civil registration in the early 1870s. Thereafter, registers are closed by law to all but direct descendants of those mentioned in the acts. The only series of signed documents found for the Badenese communities were contracts made on the occasions of interfaith marriages and acts of paternity acknowledgment *(Vaterschafterkenntnisse).*

SUPPLEMENTAL INFORMATION

Population. Information about the population of the sample communities came from a variety of sources. For Vaucluse, manuscript censuses were available for An IV, 1806, 1836, and every five years thereafter. Earlier information was taken from Expilly's dictionary and from church surveys. The manuscript census was also used for information about reported child employment patterns. For the Badenese communities, a police census of 1807 gave population totals by religious and age divisions. Later figures came from Heunisch's published statistics. Urban figures came from E. Kayser, ed., *Badisches Städtebuch.*

Industry. Since really precise information about the occupational breakdown of the populations of each community was not systematically available, a rough classification system was established that could be used on the basis of descriptive information. The extreme categories were: 1) communities which, in the absence of any information to the contrary, were assumed to be virtually completely agricultural, and 4) those in which at least the majority of the population was engaged in occupational sectors other than agriculture. The intervening categories were more difficult to categorize: the classification 2) was reserved for those where there was some minimal evidence of any nonfarming population—where there were, for example, a few mills or a weekly market; category 3) included those communities that were predominantly agricultural but had clearly supported substantial populations in other industries, like cottage manufacturing, artisanal production, mining, etc. Information for categorization was drawn from statistical memoirs, regional dictionaries, marriage records, and manuscript censuses.

Communal budgets. Information on budgets was used to supplement educational archives in determining the level of communal expenditures on schooling. For Vaucluse, these budgets are in Series O, Departmental, for the nineteenth century and in Series H of the National Archives for earlier periods. For Baden, this information came from the published *Beiträge zur Statistik des Grossherzogthums Baden.*

Notes

CHAPTER 1

1. The term "schooling society" refers, of course, to the title of the well-known assault upon the contemporary school system by Ivan Illich, *Deschooling Society* (New York, 1971). Borrowing his phrase in reverse by no means implies a borrowing of his basic frame of analysis, but his provocative critique of the logic of schooling in the contemporary world is one of the works that first set me to thinking about the origins of the modern school system.

2. Chapter II will provide a fuller account of the nature of elementary instruction in early modern Europe, but I can call attention here to several important recent studies of it. For France, F. Furet and J. Ozouf's *Lire et écrire: l'alphabétisation des français de Calvin à Jules Ferry*, 2 vols. (Paris, 1977), is an admirable synthesis of research on literacy trends and pays a great deal of attention to schooling as well. The book has recently been translated into English as *Reading and Writing: Literacy in France from Calvin to Jules Ferry* (Cambridge, 1982). David Cressy's *Literacy and the Social Order: Reading and Writing in Tudor and Stuart England* (Cambridge, 1980) provides an account of the history of literacy in early modern England, and is also notable for its sensitivity to the social and institutional contexts of learning. For a thought-provoking account of a program for teaching to read in the absence of schools, see E. Johansson, ed., *The History of Literacy in Sweden in Comparison with Some Other Countries* (Teheran, 1977). An important new interpretation of the place of pedagogy in the Reformation is provided by G. Strauss in *Luther's House of Learning: Indoctrination of the Young in the German Reformation* (Baltimore, 1979).

3. The historical literature on the subject of school reform in the late eighteenth and early nineteenth centuries is a large one. The best recent bibliography pulling together the various approaches to the history of schooling and literacy in the West is Harvey J. Graff's *Literacy in History: An Interdisciplinary Research Bibliography* (New York, 1981). Although much of the history of education written before the 1960s or so tended to focus on the evolution

of educational policy of pedagogic theory, much of the recent historical examination of education has been influenced by the emergence of social history. Many of the newer studies focus more on the actual operation of schools and the connections between schooling patterns and the evolution of social relationships. For example, T. W. Laqueur's *Religion and Respectability: Sunday Schools and Working-Class Culture, 1780–1850* (New Haven, 1976) delves into the records of the functioning of urban Sunday schools and of their place in popular culture; A. J. LaVopa's *Prussian Schoolteachers: Profession and Office, 1763–1848* (Chapel Hill, 1980) looks at the recruitment, training, practices, and situation of teachers; H. Chisick's *Limits of Reform in the Enlightenment: Attitudes towards the Education of the Lower Classes in 18th-Century France* (Princeton, 1980) recasts the attitudes of the *philosophes* about popular education in the perspective of their social position and vested interests.

4. Perhaps the best known account of evolving attitudes about the need for popular discipline in this era is M. Foucault's *Discipline and Punish* (New York, 1979). But a number of historians have pointed to the early industrial epoch's attention to new techniques for control. See, for example, E. P. Thompson, "Time, Work Discipline and Industrial Capitalism," *Past and Present* 38 (1967), or U. Aumüller, "Industrieschule und ursprüngliche Akkumulation in Deutschland," in K. Hartmann *et al.*, eds., *Schule and Staat im 18. und 19. Jahrhundert* (Frankfurt a.M., 1974).

5. M. Pazzis, *Mémoire statistique sur le département de Vaucluse* (Carpentras, 1808).

6. There has been much discussion recently about the scale and nature of the illegitimacy rise in early industrial Europe. See, for example, E. Shorter, "Female Emancipation, Birth Control and Fertility in European History," *American Historical Review* 78 (1973): 605–640; L. A. Tilly, J. Scott, and M. Cohen, "Women's Work and European Fertility Patterns," *Journal of Interdisciplinary History* 6 (1976): 447–476; W. R. Lee, "Bastardy and the Socioeconomic Structure of South Germany," *Journal of Interdisciplinary History* 7 (1977): 403–425.

7. GLA: 435/798.

8. P. Burke discusses what he terms the "discovery of the people" in his *Popular Culture in Early Modern Europe* (New York, 1978), pp. 3–22. There is an interesting discussion of the use of the French term *le peuple* in H. Chisick, *Limits,* pp. 48ff. For a related discussion in the German context, see W. Conze, "Vom 'Pöbel' zum 'Proletariat'" in *Vierteljahrsschrift für Sozial- und Wirtschaftsgeschichte* 41 (1954): 333–364.

9. ADV:T, I.P., 3.

10. For a thorough discussion of the debate over popular schooling beginning in the 1760s in France, see H. Chisick's *Limits of Reform,* cited above. C. Kaestle describes the triumph over obscurantism in the Anglo-American context in his article "'Between the Scylla of Brutal Ignorance and the Charybdis of a Literary Education': Elite Attitudes toward Mass Schooling in Early Industrial England and America," in L. Stone, ed., *Schooling and Society* (Baltimore, 1976). In addition to these works, and that of M. Foucault cited earlier, see also R. Johnson, "Social Control in Early Victorian England," *Past and Present,* 49 (1970): 96–119 and the discussion of educational ideology and policy in the context of early industrial Canada in H. Graff, *The Literacy Myth* (New York, 1979).

11. Studies attempting to assess the history of schooling from the popular perspective are beginning to appear. See, for example, M. J. Maynes, "Work or School? Youth and the Family in the Midi in the Early Nineteenth Century," in P. J. Harrigan and D. Baker, eds., *The Making of Frenchmen* (Waterloo, Ont., 1980); D. Levine, "Education and Family Life in Early Industrial England," *The Journal of Family History* 4 (1979): 368–380; B. Eklof, "Peasant Sloth Reconsidered: Strategies of Education and Learning in Rural Russia Before the Revolution," *Journal of Social History* 14 (1981): 355–385.

12. For a fuller discussion of this issue, see H. J. Graff, *The Literacy Myth,* cited above.

13. S. Thrupp, "Diachronic Methods in Comparative Politics," in R. Holt and J. B. Turner, eds., *The Methodology of Comparative Research* (New York, 1970).

14. A list of the sample communities can be found in Appendix I.

15. The sample communities in Vaucluse and Baden were chosen using a stratified sampling strategy. A stratified rather than a random sample was constructed in order to insure that a minimum number of communities in each size category would be included. Since community size is an important variable in the analysis of school provision and demand for schooling, the

sample had to include enough examples of larger and smaller communities to allow for comparison. Because of this sampling technique, however, it must be kept in mind that the entire sample cannot be taken as representative of the population of the regions as a whole.

All communities were classified for sampling purposes according to their mid-nineteenth-century populations. A number of communities in each region was selected from each size category as follows:

16. AN: F[17]9824. Letter from the *recteur* of the Académie of Nîmes to the minister of education, June 10, 1838, describing the suppression of the *école primaire supérieure* of Avignon.

Size Category of Community	*Arrondissements of Avignon and Apt*		*Kreise of Mannheim, Ladenburg Sinsheim, Heidelberg, Wiesloch*	
	Number of Communities		*Number of Communities*	
	Total	*Sample*	*Total*	*Sample*
Less than 500	21	5	10	4
500–2,000	35	8	47	10
2,000–10,000	13	6	8	4
10,000+	1	1	2	2
Total	70	20	67	20

17. A. Brun, *Recherche historique sur l'introduction du français* (Paris, 1923), p. 17.

18. F. Benoit, ed., *Voyage en Provence d'un gentilhomme polonnais* (Marseille, 1830).

19. F. Brunot, *Histoire de la langue française* (Paris, 1926), vol. 9, p. 65.

20. M. Pazzis, *Mémoire,* p. 47.

21. M. Agulhon has described this general pattern of population distribution and its social, cultural, and political consequences in *The Republic in the Village,* translated by J. Lloyd (Cambridge, 1982), a study of the Provençal département of the Var.

22. France, Bureau de la Statistique Générale, *Statistique de la France* (Paris, 1837).

23. P. Seignour, *La Vie économique en Vaucluse de 1815 à 1848* (Aix-en-Provence, 1957), p. 22.

24. Ibid., pp. 37ff.

25. M. Pazzis, *Mémoire,* p. 323.

26. P. Simoni, "Un canton rural au xixe siècle" (Thèse de doctorat de 3ème cycle, Aix-en-Provence, 1976) is a careful study of the canton of Apt. A broader overview of the economy and political life of the Alpine region of France, of which Vaucluse formed the southern border, can be found in P. Vigier, *La Seconde République dans la région Alpine* (Paris, 1963).

27. ADV:E, État Civil, Sorgues.

28. Loyd Lee has provided an analysis of the administrative difficulties encountered by state bureaucrats in Baden, and the strategies they employed, in "Liberal Constitutionalism as Administrative Reform: The Baden Constitution of 1818," *Central European History* 8 (1975): 91–112.

29. The boundaries of all these administrative units—Kreise, Landkreise, Stadtkreise—were changed continually throughout the eighteenth and nineteenth centuries. Maps and boundaries used here are those in force at the time of the archival reorganization of the late nineteenth century, unless otherwise noted. The use of individual communities as the prime unit of analysis circumvents problems inherent in the use of any of these larger units.

30. K. Brunner, *Die Badische Schulordnungen* (Berlin, 1902), p. 269.

31. GLA: 377/7930. One example of this sort of conflict is a letter of complaint from the schoolteacher of Neidenstein, written in 1833. The teacher reported that the father of one of his pupils was refusing to buy German schoolbooks for his son, claiming that he preferred that his son be taught in Hebrew. GLA: 377/7930.

32. A. Heunisch, *Das Grossherzogthum Baden* (Heidelberg, 1857), p. 240.

33. Ibid., p. 57.

34. Ibid., 292.

35. W. Fischer, "Ansätze zur Industrialisierung in Baden, 1770–1870," *Vierteljahresschrift für Sozial- und Wirtschaftsgeschichte* 47 (1960): 186–231.

36. K. Ziegler, *Ortschronik Neidenstein* (Neidenstein, 1962).

37. H. Brunn, *1200 Jahre Schriesheim* (Mannheim, 1964).

38. For a study of indications of secularization in Provence in the eighteenth century, see M. Vovelle, *Piété baroque et déchristianisation en Provence au 18e siècle* (Paris, 1973). Agulhon, in his study of the Var cited earlier, found popular religiosity strong in the 1820s despite the institutional interruptions in Christian practice during the revolution. He sees a spontaneous dechristianization taking place in that département in the course of the early nineteenth century, however. See *The Republic*, pp. 96–111.

39. A. Heunisch, *Das Grossherzogthum*, p. 243.

40. Sources of information about religious affiliation included A. Heunisch, *Das Grossherzogsthum*, p. 755; GLA: 313/2816; Baden-Württemberg. Staatliche Archivverwaltung, Die Stadt- und Landkreise Mannheim und Heidelberg (Karlsruhe, 1966).

41. GLA: 388/74.

CHAPTER 2

1. For a discussion of schooling and literacy trends throughout Provence in the late decades of the ancien régime, see M. Vovelle, "Y-a-til eu une révolution culturelle . . . ?" *Revue d'histoire moderne et contemporaine* 22 (1975): 89–141. The newly translated work of F. Furet and J. Ozouf, *Reading and Writing: Literacy in France from Calvin to Jules Ferry* (Cambridge, 1982), provides a valuable general survey of the quantitative evidence about literacy and schooling trends in France between the mid-sixteenth and the late nineteenth centuries.

2. AN: H1248,1250.

3. A great number of archival sources were compiled for information about the Badenese communities during the ancien régime. See Appendix II for more detail.

4. GLA: 213/2664, 2665, 2645 all contain records of *Nebenschulen.*

5. For a fuller discussion of regional differences and changes over time in methods of school finance, see M. J. Maynes, "The Virtues of Archaism: The Political Economy of Schooling in Europe, 1750–1850," *Comparative Studies in Society and History,* 21 (1979): 611–625, as well as F. Furet and J. Ozouf, *Reading and Writing.*

6. R. Rey, "L'Enseignement primaire et les écoles publiques dans les états pontificaux . . . avant 1789," *Mémoires de l'Académie de Vaucluse* 11 (1892): 30.

7. ADV: E, Bedarrides, 5.

8. MP: AIP, 6.

9. MP: AIP, 6.

10. AN: H1248, 1250.

11. ADV: H, 3; MP: AIP, 6; M. Feuillas, "L'Enseignement à Avignon au xviiie siècle" (*Mémoire de Maîtrise,* Aix, 1959).

12. K. Ziegler, *Ortsgeschichte Neidenstein* (Neidenstein, 1962), p. 78.

13. GLA: 204/1807.

14. MP: AIP, 6.

15. GLA: 77/1914.

16. ADV: 1L, 256: 2L, 78.

17. V. Carrière, *Introduction aux études d'histoire ecclésiastique locale* (Paris, 1936), pp. 289ff.

18. GLA: 63/144; 77/1913–1917, 9838; 382/242.

19. The essays in C. Tilly, ed., *The Formation of National States in Western Europe* (Princeton, 1975) have contributed to the formulation of concepts related to state building used here and elsewhere in this study. Of special importance are essays by G. Ardant, "Financial Policy and Economic Infrastructure of Modern States"; R. Braun, "Taxation, Socio-political Structure, and Statebuilding: Great Britain and Brandenburg-Prussia"; and C. Tilly, "Food Supply and Public Order in Modern Europe."

20. R. Collier, *La Vie en Haute Provence de 1600 à 1850* (Digne, 1973), p. 474.
21. ADV: Archives Communales de Sorgues, BB17.
22. Collier, p. 475.
23. GLA: 77/3120.
24. GLA: 77/6102. For a discussion of the operation of this examination system elsewhere, see K. Lockridge, *Literacy in Colonial New England* (New York, 1974).
25. The practice has often been cited. See, for example, *La Vie,* p. 476; M. Vovelle, "Y a-t-il eu . . . ," pp. 128ff.
26. Collier, *La Vie,* p. 470.
27. Ibid., p. 471.
28. Ibid., p. 473; Rey, "L'Enseignement," p. 18; GLA: 377/756.
29. GLA: 77/6098.
30. GLA: 229/94983.
31. GLA: 204/1819.
32. There is an interesting discussion of the interpretation of historical evidence about schooling and skills in D. and L. Resnick, "The Nature of Literacy: An Historical Explanation," *Harvard Educational Review* 47 (1977): 370–385.
33. Rey, "L'Enseignement," p. 30.
34. ADV: Archives Communales de Sorgues, BB16.
35. MP: AIP, 6.
36. MC: Ms. 1972.
37. For a discussion of the general impact of the revolution on educational endowments, see A. Prost, *L'Enseignement en France, 1800–1967* (Paris, 1968). F. Furet and J. Ozouf discount the impact of the revolution on educational practice (though not on ideology) in *Reading and Writing,* Chapter 2.
38. MP: AIP, 6.
39. ADV: 2L, 96.
40. ADV: 1L, 337.
41. ADV: 1L, 1, 15.
42. AN: H1248, 1250; ADV: 50, 51.

CHAPTER 3

1. There is a large and growing literature on the subject of the social interests represented by the various governments of the European states, especially of France, in the period from 1789 to 1848. C. Lucas's recent article, "Nobles, Bourgeois and the Origins of the French Revolution," in *Past and Present* 60 (1973): 84–126 both sorts through the various contributions to the debate on the social character of the first French Revolution and adds a new perspective of his own. For 1830, C. Johnson's "The Revolution of 1830 in French Economic History" is particularly helpful, as is the rest of the collection of articles in which it is included: J. Merriman, ed., *1830 in France* (New York, 1975). G. Rudé's *Debate on Europe 1815–1850* (New York, 1972) provides a guide to the literature on the 1848 revolts, as well as to other historiographic debates about this epoch.
2. Cited in F. Ponteil, *Histoire de l'enseignement en France* (Paris, 1966), p. 33.
3. MP: AIP, 6.
4. F. v. Rochow, *Geschichte meiner Schule* (Leipzig, 1890), p. 6.
5. For an excellent recent study of the process of school reform in Prussia, see A. Leschinsky and P. M. Roeder, *Schule im historischen Prozess* (Stuttgart, 1976).
6. K. Brunner, *Die Badische Schulordnungen* (Berlin, 1902), p. 269.
7. GLA: 313/3471.
8. GLA: 377/7930.
9. J. F. Wehrer, *Das Volkschulwesen . . . im Grossherzogsthum Baden* (Karlsruhe, 1837).
10. For a detailed history of national educational policy in France, see M. Gontard, *L'Enseignement primaire en France de la Révolution à la loi Guizot* (Paris, 1959) and *Les Ecoles primaires de la France bourgeoise* (Toulouse, 1964). There is a specific discussion of the educa-

tional legislation of the revolutionary period in H. C. Barnard, *Education and the French Revolution* (Cambridge, Mass., 1969).

11. M. Gontard, *L'Enseignement,* p. 300.

12. ADV: T, Fonds 3, 1; AN: F^{17} 10179.

13. ADV: T, Fonds 3, 2.

14. ADV: T, Fonds 3, 3bis.

15. ADV: T, Fonds 3, 3bis.

16. ADV: T, Fonds 3, 3bis.

17. Some of the French educational reforms were consciously patterned on the German model. Victor Cousin's trip to Germany was an important source of information about the German school systems. His observations were published in France under the title *État de l'instruction primaire dans la royaume de la Prusse à la fin de l'année 1831* (Paris, 1832). For a description of the contemporary educational reformers of England and the United States, see C. Kaestle, "Between the Scylla of Brutal Ignorance and the Charybdis of a Literary Education: Elite Attitudes toward Mass Schooling in Early Industrial England and America," in L. Stone, ed., *Schooling and Society* (Baltimore, 1976).

18. See F. Paulsen, *German Education: Past and Present* (London, 1908), pp. 136ff.

19. GLA: 77/6100.

20. H. Derwein, *Handschuhsheim und seine Geschichte* (Heidelberg, 1933), p. 140.

21. J. F. Wehrer, *Das Volksschulwesens . . . in Grossherzogsthum Baden* (Karlsruhe, 1837). Ordinance of May 13, 1803.

22. GLA: 231/1322.

23. See below, Chapters VI and IX.

24. ADV: T, IA, 102.

25. Historical evidence about the impact of compulsory schooling laws is mixed. The economists W. Landes and L. Solomon argue in their study of these laws in the United States that few states passed such laws before the majority of their residents were already complying with the minimal educational requirements they stipulated. They argue that the laws themselves had very little independent impact on behavior. See their article, "Compulsory Schooling Legislation: An Economic Analysis," *Journal of Economic History* 32 (1972): 54–91. The history of educational legislation in France would corroborate this finding, since by the time of the passage of obligation laws during the Third Republic, the majority of French children were enrolled in school. The Badenese case is more problematic. Majority school enrollment was achieved in the prestatistical era, but the unsystematic record does suggest that the enforcement of obligation laws was instrumental in bringing about the early accomplishment of universal enrollment. Still, it is also true that the passage of these laws may have preceded by quite a long time their serious enforcement. By the time of the intensification of the laws in the late eighteenth and early nineteenth century, a very high proportion of boys and girls were already attending school. For a discussion of the political and ideological origins of the educational policy of radical republicans, see K. Auspitz, *The Radical Bourgeoisie* (Cambridge, 1982).

26. A. Heunisch, *Geographisch-Statistisch-Topographische Beschreibung des Grossherzogthums Baden* (Heidelberg, 1833), pp. 237ff.

27. There is a discussion of the debate over the proper role of the churches in school supervision that occurred at the end of the eighteenth century in E. Fooken, *Die geistliche Schulaufsicht und ihre Kritiker* (Wiesbaden-Dotzheim, 1967). For a description of the creation of the Badenese state, see R. Haebler, *Ein Staat wird aufgebaut* (Baden-Baden, 1948), and L. Gall, *Der Liberalismus als regierende Partei* (Wiesbaden, 1968).

28. GLA: 77/6104.

29. ADV: 2L, 96.

30. ADV: T, diverse Fonds and Cartons.

31. ADV: T, Fonds 3, 1bis.

32. ADV: T, Fonds 3, 1bis.

33. ADV: T, Fonds 3, 3.

34. There has been very little detailed examination of the corps of inspectors who generated so many of the records about primary schooling. P. Gerbod, in his study "Les Inspecteurs généraux et l'inspection générale de l'instruction publique de 1802 à 1882," *Révue*

historique 236 (1966): 79–106, focuses on the higher echelons of the school bureaucracy, and mostly on inspectors of secondary schools. He does note, however, that the earliest inspectors of the primary schools recruited in the 1830s were often drawn from the ranks of retired secondary school teachers.

35. For a more detailed account of the political and religious polarization so characteristic of the Midi in this epoch, see M. Agulhon, *The Republic in the Village* (Cambridge, 1980).

CHAPTER 4

1. There have been a number of recent studies of the teaching corps. A. J. LaVopa's *Prussian Schoolteachers: Profession and Office* (Chapel Hill, 1980) is a fine analysis of the changing role and status of teachers in the largest German state. Work on French teachers has concentrated mostly on the Third Republic. See, for example, B. Singer's "The Teacher as Notable in Brittany, 1880–1914," *French Historical Studies* (1976), pp. 634–659.

2. Discussion here will focus primarily upon male schoolteachers, in part because there are better records on the official teachers being groomed for their new task by the educational bureaucracies, in part because male teachers did dominate in the field of primary instruction in this epoch. This is, of course, a transitional phenomenon. There were female teachers in large numbers in early modern Europe (hence the common name "dame school" for primary school in at least the English context). Women would also come to dominate in the field of primary instruction toward the end of the nineteenth century as the changing structure of employment opportunities for educated men led them to pursue more lucrative posts at the same time when many women, often middle-class in origin, began to seek respectable employment in the face of the necessity to support themselves. See, for example, J. Albisetti, "Women and the Professions in Imperial Germany," presented at "Condition and Consciousness: An International Conference on German Women in the Eighteenth and Nineteenth Centuries," held in Minneapolis, Minnesota, April 15–17, 1983.

3. GLA: 388/42.

4. GLA: 229/57428; 356/751.

5. GLA: 204/1807; 362/1652.

6. GLA: 204/1808, 1825; 213/2644, 2662.

7. A. Heunisch, *Beschreibung*, p. 238.

8. ADV: 5 O, 102, 103.

9. A. Heunisch, *Beschreibung*, p. 238; *Das Grossherzogthum,* p. 578.

10. ADV: T, Fonds 3, 3.

11. GLA: 377/755.

12. ADV: T, Fonds 3, 3bis.

13. Individual actions like those of Willis Leitzeifer, who was suspended from his teaching post in Wiesloch because he refused to ring the church bell, or the *instituteur* of the *école mutuelle* who was chided in the inspection report of the Vauclusan inspector in 1838 for his refusal to conduct his pupils to religious services, fed into broader reform movements calling for the secularization of the schools. This demand was prominent in the action of 1848/49 in Baden. GLA: 388/31; ADV: T, Fonds 3, 3.

14. GLA: 213/2623.

15. GLA: 229/72099.

16. Teaching by religious orders was, naturally, more disrupted than lay teaching. At the time of the reestablishment of the Brothers of the Christian Schools in the first decade of the nineteenth century, the *recteur* of Nîmes complained that only six members of this once flourishing order remained in Vaucluse. Two of these were too old to teach, one was already teaching, another was willing to begin teaching again; one was a married woolen manufacturer, and the last was a convicted sodomist. An: F^{17} 6286.

17. ADV: T, Fonds 3, 1bis; AN: F^{17} 10374.

18. ADV: T, Fonds 3, 2,3,3bis. Actually, different reports varied somewhat in their

estimates. One inspector estimated that there were around 200 *institutrices* in Vaucluse in 1835/36; he visited 146 of them. The inspector the following year found 170 *institutrices.*

19. See Appendix II for complete description of sources about the existence and condition of schools.

20. ADV: T, Fonds 3, 3bis.

21. ADV: T, Fonds 3, 3bis.

22. ADV: T, Fonds 3, 3bis.

23. ADV: T, FIA, 207.

24. GLA: 229/109025.

25. GLA: 377/965.

26. GLA: 235/21692, 21693, 21722, 26380, 26390.

27. ADV: T, Fonds 3, 3bis.

28. GLA: 356/751.

29. ADV: T, Fonds 3, 3bis.

30. For studies of various aspects of the professionalization of the teaching corps in the nineteenth century, see, in addition to the works by B. Singer and A. J. LaVopa cited in Note 1 above, P. V. Meyers, "Professionalization and Societal Change: Rural Teachers in Nineteenth-Century France," *Journal of Social History* 9(1976): 542–588. An earlier, more general study, G. Duveau's *Les Instituteurs,* remains provocative despite being unsystematic (Paris, 1957).

31. GLA: 204/1824.

32. Local officials in Mannheim estimated that only about 240 of 600 school-aged children of the Reformed community were in the official schools at the turn of the century, and many of the rest were in other schools. By 1824, fully 850 of the 1000 or so school-aged children were in the official schools and 120 or so in the "*Wart-* or *Nebenschulen.*" GLA: 63/38; 435/1463.

33. In the late 1820s, the communities of Avignon, L'Isle, and Cucuron all refused the request of the académie to aid in the opening of a départemental normal school. ADV: T, Fonds 1, 1.

34. ADV: T, FIA, 84.

35. ADV: T, FIA, 84.

36. ADV: T, Fonds 3, 3bis.

37. ADV: T, FIA, 102.

38. ADV: T, Fonds 3, 2bis.

39. ADV: T, Fonds 3, 3.

40. ADV: T, Fonds 3, 3.

41. ADV: T, Fonds 3, 4.

42. The sources are scattered; among others, for example, GLA: 229/38, 38401.

43. A. Heunisch, *Geographisch . . . Beschreibung,* pp. 147ff.

44. Cited in H. Heyd, *Geschichte der Entwicklung des Volksschulwesens* (Buhl, 1900).

45. GLA: 213/2625.

46. GLA: 213/2626.

47. GLA: 213/2570.

48. GLA: 213/2570.

49. GLA: 235/26318.

50. GLA: 235/2173.

51. GLA: 204/1787.

52. GLA: 235/23025.

53. GLA: 235/21685.

54. ADV: T, Fonds 3, 2bis.

55. ADV: H, Freres, 1.

56. ADV: T, Fonds 3, 3.

57. For a discussion of the political dimension of the controversy between supporters of the *Frères* and those of the *mutuelles,* see below, Chapter V. G. Duveau has suggested that the style of teaching in the *mutuelle* schools, which allowed pupils a certain leadership role, may have helped to develop the kinds of skills later valuable for the self-organization of the working class. See *Les Instituteurs* (Paris, 1957).

58. K. Brunner, *Die Badische Schulordnungen,* p. 302.
59. ADV: T, Fonds 3, 3bis.
60. ADV: T, Fonds 3, 3.
61. ADV: T, Fonds 3, 3.
62. ADV: T, Fonds 3, 2bis.
63. GLA: 235/19266.
64. MC: Ms. 1972.
65. ADV: T, Fonds 3, 3.
66. *Alphabet et premier livre de lecture* (Paris, 1847), pp. 44–59.
67. ADV: T, Fonds 3, 3.

CHAPTER 5

1. ADV: T, Fonds 3, 3.
2. ADV: T, Fonds 3, 3.
3. ADV: T, Fonds 3, 3.
4. ADV: T, Fonds 3, 3.
5. ADV: T, Fonds 3, 3.
6. F. Furet and J. Ozouf, *Lire et écrire: l'alphabétisation des français de Calvin à Jules Ferry* (Paris, 1977), vol. 1, pp. 185–186.
7. ADV: Archives Communales de Sorgues, 1L1, 15.
8. AN: H1248, 1250; ADV: 50, 51.
9. ADV: T, Fonds 3, 3bis.
10. K. Keller, *Waldangellochs Vergangenheit* (Eppingen, 1935).
11. GLA: 63/144; 77/9838; 388/242.
12. Examples of local disputes are recorded in GLA: 156/59; 356/2182. For a description of the reform of teaching salaries, see above, Chapter III. It should be noted here that even the most progressive teachers were not prepared to commit themselves entirely to the cash nexus for the simple reason that the inflation that characterized the late eighteenth and early nineteenth centuries made such a transition frightening. In a petition submitted to the Frankfurt Assembly in 1848, a group of Badenese teachers made a series of proposals drastically to alter the means of reimbursement of teachers. They requested, however, that farmlands remain attached to the teaching posts because "the worth of a money salary [was] too subject to change." GLA: 235/29580.
13. GLA: 356/78.
14. The political activism of schoolteachers in Germany, and especially in the Southwest, during the *Vormärz* and the 1848 revolts has been noted but never adequately studied. An analysis of the conditions and political organizations of Badenese schoolteachers in this epoch is currently in progress. It will be the subject of a doctoral dissertation by Werner Freund of the Department of Sociology of the University of Heidelberg. For a study of the reform of teaching in Prussia, see A. J. LaVopa, *Prussian Schoolteachers: Profession and Office* (Chapel Hill, 1980).
15. ADV: T, Fonds 3, 3.
16. For an account of opposition of this sort in some communities in the canton of Apt, see P. Simoni, "Un Canton rural au XIXe siècle," doctoral thesis (Aix-Marseille, 1976), pp. 460ff.
17. AN: F^{19} 6257.
18. ADV: T, Fonds 3, 3bis.
19. AN: F^{17} 11772. For a description of the method of teaching, see above, Chapter IV.
20. AN: F^{17} 10179.
21. ADV: T, Fonds 3, 3bis.
22. AN: F^{17} 9824.
23. In contrast with the ambivalent support for lay instruction offered by the July Monarchy government, the radical republicans of the Third Republic would wholeheartedly take up

the lay cause. For an analysis of the political, ideological, and organizational roots of this later policy, see K. Auspitz, *The Radical Bourgeoisie: the Ligue de l'Enseignement and the Origins of the Third Republic, 1866–1885* (Cambridge, 1982).

24. AN: F^{17} 9824. The term "Carlist" here referred to the Catholic, legitimist camp in the Spanish political struggle of the 1830s.

25. There is a description of the role of church administrators and a mention of the early opposition to them in Chapter III.

26. GLA: 377/227.

27. Not all of the members of these communities agreed with the change. As late as 1853, there were three Lutheran families of the town of Nussloch who refused to send their children to the Evangelical school and were fined for their refusal. GLA: 356/1015.

28. GLA: 377/7930.

29. GLA: 231/1324.

CHAPTER 6

1. AN: F^{17} 9372.

2. AN: F^{17} 9372.

3. For a good discussion of the early *Schulzwang* laws, and the coercive element in Reformation-era schools, see K. Hartmann *et al., Schule und Staat im 18. und 19. Jahrhundert* (Frankfurt, 1974). On the aim of Lutheran pedagogical reform, see G. Strauss, *Luther's House of Learning* (Baltimore, 1978).

4. GLA: 77/6100.

5. GLA: 435/827.

6. GLA: 435/320.

7. ADV: T, FIA, 102.

8. ADV: T, Fonds 3, 3.

9. ADV: T, Fonds 3, 3.

10. AN: F^{17} 12203.

11. ADV: T, Fonds 3, 3bis.

12. AN: F^{17} 9335.

13. ADV: T, Fonds 3, 3bis; FIA, 102.

14. GLA: 77/6093.

15. GLA: 77/6093.

16. GLA: 77/7187.

17. ADV: T, Fonds 3, 3bis.

18. ADV: T, Fonds 3, 3bis.

19. The family economy model on which this chapter is based draws much of its outline from the work of J. Scott and L. Tilly. See, for example, "Work and the Family in Nineteenth-Century Europe," *Comparative Studies in Society and History* 17 (1974): 36–64, and *Women, Work and Family* (New York, 1978). M. Anderson's *Family Structure in Nineteenth Century Lancashire* (Cambridge, 1971) was also helpful in describing the workings of the family economy in an urban context.

20. P. Seignour, *La Vie économique*, pp. 180–182.

21. See P. Simoni, "Un Canton rural," pp. 422ff.

22. P. Seignour, *La Vie économique*, p. 182.

23. The situation was not unique to Vaucluse, of course. J. Simon estimated that in Paris as late as the 1860s, only a tenth of working-class families could survive on the wages of the head of household alone. See *Ouvrier de huit ans* (Paris, 1867).

24. A. Heunisch. *Das Grossherzogsthum Baden*, pp. 274–275.

25. A good general account of the crisis faced by German artisans in the *Vormärz* period can be found in T. Hamerow, *Restoration, Revolution, Reaction* (Princeton, 1958).

Just which members of the family would be sent to work depended, of course, on the composition of the household and the availability of employment. Scott and Tilly point out in their history of women and work in France and England that when children were too young to work, mothers often had to, but as soon as the children were old enough to work, mothers would return to their household labors. *Women, Work and Family,* their study, is cited above in Note 19.

26. ADV: T, Fonds 3, 3bis, 4.
27. ADV: T, Fonds 3, 4bis.
28. A. Perdiguier, *Mémoires d'un compagnon* (Moulinas, 1914).
29. GLA: 235/15531.
30. GLA: 235/20101.
31. GLA: 77/6093.
32. M. Vovelle, "Y-a-til eu une révolution culturelle au xviiie siècle?" *Revue d'histoire moderne et contemporaine* 22 (1975): 98–141, and I. Davey, "The Rhythms of Work and the Rhythms of School" (unpublished manuscript), illustrate the same pattern in Haute Provence and rural Ontario, respectively.
33. GLA: 356/1059.
34. GLA: 235/20101. See below, Chapter VI, for a description of the *Industrieschulen.*
35. ADV: T, Fonds 3, 3bis.
36. AN: F^{12} 4705.
37. *Universallexikon von Grossherzogthum Baden* (Karlsruhe, 1843).
38. GLA: 77/6102; HStA: 253.
39. The following table lists the sex ratios (girls/boys) of pupils in all of the sample community schools for which such data were available. Although there were some suspiciously low ratios around the turn of the century, by the 1820s all ratios fall into the bounds of what one might expect on the basis of sex distribution probabilities, with the possible exception of the Heidelberg Reformed community, where in 1821 the enrollments of girls were actually significantly higher than those of boys:

Community	*Date*	*Boys enrolled*	*Girls enrolled*	*Ratio of girls to boys*
North Badenese Lutheran communities	1802	708	592	.84
Daisbach (Lutheran)	1809	29	31	1.07
Waldangelloch (Lutheran)	1810	70	55	.79
Mannheim (Reformed)	1811	174	113	.65
Heidelberg (Reformed)	1821	41	59	1.44
Mannheim (Lutheran)	1824	177	172	.97
Muhlhausen (Catholic)	1837	91	79	.87
Schriesheim (Evangelical)	1844	99	100	1.01
Walldorf (Jewish)	1844	15	13	.87
Mannheim (Catholic)	1849	407	416	1.02

40. GLA: 213/2644.
41. GLA: 229/94987.
42. F. Benoit, *La Provence et le Comtat Venaissin* (Aubanel, 1975), pp. 136–137.
43. GLA: 435/1464.
44. For a discussion of evidence about the ages of pupils in elementary schools, see below, Note 5, Chapter IX.
45. ADV: T, Fonds 3, 1, 4.
46. ADV: T, Fonds 3, 4bis.
47. The following graph illustrates the distribution of child and adolescent employees in six of the Vauclusan sample communities in 1836. The distribution is calculated for all persons aged twenty or under reported as having an occupation. All census evidence is from the *Listes nominatives* of the 1836 census in ADV: Série M. In most communities, about a third of all

teenagers were reported as employed. Although underreporting is almost a certainty, the argument about the age distribution of child employees in different sectors should not be affected, since, if anything, underreporting was probably more common for the younger, more sporadic workers and those employed in agriculture. A more detailed argument about ages of employment in Vaucluse is presented in my article, "Work or School? Youth and the Family in the Midi in the Early Nineteenth Century," in D. N. Baker and P. J. Harrigan, eds., *The Making of Frenchmen: Current Directions in the History of Education in France, 1679–1979*, pp. 115–134.

Distribution of Employees Age 20 and Below by Age Group and Occupational Sector: Six Vauclusan Communities, 1836

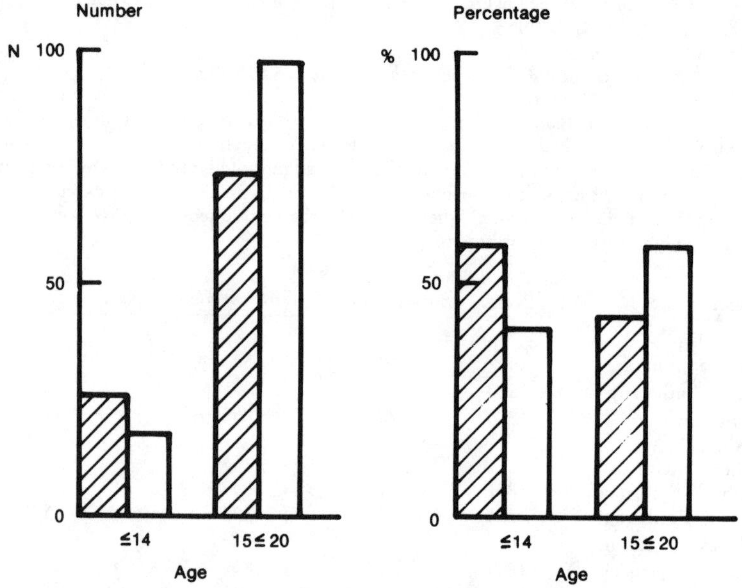

Key: Hatched areas represent the child and teenage employees in agricultural occupations. Blank areas represent the non-agricultural employment sector.

48. The evidence about apprenticeship is drawn from a sample of contracts of apprenticeship from the notarial archives for several Vauclusan communities. These contracts are preserved in ADV: 8U. For a discussion of the apprentices in the Badenese *Gewerbeschulen*, see below, Chapter VII.

49. GLA: 77/9839. As described in Appendix II, the earliest reports of school-aged populations are distorted by the apparent misunderstanding of the concept. Local officials often left out certain kinds of children who they felt would be unlikely to attend school, in particular the very poor and girls. For example, of the thirty-five communities of the Lutheran dioceses of

north Baden who reported their school attendance in 1802, fourteen reported school attendance at 100 percent of school-aged children, but at the same time gave values to the latter population that would have entailed improbable sex ratios. These communities were excluded for the purpose of obtaining age-specific enrollment rates, although it is possible that in exluding them some actual cases of universal enrollment have been left out of consideration. The reports of the remaining twenty-one communities, which yield realistic sex ratios, seem more accurate.

50. The Mannheim Police Poor School was a special institution that allowed the children of the poor to combine work and schooling. (For a more complete description of institutions like this and their role in the school system, see below, Chapter VII.) Because of the special character of the school, the same types of constraints did not operate as in the regular schools. Two-thirds of the 122 pupils enrolled in 1848 were girls; most were enrolled in the first two grades. The pattern of truancy of the pupils also reflects the socioeconomic position of the poor households from which they were drawn. Although the numbers are too small to support much analysis, the relationship between socioeconomic origin and truancy is nonetheless interesting. Children from female-headed households were the most truant, followed by the children of unskilled and semiskilled fathers. Sons of artisans were rarely truant, but their daughters frequently were. The least truant of all, not surprisingly, were the children from the city's orphan asylum, whose time was controlled by a cooperating institution rather than by a family whose demands often conflicted with those of the school. This evidence, scant as it is, does support the view that children were more likely to be truant the more in demand their services to their families were and the less likely their schooling was to contribute to their preparation for the future. GLA 213/2570.

Truancy by Parental Occupation: Mannheim Poor School, 1848/49

Head of Family	*Average Number of Days Truant of Children*			
	Boys	*Girls*	*Total*	*n*
Orphan Asylum	—	0	0	8
Female	30.5	23.6	25.2	19
Unskilled or semiskilled	17.9	17.8	17.8	37
Skilled	4.6	14.2	10.9	38
Other	13.3	2.8	7.4	20

51. GLA: 231/1322.
52. AN: F^{17} 9372.
53. ADV: T, Fonds 3, 3bis.
54. GLA: 213/2645; 229/94906.
55. GLA: 213/2569; 235/21685,22714; 435/14630.
56. GLA: 435/320.
57. K. Brunner, *Die Badische Schulordnungen,* p. 301.
58. GLA: 63/1; 229/38388.
59. ADV: T, Fonds 3, 4bis.
60. ADV: T, Fonds 3, 3.
61. ADV: T, Fonds 3, 3bis.
62. ADV: T, Fonds 3, 3bis.
63. ADV: T, Fonds 3, 3bis.
64. By 1796, the cost of wood had risen so much that it took around 75 gulden worth of wood to heat a classroom for the winter. Firewood payments never came close to this amount. In one school, for example, *Holzgeld* fees totaled only 16 gulden. GLA: 204/2693.
65. GLA: 204/2693.

66. GLA: 235/21687.
67. GLA: 235/21687.
68. GLA: 235/21079.
69. HStA: 260.
70. ADV: T, Fonds 3, 3bis.
71. Ariès opened the subject of childhood to social-historical analysis in his *Centuries of Childhood: A Social History of Family Life,* R. Baldick, tr. (New York, 1962). His argument is not entirely clear and systematic, but he does suggest that there was a relationship between the revival of interest in schooling in the seventeenth century and the adoption of new attitudes toward family evidenced by the use of contraception. His evidence is almost exclusively drawn from elite sources, but among these families, at least, Ariès argues that as the number of children in each family was limited, families became more willing to invest lavish resources in each child. Ariès claims, however, that the attitudinal changes preceded the general decline in infant and child mortality and so could not have been simply caused by them. The case has been restated by C. Tilly, who pointed out that declining mortality rates may well have affected the children of the upper clases long before the general decline and may in fact have been the motor for attitudinal changes in the elite. Then, as mortality declined more generally, and as families adjusted their fertility to the new conditions, there was a more general tendency to reduce the number of children in each family and to value each child more, since "an investment of attention, love and money in a young child began to have a reasonable chance of return for the parents and for the family as a whole." "Population and Pedagogy," *History of Education Quarterly,* 13 (1973): 113–129. Tilly's version of the argument would predict that increased interest in schooling would accompany a downward trend in child mortality.
72. For a discussion of available evidence on fertility trends, see E. van de Walle, *The Female Population of France* (Princeton, 1974).
73. For evidence about fertility patterns in Germany, including the Badenese village of Grafenhausen, which was the site of the precocious fertility decline, see J. Knodel, "Natural Fertility in Pre-industrial Germany," *Population Studies,* 32(1978): 481–510.
74. For a description of the construction of the indexes of infant and child mortality, see Appendix II.
75. For a discussion of evidence about the incidence and disappearance of smallpox in these regions, see Note 77, below.
76. The values of the two indexes of infant and child mortality (unweighted means of the sample communities) were as follows:

	Baden	*Vaucluse*	*Student's T*
1800–1804			
Infant Mortality[a]	.24	.21	−1.6
Child Mortality[b]	.23	.28	1.2
1840–1844			
Infant Mortality	.24	.23	−0.7
Child Mortality	.17	.29	4.3*

[a]Number of deaths of infants below one year of age, divided by the total number of live births for each of the sample communities.
[b]Total number of deaths of persons aged one to twenty, divided by the total number of survivors to age one in each community.
*Significant at the .05 level.

77. Where cause-of-death reports were written during this epoch, their evidence suggests that the most commonly listed cause of death for infants was "gout" *(Gichtern),* which probably referred to a digestive problem of some sort. Causes of death listed for young children were usually infectious diseases, either respiratory infections or epidemics. In Mannheim in 1762, dysentery was the largest killer of toddlers. In the early 1780s there were a number of

epidemics: dysentery (Ruhr) in 1781, smallpox (Blättern) in 1782, measles (Rödeln) in 1783. Cause-of-death records were kept continuously in the town of Wiesloch from 1790 to 1810. During this period there were three smallpox epidemics, with that of 1805 being the most severe; during this last epidemic twenty-five children between the ages of two and seven died. A large number of Badenese parishes began to keep cause-of-death records in the 1820s under the instructions of the state. From them one can learn, for example, that measles killed twelve children in Schriesheim in 1822 and that scarlet fever reportedly took the lives of six children in Walldorf in 1824. But by the time of these reports, smallpox was apparently in abeyance. The state of Baden had undertaken measures to end the disease; inoculation was introduced at the end of the eighteenth century. By 1808 the first law was passed requiring the vaccination of certain classes of schoolchildren. By 1815 parents were required under penalty of fine to vaccinate their children when these reached their first birthday. During the first quarter of the nineteenth century a half million Badenese citizens were vaccinated. The effects of medical intervention on the recession of smallpox are still a debatable issue. Contemporary observers certainly thought they were significant. One medical report issued in 1827 attributed to the vaccination program the saving of one hundred thousand lives. A Badenese medical man traveling in France in 1825 was appalled by the number of smallpox victims there during that epidemic year. He claimed that the deaths were avoidable and persisted only because vaccination was still voluntary in France. The most recent findings of medical historians are in disagreement about the course of the disease in Europe: some historians emphasize the impact of medical intervention; others the natural course of relationships between disease-causing agents and their human hosts. For the nineteenth-century statistics and discussion, see: GLA: 390/2944, 6093; Baden, Statistisches Landesamt, *Beiträge zur Statistik* 2(1856); F. Roller, "Ein Fall von Variola Vaccinatorum" *Annalen für den gesammten Heilkunden* 1(1827) and "Geschichtliche Darstellung der in dem Grossherzogsthum Baden von 1801 bis 1825 geschehene Schutzpocken—Impfung, und deren Resultate," *Annalen für den gesammten Heilkunden* 1 (1827). For the debate among historians, see T. McKeown, R. Brown, and R. G. Record, "An Interpretation of the Modern Rise in Population in Europe," *Population Studies* 26 (1972): 345–382; P. Razzell, "An Interpretation . . . a Critique," *Population Studies* 28 (1974): 5–18. More recent studies of the problem, still producing conflicting results based on the histories of the disease in Sweden, Finland, and Switzerland, are included in A. Imhof, ed; *Mensch und Gesundheit in der Geschichte* (Husum, 1980).

78. Measurement of the impact of child mortality on parental interest in schooling is complicated by the multi-colinearity of a number of critical variables: region, child mortality level, community size, and school attendance. Zero-order correlations between child mortality index and reported proportion of school-aged children attending school in the late 1830s were as follows:

Vaucluse	*Baden*	*Total*
−.27	−.25	−.54

The correlation for the entire sample is significant at the .05 level. The other correlations are weak, but in the expected direction. The correlation increases slightly when community size is controlled for, since both school attendance and mortality were typically higher in urban than in rural areas.

79. A number of recent authors have argued this point. See, for example, P. Bourdieu and J.-C. Passeron, *La Réproduction* (Paris, 1970); C. Jencks, *Inequality* (New York, 1972); S. Bowles and H. Gintis, *Schooling in Capitalist America* (New York, 1976).

80. One of the sources of evidence for the rise in peasant interest in schooling is the increased literacy that can be noted in the late eighteenth century—that is, before the era of school reform. Literacy trends will be discussed more fully below, in chapter 9.

81. ADV: T, Fonds 3, 3bis.

82. ADV: T, Fonds 3, 3bis.

83. ADV: T, Fonds 3, 3bis.

84. Of the sixty-nine communities in the arrondissements of Avignon and Apt included in the report of 1836/37, thirteen had no school, and twenty-six had only a school for boys. Of these latter, fifteen had some girl pupils but the other eleven had none. It is clear that the existence of a separate girls' school was associated with higher relative attendance of girls. The ratio of girls to boys in school in those communities where there was a separate girls' school was .72. In communities where there was only one school, the ratio was .17.

85. ADV: T, Fonds 3, 3bis.

86. ADV: T, Fonds 3, 4.

87. A. Perdiguier, *Mémoires,* p. 4.

88. See Note 48, above.

89. ADV: 9M, 11.

90. For a more detailed discussion of the establishment of *Gewerbeschulen,* see below, Chapter VII.

91. Seventy-eight of the 316 pupils at the *Gewerbeschule* of Mannheim in 1844 were journeymen, as were 86 of the 156 pupils in Heidelberg. GLA: 362/1616; HStA: 273/1.

92. ADV: T, Fonds 3, 3.

93. For a fuller discussion of the question of access to secondary schooling, see below, Chapter VIII.

94. There is little evidence directly touching on the question of the destinies of primary-school graduates. Some of the proponents of schooling in Vaucluse did like to point to examples of pupils who made good because of their learning. Inspectors applauded the success of the *instituteur* who managed to send a pupil or two on to the *école normale* in Avignon, or to the *école des arts et métiers.* The director of the monitorial school in Avignon claimed that in the very first year of the school's existence, "several pupils received offers of employment in offices, and two [were] hired" (ADV: T, Fonds 3, 3, 3bis.). An occasional primary-school graduate even went on to secondary school, even if the overwhelming majority simply took up the sort of work they would have without elementary schooling. The only systematic records of pupils' destinations upon leaving school were the quarterly reports of the monitorial schools, records that indicated the number of pupils who left and their motives for leaving. In the thirty-two such quarterly reports that have survived, there were only three instances of pupils reportedly leaving for secondary education,,and one to take a clerical job. The vast majority left to work in the fields, or simply "to work." A few left to attend other elementary schools, or to be apprenticed. The rest left because of illness or death, a family move or expulsion. (ADV: Fonds 3,3.) It is interesting to note, however, that meritocratic thinking was already pervading the reports of the French inspectors and teachers in some instances, or else they would not have been interested in these questions. In Baden there was never a question of proving that primary schooling could improve one's chances of social mobility. Even in France, as I have argued, this ideal was not given the official stamp of approval until the Third Republic, but indications of its influence can be detected earlier in these sorts of accounts, as well as in some of the research about secondary schooling during the Second Empire, which will be discussed below in Chapter VIII.

CHAPTER 7

1. GLA: 235/22776.
2. GLA: 235/22776; 362/1596.
3. GLA: 235/22715.
4. GLA: 235/22715.
5. GLA: 235/22716.
6. ADV: J, 3.
7. ADV: T, FIA, 102.
8. MC: Ms. 3003.
9. ADV: T, Fonds 3, 3.
10. For a fuller discussion of these institutions, see below, chapter 8.

11. GLA: 362/1595.
12. GLA: 235/22715.
13. GLA: 231/1591.
14. GLA: 233/32560.
15. AN: F^{17} 4704.
16. For a discussion of the interactions of parents, factory owners, and school officials over the issue of the schooling of factory children in southern Baden, the work of W. Trapp is useful. See, for example, his "Liberal *Volksschulpolitik* in der 2. Hälfte des 19. Jahrhunderts—untersucht am Beispiel des Amtsbezirks Konstanz/Baden" (unpublished *Arbeitspapier*, Konstanz, 1974).
17. ADV: T, Fonds 3, 3bis.
18. AN: F^{17} 4714.
19. GLA: 235/1334.
20. GLA: 235/1344.
21. GLA: 235/1344.
22. GLA: 235/32520.
23. GLA: 235/1344.
24. AN: F^{17} 4704.
25. F^{12} 4704; GLA: 233/32520.
26. HStA: 264. Trapp, cited above in Note 16, argues that factory-school legislation remained essentially unenforced in Konstanz during at least the first two decades after its passage because factory owners depended on child labor for survival during this period and authorities were unwilling to jeopardize their ventures.
27. The evolution of the concept of "school-aged population" appears in records in both regions. In Baden, the concept of school age was legally established by the end of the eighteenth century. The earliest school ordinances had often been vague, but the *Landschulordnung* for Baden-Baden in 1770 required parents to send their children to school "as soon as they have reached their sixth year . . . until the completion of their thirteenth year." (Brunner, *Die Badische Schulordnungen*, p. 212.) The Badenese *Trivialschulordnung* of 1803 specified seven to thirteen years for girls and seven to fourteen years for boys as the "defined school age." (Brunner, p. 301.) Still, early local reports about *schulfähige Kinder* reveal that local authorities were not always sure of the meaning of the concept. The Lutheran school tables of 1802, for example, show that authorities sometimes reported 100 percent school attendance of school-aged children, giving enrollment figures that show improbable sex ratios and suggest underreporting at least of girls and possibly other categories of school-aged children. The following table illustrates the pattern of underreporting, a pattern similar to that found twenty years later

Badenese Lutheran communities, 1802

	Reported proportion of school-aged children enrolled in school		Ratio of girl to boy pupils
	Age 6–9	*Age 9–15*	
In communities reporting 100% enrollment of *schulfähige Kinder*	1.00	1.00	.66
In communities reporting less than 100% enrollment	.91	.78	1.11

Vauclusan sample communities, 1823

Size of community	*Reported proportion of school-aged children enrolled in school*	*Ratio of girls to boys in reported population susceptible*
Less than 500	.36	.62
500–2,000	.42	.71
2,000–10,000	.53	.77
10,000+	.78	1.00

in the Vauclusan sample communities.

In Vaucluse consistent misreporting of the *population susceptible* remained a problem throughout the first half of the nineteenth century. Not only was there a serious underreporting of girls, but local officials held assumptions about the concept that made returns even for boys dubious; they often interpreted the term *population susceptible* to mean those for whom schooling was likely or appropriate. Thus, in 1821 there were two local estimates made at different times of the year, and one national estimate, all of which were quite different. In August of that year, at the height of the agricultural work season, local officials in the twelve Vauclusan sample communities for which reports were found estimated a total *population susceptible* of 2,017 children; in October of the same year, local estimates totaled 2,964; the national estimate amounted to 4,067 children. (ADV:T, Fonds 3, 1; AN: F^{17} 10382.) To overcome these reporting problems, central authorities first simply took a fixed proportion of the total population of each commune as the number of school-aged children. Later figures were derived from the annual number of reported births. It was only in the mid-1830s that new efforts were made to collect direct information about the number of children in a defined age range, usually either five to twelve years or six to thirteen years. The derivation of estimated school-aged populations used in this study to compare with the dubious official figures is described in Appendix II.

28. For a discussion of the reevaluation of the child's personality during the Enlightenment, see G. Snyders, *La Pédagogie en France aux xviie et xviiie siècles* (Paris, 1965).
29. ADV: T, FIA, 102.
30. GLA: 231/1319.
31. GLA: 235/16423.
32. GLA: 231/1319.
33. ADV: T, FIA, 102.
34. GLA: 231/1319.
35. GLA: 362/1596, 1599.
36. AN: F^{17} 10031.
37. GLA: 135/21685.
38. ADV: T, Fonds 3, 3.
39. GLA: 235/21685, 22714. M. Vinovskis and D. May have noted the same trend toward disappearance of the very youngest children from classrooms in early-nineteenth-century Massachusetts. They believe that new theories about the possible harmful effects of early schooling were responsible for this withdrawal, but I found no evidence of such considerations in the regions I studied. See "A Ray of Millennial Light: Early Education and Social Reform in the Infant School Movement in Massachusetts, 1826 to 1840" (Multilithed, Ann Arbor, 1975).
40. T. Laqueur's "The Cultural Origins of Popular Literacy in England, 1500–1850," *Oxford Review of Education* 2(1976): 255–275, and his book *Religion and Respectability* (New Haven, 1976) describe these institutions in the English context.
41. ADV: T, Fonds 3, 3bis.
42. ADV: T, Fonds 3, 4.
43. ADV: T, FIA, 102.
44. ADV: T, FIA, 102; GLA: 362/1506.
45. ADV: T, FIA, 207.
46. ADV: T, FIA, 102.

47. For reference to the comments about moral upheaval observed during this epoch, see for example, E. Shorter, *The Making of the Modern Family* (New York, 1975), pp. 79ff. For a study that also discusses evidence about beliefs in moral progress, see W. Roessler, *Die Entstehung des modernen Erziehungswesens in Deutschland* (Stuttgart, 1961).

48. GLA: 229/113589.

49. GLA: 435/798, 829.

50. GLA: 313/3482.

51. GLA: 388/74.

52. GLA: 388/74.

53. GLA: 388/74.

54. ADV: T, FIA, 102.

55. ADV: T, FIA, 102.

56. ADV: T, Fonds 3, 3bis. Males between the ages of fifteen and twenty-four comprised about 9 percent of the Vauclusan population in 1851. In the cities the proportion was probably somewhat higher because of migration patterns. The age distributions of pupils in the night classes at Carpentras suggest that total evening-school enrollments amounted to between 10 and 15 percent of the urban male population in the age group in question. If enrollments in the courses in chemistry, mathematics, and design are added, the total for the city of Avignon could amount to as many as a quarter of the young men in that city.

57. For a more complete discussion of this question, see below, Chapter VIII. The most careful historical study of the connections between literacy and economic well-being is H. J. Graff's *The Literacy Myth* (New York, 1979), set in the context of mid-nineteenth-century Canada. See also M. Sanderson's "Literacy and Social Mobility in the Industrial Revolution in England," *Past and Present* 56 (1972): 75–104, and T. Laqueur's response, "Literacy and Social Mobility in the Industrial Revolution in England," as well as Sanderson's "Rejoinder," in *Past and Present* 64(1974): 96–112.

CHAPTER 8

1. Refer to H. Chisick, *The Limits of Reform in the Enlightenment,* for a discussion of eighteenth-century attitudes about schooling and mobility. There are several recent works that include discussions of patterns of secondary-school enrollment in the nineteenth century. See, for example, R. S. Elkar, *Junges Deutschland in polemischem Zeitalter* (Düsseldorf, 1979) and P. J. Harrigan, *Mobility, Elites and Education in French Society of the Second Empire* (Waterloo, Ontario, 1980).

2. GLA: 235/16138. The *Industrieschulen,* designed to supplement the economic activities in which children were already engaged, met only during that time of the year when children were most likely to be idle. "The time of the opening of such schools [was] established after the end of the fieldwork, thus in the month of November, and [they were to continue] until March when fieldwork again reaches an active pace."

3. GLA: 235/16138.

4. GLA: 313/3484.

5. H. Zander *et al.,* "Zur Methodenproblematik in der Analyse der Volksschulentwicklung," in K. Hartmann *et al.,* eds. *Schule und Staat im 18. und 19. Jahrhundert,* pp. 287ff.

6. GLA: 231/1327.

7. GLA: 362/1616; 377/8190; HStA: 273/1.

8. GLA: 362/1616.

9. This potential for interference became obvious, for example, when a guild wished to grant *Ledigsprechung* to an apprentice who had failed to attend or graduate from a *Gewerbeschule,* or when *Gewerbeschule* officials claimed that masters should not take as apprentices boys who were not well enough educated to be admitted to classes in the school. (GLA: 377/8190.) Although the challenges artisans faced as a result of industrial reorganization were certainly more threatening, the early state inroads into industrial education also presented a threat to workers' control over industrial training, and hence over access to their trade.

10. GLA: 362/1616. A few pupils stayed on for many years. The distribution of pupils in the Mannheim *Gewerbeschule*, according to the duration of their enrollment in 1844 was:

Number of Years	*Number of Pupils*
1	266
2	30
3	21
4	5
5	1

11. For example, the directors of the *Gewerbeschule* of Mannheim complained to the *Bezirksamt* in 1841 that there were apprentices who were not enrolled in the school and whose masters were refusing to comply with the law or pay fines for its infringement. Many enrolled apprentices were frequently absent, particularly those in the construction trades. (GLA: 362/1616.) Similar complaints came from the *Gewerbeschule* in Sinsheim in 1846. There the directors demanded that the *Bezirksamt* discipline uncooperative apprentices and masters. (GLA: 377/8190.)

12. ADV: T, Fonds 3, 3.

13. For a discussion of the teaching of these orders, see W. J. Battersby, *History of the Institute of the Brothers of the Christian Schools* (London, 1960); P. Lallemand, *Histoire de l'éducation dans l'ancien Oratoire de la France* (Paris, 1888); F. Ponteil, *Histoire de l'enseignement en France* (Paris, 1966), pp. 37ff.

14. There is a brief discussion of the debate over the classics in July Monarchy France in L. Trenard, "L'enseignement sécondaire sous la Monarchie de Juillet," *Revue d'histoire moderne et contemporaine* 12 (1965): 81–134.

15. AN: F^{17} 10374.

16. J. Behaghel, *Geschichte und Statistik des Lyceums zu Mannheim* (Mannheim, 1857).

17. ADV: 1G, 23. F. de Dainville's "Effectifs des collèges et scolarisation aux xviie et xviiie siècles dans le Nord-est de la France," *Population* 10 (1955): 455–488, discusses enrollment patterns in some of the Jesuit collèges of northern France. See also Note 31, below.

18. M. Pazzis, *Mémoire*, p. 219; AN: F^{17} 10374; GLA: 362/1591.

19. GLA: 356/696.

20. GLA: 435/1464.

21. GLA: 435/1464.

22. V. Cousin, *État de l'instruction primaire dans le royaume de la Prusse* (Paris, 1833).

23. AN: F^{12} 4830.

24. ADV: T, Fonds 3, 3bis.

25. Opposition to the founding of an *école primaire supérieure* in the municipal council of Avignon is recorded in AN: F^{17} 9824.

26. AN: F^{17} 10180.

27. AN: F^{17} 9824.

28. GLA: 356/690.

29. ADV: T, Fonds 3, 3.

30. ADV: T, FIA, 102.

31. K. Hausen's "Family and Role Division: The Polarisation of Sexual Stereotypes in the Nineteenth Century," in R. J. Evans and W. R. Lee, eds., *The German Family* (London, 1981), offers some insights into broader transformations in gender ideology that were reflected in educational policies affecting girls. See also F. Mayeur, *L'Éducation des filles en France au XIXe siècle* (Paris, 1979) for a more detailed analysis of French policy.

32. The Jesuit collège in Avignon, for example, generally enrolled more than five hundred pupils between the mid-sixteenth and the mid-eighteenth centuries. The highest recorded enrollment, toward the end of the sixteenth century, was over fifteen hundred pupils! These early records suggest that a substantial proportion, probably around a half, were local day pupils. In

other words, the relatively high enrollments of this epoch are not to be explained simply in terms of the smaller number of educational establishments. Similarly, in Heidelberg, enrollment in the Catholic Latin school in the early eighteenth century was about three times that of Catholic pupils in the city's lyceum in the middle of the nineteenth century. J. Girard, "L'ancien église du collège des Jesuits . . . ," *Mémoires de l'Académie de Vaucluse,* Série 2, 33 (1933): 81–110; F. Frey, *Aus der Geschichte des Erziehungswesens in Heidelberg* (Heidelberg, 1964).

33. The years ten through sixteen were chosen since most boys enrolled in secondary schools fell into this age range. The French government at this time often used the eight-to-eighteen-year range, which would make differences between Baden and Vaucluse diminish markedly, since there were far more eight-to-ten-year-olds in secondary schools in Vaucluse than in Baden.

34. ADV: T, Collèges, 1–6; France, Ministère de l'Instruction Publique, *Rapport au Roi* (Paris, 1843).

35. D. Julia and W. Frijhoff, *École et société dans la France d'Ancien Régime* (Paris, 1975), pp. 63ff.

36. MStA: KFG, 40/1971; J. B. Behaghel, *Geschichte.*

37. For a discussion of the various ways in which schooling can be related to career mobility, see R. Turner, "Modes of Ascent through Education," in R. Bendix and S. M. Lipset, eds., *Class, Status and Power: A Reader in Social Stratification* (New York, 1953).

38. A. Heunisch, *Beschreibung,* pp. 296–298; France, *Statistique de la France* (Paris, 1854).

39. For a discussion of the role of secondary education in social mobility in France in the second half of the nineteenth century, see P. J. Harrigan, *Mobility,* and R. Gildea, "Education and the Classes Moyennes in the Nineteenth Century," in P. J. Harrigan and D. S. Baker, eds., *The Making of Frenchmen* (Waterloo, Ontario, 1980).

40. ADV: T, Fonds 3, 4; GLA: 235/16092; 356/696; 362/1616; HStA: 274/1; MStA: KFG, 40/1971.

41. ADV: T, Collèges, 1–2

42. ADV: T, Collèges, 1–6.

43. HStA: 274/1; MStA: KFG, 40/1971.

44. ADV: D, 344.

45. AN: F^{17} 7396.

46. ADV: T, FIA, 37.

47. GLA: 362/1591.

48. A. M. Bastit, "Personnel et élèves du Lycée d'Avignon de sa fondation à 1850" (unpublished master's thesis, Aix, 1973).

49. In the 1830s, a group of town citizens and pupils' fathers signed a petition supporting the principal of the collège. Of those who indicated their occupation, about half were artisans, the other half professionals and notables. ADV: T, Collèges.

50. ADV: T, Collèges, 6.

51. GLA: 435/847.

52. W. Hohler, *Das Realgymnasium Mannheim, 1840–1910* (Mannheim, 1911).

53. GLA: 435/870.

54. GLA: 213/3072; MStA: KFG, 40/1971. R. Elkar finds a similar trend in his study of recruitment into the *Gelehrtenschulen* of Schleswig-Holstein. See *Junges Deutschland in polemischem Zeitalter* (Düsseldorf, 1979).

55. M. Katz makes a similar argument about the interests behind the public subsidy of secondary education in Massachusetts in the nineteenth century in his *The Irony of Early School Reform* (Cambridge, Mass., 1968) and about the decreasing advantages of primary education in an era of educational expansion in "Who Went to School?" *History of Education Quarterly* 12 (1972): 432–454.

56. ADV: T, Collèges, 6.

57. In the four bourgs, communities of between 2,000 and 10,000 population, in the Vauclusan sample, growth averaged less than 2 percent a decade during the first half of the nineteenth century.

58. ADV: T, FIA, 63.
59. ADV: T, Collèges, 2.
60. AN: F^{17} 8125.
61. ADV: T, Collèges, 6.
62. GLA: 356/696.
63. GLA: 435/871.
64. There is a growing literature on the reproductive role of educational institutions in the contemporary industrial world. See, for example, P. Bourdieu and J.-C. Passeron, *Les Héritiers* (Paris, 1964) and *La Réproduction* (Paris, 1970); E. Altvater and F. Huisken, eds., *Materielen zur politische Ökonomie des Ausbildungssektors* (Erlangen, 1971); S. Bowles and H. Gintis, *Schooling in Capitalist America* (New York, 1976), and C. Jencks, *et al.*, *Inequality* (New York, 1972).

CHAPTER 9

1. For a discussion of the changing concept of "school age," see Chapter VII, Note 27.
2. Again, the evidence is too sparse to make a strong argument, but for those schools for which age data on pupils have survived, enrollments are nearly always lower among the older pupils within the school-age range. Since the probability of surviving beyond the end of the school years once the age of five was reached was on the order of 95 percent, mortality alone would account for very little of this thinning of the ranks. The following chart shows the evidence for schools in the sample communities of Baden:

		Number Enrolled by Age or Age Group				
Community	*Year*	*Below age 7*		*7–10*		*11–14*
Heidelberg	1729	17		45		25
			6–9		*9–15*	
21 Lutheran communities	1802		91%		78%	
			9–11		*12–14*	
Mannheim	1811		162		91	
		Below age 7		*7–10*		*11–14*
Waldangelloch	1810	12		65		46
Mannheim poor school	1849	6		48		51

(GLA: 77/9839; 204/1819; 213/2570; 220/109025; 235/22776.) Note both the dropoff at older ages in all but the last case, and the continued presence in the classroom of younger children.

3. The following table summarizes information about truancy levels in several schools in the Badenese sample communities:

Community	*Date*	*Annual number of unexcused absences per 100 pupils*	
		Boys	*Girls*
Waldangelloch	1809/10	4,000	3,400
Sinsheim	1812		350
Mannheim	1811	4,000	
Mannheim	1849	1,500	1,400
Mannheim	1896/97	35	18

Source: GLA: 229/109025, 377/966, 213/2570, 235/22776; MStA: Volksschule "Ersatz."

4. AN: F[17] 155. The results of the surveys were as follows:

Community size	*Number of teachers reporting average age of entry of:*					
	4	*5*	*6*	*7*	*8*	*n*
Less than 2,000	0	7	1	0	1	9
More than 2,000	4	12	2	2	0	20
Total	4	19	3	2	1	29

Community size	*Number of teachers reporting an average duration of schooling of:*			
	4 Years	*4–5 Years*	*6 years or more*	*n*
Less than 2,000	1	4	5	10
More than 2,000	7	5	8	20
Total	8	9	13	30

5. With few exceptions, registers indicated that the number of pupils diminished with each successive grade level. For example, the following chart lists the enrollments by grade in each of the various kinds of primary schools in the city of Mannheim in 1849:

Grade, Ordnung, etc. (lowest to highest)		*Number of pupils*
Police poor school	1	51
	2	40
	3	31
Free school	1	49
	2	33
	3	25
Einfache Volksschule	1	133
	2	90
	3	100
Erweiterte Volksschule	1	171
	2	130
	3	124
	4	110
	5	98

6. ADV: T, Fonds 3, 3.
7. GLA: 235/22715.
8. The *actes de mariage* in French parish registers and the later *Etat Civil* can be used to yield evidence about the historical prevalence of the ability to sign. For Baden, there was no comparable series, since marriage acts were unsigned until the time of introduction of civil registration in the 1870s. Inferences can be drawn from other series of signed documents like those mentioned in the text, but their selectivity is obviously greater. For a discussion of the analysis of signature data, see R. Schofield, "The Measurement of Literacy in Pre-industrial England," in J. Goody, ed., *Literacy in Traditional Societies* (Cambridge, 1969), and F. Furet and V. Sachs, "La Croissance de l'alphabétisation," *Annales, E.S.C.* (1974): 714–737.
9. H. Brunn, *1200 Jahre Schriesheim* (Mannheim, 1964), p. 254.
10. GLA: 229/16521.
11. MStA: Kirchenbücher.
12. A. Heunisch, *Das Grossherzogthum Baden*, p. 542.
13. Marriage registers are closed by law in Germany to all but the direct descendants of contracting parties. The *Amtsvorstand* of the city of Mannheim was kind enough to allow me to peer over his shoulder as he perused the marriage acts for the early 1870s. As he had assured me, the inability to sign was virtually unheard of by this epoch. Not only did brides and bridegrooms sign, but so did their parents and witnesses in most cases.
14. GLA: 235/22715; ADV: T, Fonds 3, 3bis.
15. For a description of literacy patterns in other areas of southeastern France, see M. Vovelle, "Y-a-til eu une révolution culturelle . . . ?" *Revue d'histoire moderne et contemporaine* 23 (1975): 89–141, and J. Sanchez, "La Culture populaire au xviiie siècle" (*Mémoire de maîtrise*, Aix, 1973).
16. L. Maggiolo, *Statistique de l'enseignement primaire* (Paris, 1880); M. Fleury and L. Valarmy, "Le Progrès de l'instruction primaire," *Population* 12 (1957): 71–92.
17. GLA: 65/1612.
18. The following table indicates the rank-order correlations between the proportion of school-aged children reportedly enrolled in school and the proportion of brides and grooms able to sign at marriage in the Vauclusan sample communities, 1800–1840:

	Community Literacy			
	Male		*Female*	
	1800	*1840*	*1800*	*1840*
Proportion of school-aged children reportedly enrolled in school	.18	.48*	.20	.60**

* = .05 level of significance
** = .01 level of significance

19. A. Heunisch, *Das Grossherzogsthum Baden*, p. 288.
20. G. Gabrielli, *Manuel du Provençal* (Aix, 1836).
21. E. Weber argues in *Peasants into Frenchmen* (Stanford, 1976) that the essential cultural transformations of the French countryside occurred only after the middle of the nineteenth century, and that prior to that time traditional local cultures flourished unaltered. The evidence from Vaucluse would certainly cast doubt on this chronology, as would the results of numerous local studies of demographic behavior, literacy, and economic life in other rural areas of France.
22. AN: F^{17} 9335. It is interesting to note in this connection that school inspectors' reports showed that inspectors were quite satisfied with the written work of pupils in Vaucluse even while they criticized their spoken French. The following table illustrates this pattern: in the arrondissement of Apt in 1832:

	Number of classes in which			
	evaluations of notebooks were:		*evaluations of responses were:*	
Size of Community	*Good or satisfactory*	*Bad or unsatisfactory*	*Good or satisfactory*	*Bad or unsatisfactory*
Less than 2,000	7	2	2	7
More than 2,000	17	1	7	11
Total	24	3	9	18

Source: ADV: T, Fonds 3, 3.

23. The influence of the growing market on early modern life in Europe is the subject of study in F. Braudel, *Capitalism and Material Life* (New York, 1973). E. Labrousse *et al.* analyze specific economic and monetary trends in ancien régime France in *Histoire économique et sociale de la France*, vol. 2 (Paris, 1970). For a discussion of the relationship between literacy and market relations in contemporary societies, see J. Goody, ed., *Literacy in Traditional Societies* (Cambridge, 1968).
24. It should be noted that there was very little relationship in the Badenese communities between the predominance of agriculture and literacy levels, since the variance in the latter was so low. All communities, whether agricultural or industrial, had high levels of school enrollment.

25. The impact upon literacy change of the rising levels of literacy within the agrarian sector as opposed to shifts from agricultural into other sectors can be demonstrated by means of a hypothetical calculation. In effect, what the calculation does is to project what community-level literacy would have been if the *only* change were the shift between sectors, on the one hand, or the changing levels of literacy within sectors, on the other. The data are drawn from the civil registers of three different communities: the village of Merindol, the bourg of Cadenet, and the milltown of L'Isle-sur-la-Sorgue for 1800–1860. The literacy as indicated by the ability to sign among brides and grooms in the different occupational sectors was as follows:

	Agricultural sector		*Other sectors*		*Total*	
Community, year	*Males*	*Females*	*Males*	*Females*	*Males*	*Females*
Merindol, 1820[a]						
% in sector	67	75	33	25	100	100
% able to sign	25	10	50	14	33	11
Merindol, 1860						
% in sector	57	74	43	26	100	100
% able to sign	69	41	90	50	78	43
Cadenet, 1800						
% in sector	72	70	28	30	100	100
% able to sign	20	0	76	8	30	3
Cadenet, 1860						
% in sector	53	60	47	40	100	100
% able to sign	37	29	88	60	61	41
L'Isle, 1800						
% in sector	61	64	39	36	100	100
% able to sign	28	10	74	49	46	24
L'Isle, 1860						
% in sector	68	50	32	50	100	100
% able to sign	54	17	93	45	66	31

[a]The year 1820 was used for Merindol since earlier registers did not indicate the occupation of brides or their families.

The standardization procedure yields the following projections for literacy change caused by sectoral change alone and intrasectoral rise in literacy alone.

			Projected % increase in ability to sign, 1800–1860, if:					
	% able to sign, 1800		*Only intrasectoral rise occurred*		*Only sectoral change occurred*		*Actual % increase in ability to sign, 1800–1860*	
Community	*Male*	*Female*	*Male*	*Female*	*Male*	*Female*	*Male*	*Female*
Merindol	33	11	43	33	3	0	45	32
Cadenet	30	3	21	35	12	0	31	38
L'Isle	46	24	23	2	−3	6	20	7

In the bourg of Cadenet, the decline in the agricultural sector had some effect upon the male literacy rate, but the impact of growing literacy within each sector was more important. The effect of the rising literacy among peasants is even more striking in the case of the village of

Merindol, a center of agriculture and, until its disappearance from the region, rural textile production. In these two communities, women were moving less quickly than men out of agriculture, and sectoral shifts were apparently insignificant in accounting for the rise in female literacy. In the milltown of L'Isle, on the other hand, female literacy rates within each sector stagnated, and those of men were less dynamic than elsewhere. The shift into manufacturing was associated with some increase in female literacy (although not so for men) but it should be noted that in this milltown the rise that did occur was modest in comparison with the other communities.

26. The view that advanced educational levels of a people are an independent causal factor in the process of economic development is argued, for example, in C. A. Anderson and M. J. Bowman, "Education and Economic Modernization," in L. Stone, ed., *Schooling and Society* (Baltimore, 1976), and D. McClelland, "Does Education Accelerate Economic Growth?" *Economic Development and Cultural Change,* 14 (1966): 257–278. For theoretical and historical criticism of this view, see P. Lundgreen, *Bildung und Wirtschaftswachstum im Industrialisierungsprozess des 19. Jahrhunderts* (Berlin, 1973) and D. Hinrichsen and K. Kohler, "Bürgerliche Theorien—Darstellung und Kritik," in E. Altvater and F. Huisken, eds., *Materielen zur politischen Ökonomie des Ausbildungssektors* (Erlangen, 1971).

27. L. Stone found a similar stagnation in urban literacy rates in late-eighteenth- and early-nineteenth-century England. See "Literacy and Education in England, 1640–1900," *Past and Present* 42 (1969): 61–139.

28. The following graphs illustrate trends in literacy patterns of rural residents of Vaucluse, and migrants to Avignon and several smaller towns, and natives of those communities.

Literacy of Rural Residents (Communities < 2,000) and City Natives and Migrants for Avignon

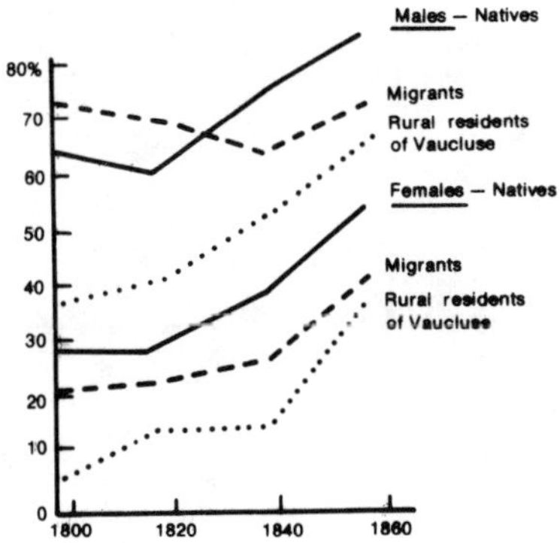

Literacy of Rural Residents (Communities < 2,000) and Town Natives and Migrants for Three Towns (Cadenet, Sorgues, and L'Isle-sur-la-Sorgue)

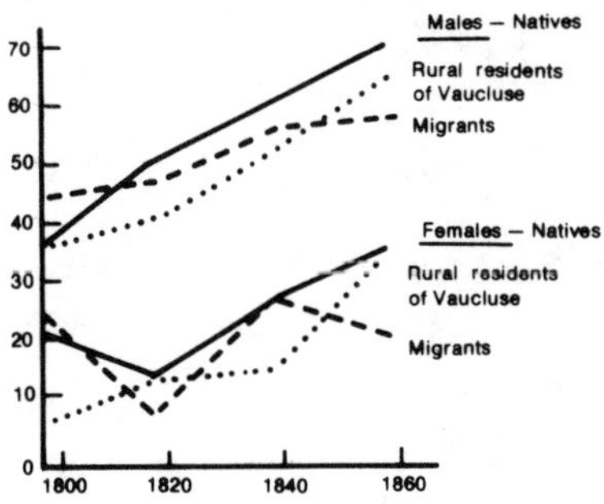

29. See Note 26 above.

30. H. Graff, *The Literacy Myth* (New York, 1979).

Bibliography

Archival Sources

A—France

Archives Nationales
- Ancien:
- Série H^1—1247–1251, Comptes des Vigueries de Provence
- Moderne:
- Série DXXIV—Comité d'Avignon
    - DXXXVIII—Comité d'Instruction Publique
    - F^{12}—Commerce et Industrie
    - F^{17}—Instruction Publique
    - F^{19}—Cultes
- Fonds Particuliers (Imprimées):
    - AD VIII—Instruction Publique

Bibliothèque Nationale
- Nouvelles Acquisitions Françaises:
- Manuscrits 5912—Enquête sur Patois, 1811–1812
    - 5913—Poésies Languedociennes
    - 20080—Enquête de 1807–1812
    - 20081—Juifs en Provence

Musée Pedagogique
    Archives de l'Instruction Primaire
        #6—Vaucluse
Archives Départementales de Vaucluse
    Série D—Université D'Avignon; Collège d'Avignon
        E—État Civil
        G—Archévêché d'Avignon
        H—Clergé Régulier
        J—Documents Extraordinaires
        L—Administration Révolutionnaire
            1L—Budgets Communaux; Écoles Centrales
            2L—District d'Apt
            4L—Instruction Publique
        M—Rencensements
        O—Archives Communales
        T—Instruction Publique:
            Fonds 1—École Normale Primaire d'Avignon
            Fonds 2—Instruction Primaire
            Fonds 3—Instruction Primaire; Organization; Fonctionnement; Salles d'Asile
            Fonds 5—École Centrale, Lycées, etc.
            Fonds de l'Inspection Académique
            Collèges
        U—Archives Judiciaires
            8U—Notaires
Archives Municipales d'Avignon
    Série F—Documents de l'Epoque Révolutionnaire
        R—Instruction Publique
Archives Communales de Cabrières d'Aigues, La Motte d'Aigues, La Coste, Merindol
    Série GG—État Civil Ancien
Archives Communales de Sorgues
    Série F—Commerce et Industrie
        7F—Travail d'Enfants; Livrets
Musée Calvet
    Manuscrits:
        #1839—Frères des Écoles Chrétiennes
        1972—Ursulines
        2566—Instruction Publique
        2535—Distribution des Prix
        3003—Conseil Municipal d'Apt
        3007—Voyages en Provence

B—Baden

Generallandesarchiv
Abteilung
63—Kompetenzenbücher
65—Handschriften
74—Akten; Baden
77—Akten; Pfalz; Generalia
204—Stadt Heidelberg
213—Stadt Mannheim
229—Akten Kleinerer Ämter und Städte und der Landgemeinden
231—Landtag
233—Staatsministerium
235—Kultusministerium
236—Innenministerium
313—Kreisregierungen
356—Bezirksamt Heidelberg
362—Bezirksamt Mannheim
377—Bezirksamt Sinsheim
388—Bezirksamt Wiesloch
390—Gestandesbücher
435—Evangelische Oberkirchenamt
Heidelberg Stadtarchiv
Uraltakten XXIV—Schulanstalten:
258–267—Volksschulen
270—Höhere Bürgerschule
273—Gewerbeschule
274—Gymnasium
Mannheim Stadtarchiv
Zugang 40/1971—Karl Friederich Gymnasium
Volksschule Ersatz
Mannheim Standesamt
Ehebücher
Badenese Church Archives:
Heidelberg: Katholisches Kirchenamt
Evangelisches Kirchenamt
Mannheim: Katholisches Kirchenamt
Karlsruhe: Evangelische Kirchenoberrat—Archiv
Taufbücher, Sterbebücher, Ehebücher

Published Sources

Baden. Statistisches Amt, *Beiträge zur Statistik der Inneren Verwaltung des Grossherzogthums Baden*, vols. 1–2. Karlsruhe, 1855–1856.

Bericht über den Stand der Gewerbeschule zu Heidelberg. Heidelberg, 1841.

Condorcet, (Marie Jean, Marquis) de. "Report on the General Organization of Public Instruction," in F. de la Fontainerie, ed., *French Liberalism and Education in the Eighteenth Century.* New York, 1932.

Cousin, Victor. *État de l'instruction primaire dans le Royaume de Prusse à la fin de l'année 1831.* Paris, 1932.

Expilly, Abbé J. J. *Dictionnaire géographique, historique et politique des Gaules et de la France,* 6 vols. Paris, 1762–1770.

France. Ministère de l'Instruction et des Beaux Arts. *Statistique de l'enseignement primaire, 1829–1877.* Paris, 1880.

France. Ministère de l'Instruction Publique. *Rapport au roi sur l'instruction secondaire.* Paris, 1843.

France. Statistique Générale. *Statistique de la France,* vol. 2, second series, *Resultats généraux du dénombrement de 1851.* Paris, 1855.

Gazier, A., ed. *Lettres à Gregoire sur les patois de France, 1790–1794.* Paris, 1880.

Heunisch, A. J. V. *Geographisch-Statistisch-Topographische Beschreibung des Grossherzogsthums Baden . . . nach Officiellen Quellen Bearbeitet.* Heidelberg, 1833.

———. *Das Grossherzogsthum Baden, Historisch-Geographisch-Statistisch-Topographisch Beschreiben.* Heidelberg, 1857.

Maggiolo, Louis. *Statistique de l'enseignement primaire.* Paris, 1880.

Mistral, Frédéric. *Mes origines: mémoires et récits.* Paris, 1906.

Pazzis, Maxim. *Mémoire statistique sur le département de Vaucluse.* Carpentras, 1808.

Perdiguier, Agricol. *Mémoires d'un compagnon.* Moulinas, 1914.

Prussia. *Die Volks- und Mittelschulen.* Berlin, 1893.

Rochow, Friedrich von. *Geschichte Meiner Schule.* Neudrucke Pädagogischer Schriften. Leipzig, 1890.

Staatliche Archivverwaltung Baden-Württemberg. *Die Stadt- und Landkreise Heidelberg und Mannheim.* Mannheim, 1966.

Universal-Lexikon vom Grossherzogsthum Baden. Karlsruhe, 1843.

Verordnungen über die Gelehrteschulen in Baden. Karlsruhe, 1837.

Villemain, M. *Tableau de l'état actuel de l'instruction primaire en France.* Paris, 1841.

Wehrer, J. F. *Das Volkschulwesens . . . in Grossherzogsthum Baden.* Karlsruhe, 1837.

Secondary Literature

Actes de 95e Congrès des Sociétés Savantes. *Histoire de l'enseignement de 1610 à nos jours.* Paris, 1974.

Agulhon, Maurice. *The Republic in the Village.* Cambridge, 1982.

Allain, Ernst. *L'Instruction primaire en France avant la Révolution.* Paris, 1881.

Alt, Robert. *Bilderatlas zur Schule- und Erziehungsgeschichte.* Berlin, 1960.

———, and W. Lemm, eds. *Zur Geschichte der Arbeitererziehung in Deutschland.* Berlin, 1970.

Altvater, E., and F. Huisken, eds. *Materielen zur politischen Ökonomie des Ausbildungssektors.* Erlangen, 1971.

Altvater, E. "Industrie- und Fabrikschulen im Frühkapitalismus," in E. Altvater and F. Huisken, eds., *Materielen zur politischen Ökonomie des Ausbildungssektors.* Erlangen, 1971.

Ambruster, G. *Geschichte des Dorfes Mühlhausen in Kraichgau.* Mühlhausen, 1971.

Aminzade, Ronald. "Class Struggles, Political Conflict and Social Change in Toulouse, France, 1830–1872." Ph.D. Thesis, Sociology, University of Michigan, 1977.

Anderson, Charles A., and M. J. Bowman. "Education and Economic Modernization in Historical Perspective," in Lawrence Stone, ed., *Schooling and Society.* Baltimore, 1976.

Anderson, Michael. "Family, Household and the Industrial Revolution," in Michael Gordon, ed., *The American Family in Social Historical Perspective.* New York, 1973.

———. *Family Structure in Nineteenth Century Lancashire.* Cambridge, 1971.

Anderson, Robert D. *Education in France: 1848–1870.* Oxford, 1975.

Ariès, Philippe. *Centuries of Childhood: A Social History of Family Life,* Robert Baldwick, trans. New York, 1962.

Aulard, A. *Napoleon Ier et le monopol universitaire.* Paris, 1911.

Auspitz, Katherine. *The Radical Bourgeoisie: The Ligue de l'enseignement and the Origins of the Third Republic, 1866–1885.* Cambridge, 1982.

Baihrel, Réné. *Une Croissance: La Basse Provence rurale.* Paris, 1961.

Baratier, Edward, *et al. Atlas historique de Provence.* Paris, 1969.

Barnard, H. C. *Education and the French Revolution.* Cambridge, 1969.

Bastit, Anne-Marie. "Personnel et élèves du lycée d'Avignon de sa fondation à 1850." Mémoire de maitrise, Aix, 1973.

Battersby, W. J. *History of the Institution of the Brothers of the Christian Schools.* London, 1960.

Behaghel, J. B. "Geschichte und Statistik des Lyceums zu Mannheim, 1807–1857," in *Jahres-Bericht des Lyceums zu Mannheim.* Mannheim, 1857.

Benoit, F., ed. *Voyage en Provence d'un gentilhomme Polonais, 1784–1785.* Marseille, 1830.

Benoit, Fernand. *La Provence et le Comtat Venaissin: arts et traditions populaires.* Aubanel, 1975.

Bien, David D. "Military Education in 18th Century France: Technical and Non-Technical Determinants," in Monte D. Wright and L. J. Paszek, eds., *Science, Technology and Warfare,* Proceedings of the Third Military History Symposium. Washington, D.C., 1971.

———. "La Réaction aristocratique avant 1789: l'exemple de l'armée." *Annales: E.S.C.* (1974), 23–48, 505–534.

Blanc, M. "Essai sur la substitution du français au provençal à Narbonne." *Extrait du bulletin historique et philologique* (1897).

Bollème, Géneviève, *et al. Livre et société dans la France du XVIIIème siècle.* Paris, 1965.

Boon, H. *Enseignement primaire et alphabétisation dans l'agglomération bruxelloise de 1830 à 1879.* Louvain, 1969.

Bourdieu, Pierre. "Cultural Reproduction and Social Reproduction," in R. Brown, ed., *Knowledge, Education and Cultural Change: Papers in the Sociology of Education.* London, 1973.

———, and Jean-Claude Passeron. *Les Héritiers.* Paris, 1964.

———. *La Réproduction.* Paris, 1970.

Bowles, Samuel, and Herbert Gintis. *Schooling in Capitalist America.* New York, 1976.

Bowman, M. J., and C. A. Anderson. *Education and Economic Development.* Chicago, 1966.

Braudel, Ferdinand. *Capitalism and Material Life,* Miriam Kochan, trans. New York, 1973.

Brown, Richard, ed. *Knowledge, Education and Cultural Change: Papers in the Sociology of Education.* London, 1973.

Brun, Auguste. *La Langue française en Provence de Louis XIV au Félibrige.* Marseille, 1927.

———. *Recherches historiques sur l'introduction du français. . . .* Paris, 1923.

Brunn, Hermann. *1200 Jahre Schriesheim.* Mannheim, 1964.

Brunner, Karl. *Die Badische Schulordnungen,* Monumenta Germaniae Paedagogica, 24. Berlin, 1902.

Brunot, F. *Histoire de la langue française des origines à 1900.* Paris, 1926.

Burke, Peter. *Popular Culture in Early Modern Europe.* New York, 1978.

Butts, R. Freeman. "Civilization-Building and the Modernization Process: A Framework for the Reinterpretation of the History of Education." *History of Education Quarterly* 7 (1967): 147–174.

———. *A Cultural History of Education: Reassessing Our Educational Traditions.* New York, 1947.

Chartier, Roger, Dominique Julia, and Marie-Madeleine Compère. *L'Education en France du xvie à xviiie siècle.* Paris, 1976.

Chevallier, Pierre, ed. *La Scolarisation en France depuis un siècle.* Paris, 1974.

———, B. Grosperrin, and J. Maillet. *L'Enseignement en France de la Révolution à nos jours,* 2 vols. Paris, 1968.

Chisick, Harvey. *The Limits of Reform in the Enlightenment: Attitudes towards the Education of the Lower Classes in Eighteenth-Century France.* Princeton, 1980.

Cipolla, Carlo M. *Literacy and Development in the West.* London, 1969.

Claeyssen, Michel. "L'Enseignement de la lecture au 18e siècle," in P. J. Harrigan and D. S. Baker, eds., *The Making of Frenchmen.* Waterloo, Ontario, 1980.

Cohen, Miriam. "Italian-American Women in New York City: Work and School," in M. Cantor and B. Laurie, eds., *Class, Sex and the Woman Worker.* Westport, Conn., 1977.

Compayre, Gabriel. *Histoire critique des doctrines de l'éducation en France.* Paris, 1885.

Connor, Walter D. "Education and National Development in the European Socialist States: A Model for the Third World?" *Comparative Studies in Society and History* 17 (1974): 326–348.

Cressy, David. *Literacy and the Social Order: Reading and Writing in Tudor and Stuart England.* Cambridge, 1980.

Cubberly, E. P. *The History of Education: Educational Practice and Progress.* Boston, 1920.

Dainville, F. de. "Collèges et fréquentations scolaires au XVIIe siècle." *Population* 12 (1957): 467–494.

———. "Effectifs des collèges et scolarité au XVIIe et XVIIIe siècles dans le Nord-est de la France." *Population* 10 (1955): 455–488.

Davey, Ian. "The Rhythms of Work and the Rhythms of School." Multilithed, Toronto, 1975.

———. "Trends in Female School Attendance Patterns." *Histoire Sociale/Social History* 8 (1975): 238–254.

de Mause, Lloyd, ed. *The History of Childhood.* New York, 1975.

Derwein, Herbert. *Handschuhsheim und seine Geschichte.* Heidelberg, 1933.

Duveau, Georges. *Les Instituteurs.* Paris, 1957.

———. *La Pensée ouvrière sur l'éducation pendant la Seconde République et le Second Empire.* Paris, 1948.

Eisenstein, Elizabeth L. "Some Conjectures about the Impact of Printing on Western Society and Thought: A Preliminary Report." *Journal of Modern History* 40 (1968): 1–56.

Eklof, Ben. "Peasant Sloth Reconsidered: Strategies of Education and Learning in Rural Russia before the Revolution." *Journal of Social History* 14 (1981): 355–385.

Elkar, Rainer B. *Junges Deutschland in polemischem Zeitalter.* Düsseldorf, 1979.

Engelsing, Rolf. *Analphabetentum und Lektüre.* Stuttgart, 1973.

Feuillas, Michel. "L'Enseignement à Avignon au XVIIIème siècle." Mémoire de maitrise, Aix, 1959.

Fischer, Wolfram. "Ansätze zur Industrialisierung in Baden, 1770–1870." *Vierteljahrschrift für Sozial- und Wirtschaftsgeschichte* 47 (1960): 186–231.

———. *Der Staat und die Anfange der Industrialisierung in Baden, 1800–1850.* Berlin, 1962.

Fleury, M., and Valarmy, P. "Le Progrès de l'instruction élémentaire de Louis XIV à Napoleon III." *Population* 12 (1957): 71–92.

Fontainerie, F. de la, ed. *French Liberalism and Education in the Eighteenth Century.* New York, 1932.

Fooken, Enno. *Die Geistliche Schulaufsicht und ihre Kritiker im 18. Jahrhundert.* Wiesbaden-Dotzheim, 1967.

Fornery, Joseph. *Histoire du Comtat Venaissin et de la ville d'Avignon.* Avignon, n.d.

"Fortsetzung der Beschreibung des epidemischen Ganges der Masern. . . ." *Annalen für die Gesammte Heilkunde* (1828).

Foucault, Michel. *Discipline and Punish.* New York, 1979.

Frey, F. *Aus der Geschichte des Erziehungswesens in Heidelberg.* Heidelberg, 1954.

Furet, François, and Jacques Ozouf. *Lire et écrire: l'alphabétisation des français de Calvin à Jules Ferry,* 2 vols. Paris, 1977. The first volume has been translated into English as *Reading and Writing: Literacy in France from Calvin to Jules Ferry.* Cambridge, 1982.

———, and Vladimir Sachs. "La Croissance de l'alphabétisation en France du xviiie à xixe siècle." *Annales, E.S.C.* (1974): 114–137.

Gall, Lothar. *Der Liberalismus als Regierende Partei.* Wiesbaden, 1968.

Gerbod, Paul. *La Vie quotidienne dans les lycées et collèges au XIXe siècle.* Paris, 1968.

———. "La Vie universitaire à Paris sous la Restauration." *Revue d'histoire moderne et contemporaine* 13 (1966): 5–38.

———. "Les Inspecteurs généraux et l'inspection générale d'instruction publique de 1802 à 1882." *Revue historique* 236 (1966): 79–106.

"Geschichtliche Darstellung der im Grossherzogthum Baden von 1801 bis 1825 geschehene Schutzpocken-Impfung und deren Resultate." *Annalen für die Gesammte Heilkunde* 1 (1827).

Gilmour, Robin. "The Gradgrind School." *Victorian Studies,* 11 (1967): 207–224.

Girard, Joseph. "L'Ancienne église du collège des Jesuits et la musée lapidaire d'Avignon," *Mémoires de l'Académie de Vaucluse,* Series 2, 33 (1933): 81–110.

Glass, D. W., and D. E. C. Eversley. *Population in History.* London, 1965.

Goldrich, David. "Peasants' Sons in City Schools: An Inquiry into the Effects of Urbanization in Panama and Costa Rica." *Human Organization* 23 (1964): 328–333.

Gontard, Maurice. *L'Enseignement primaire en France, 1789–1833.* Paris, 1959.

———. *Les Écoles primaires de la France bourgeoise.* Toulouse, 1964.

Goody, Jack, ed. *Literacy in Traditional Societies.* Cambridge, 1968.

———, and Ian Watt. "The Consequences of Literacy." *Comparative Studies in Society and History* 5 (1963).

Goubert, Pierre. *The Ancien Régime.* New York, 1969.

Graff, Harvey J. *Literacy in History: An Interdisciplinary Research Bibliography.* New York, 1981.

———. *The Literacy Myth: Literacy and Social Structure in the Nineteenth-Century City.* New York, 1979.

Grimaud, Louis. *Histoire de la liberté d'enseignement en France.* Paris, 1944–1954.

Haebler, R. G. *Ein Staat wird aufgebaut.* Baden-Baden, 1948.

Harrigan, Patrick J. "Secondary Education and the Professions in France during the Second Empire." *Comparative Studies in Society and History* 17 (1975): 349–374.

———. *Mobility, Elites and Education in French Society of the Second Empire.* Waterloo, Ontario, 1980.

———, and Donald S. Baker, eds. *Making Frenchmen: Current Directions in the History of Education in France, 1679–1979.* Waterloo, Ontario, 1980.

Hartmann, K., F. Nyssen, and H. Waldeyer, eds. *Schule und Staat im 18. und 19. Jahrhundert.* Frankfurt am Main, 1974.

Hausen, Karin. "Family and Role Division: The Polarisation of Sexual Stereotypes in the Nineteenth Century," in Evans, Richard J., and W. R. Lee, eds., *The German Family.* London, 1981.

Hautz, J. F. *Geschichte der Neckarschule in Heidelberg.* Heidelberg, 1849.

———. *Lycei Heidelbergensis.* Heidelberg, 1846.

Heubaum, Alfred. *Geschichte des deutschen Bildungswesens,* vol. 1. Berlin, 1905.

Heyd, H. *Geschichte der Entwicklung des Volksschulwesens im Grossherzogthum Baden*, 3 vols. Buhl, 1900.

Hinrichsen, D., and K. Kohler. "Bürgerliche Theorien—Darstellung und Kritik," in E. Altvater *et al.*, eds., *Materielen zur politischen Ökonomie des Ausbildungssektors.* Erlangen, 1971.

Hippeau, Celestin. *L'Instruction publique en France pendant la Révolution.* Paris, 1883.

Hohler, W. *Das Realgymnasium Mannheim, 1840–1910.* Mannheim, 1911.

Jencks, Christopher. *Inequality.* New York, 1972.

Johansson, Egil. *The History of Literacy in Sweden in Comparison with Some Other Countries.* Teheran, 1977.

Johnson, Richard. "Educational Policy and Social Control in Early Victorian England." *Past and Present* 49 (1970): 96–119.

Julia, Dominic, and W. Frijhoff. *École et société dans la France d'Ancien Régime.* Paris, 1975.

———, and Paul Pressly. "La Population scolaire en 1789." *Annales, E. S. C.* (1975), 1516–1561.

Kaestle, Carl B. " 'Between the Scylla of Brutal Ignorance and the Charybdis of a Literary Education': Elite Attitudes toward Mass Schooling in Early Industrial England and America," in Lawrence Stone, ed., *Schooling and Society.* Baltimore, 1976.

Kahan, A. "Determinants of the Incidence of Literacy in Rural Nineteenth Century Russia," in C. A. Anderson and M. J. Bowman, eds., *Education and Economic Development.* Chicago, 1966.

Katz, Michael B. *The Irony of Early School Reform.* Cambridge, Mass., 1968.

———. "Who Went to School?" *History of Education Quarterly* 12 (1972): 432–454.

Kay, Joseph. *The Social Condition and Education of the People,* vol. 1. Shannon, reedition, 1971.

Kazamanias, A. M., and E. H. Epstein. *Schools in Transition.* Boston, 1968.

Keller, Karl. *Aus Waldangellochs Vergangenheit.* Eppingen, 1935.

Keyser, Erich, ed. *Das Badische Städtebuch.* Stuttgart, 1959.

Knodel, John. *The Decline of Fertility in Germany, 1871–1939.* Princeton, 1974.

König, Helmut. *Zur Geschichte der bürgerlichen Nationalerziehung in Deutschland zwischen 1807 und 1815,* 2 parts. Berlin, 1972–1973.

———. *Zur Geschichte der Nationalerziehung in Deutschland im Letzten Drittel des 18. Jahrhunderts.* Berlin, 1960.

Labrousse, Ernest, *et al. Histoire économique et sociale de la France,* vol. 2. Paris, 1970.

Lallemand, Paul. *Histoire de l'éducation dans l'ancien Oratoire de France.* Paris, 1888.

Landes, W. M., and Solmon, L. C. "Compulsory Schooling Legislation: An Economic Analysis of Law and Social Change in the Nineteenth Century." *Journal of Economic History* 32 (1972): 54–91.

Laqueur, Thomas W. "Literacy and Social Mobility in the Industrial Revolution in England." *Past and Present* 64 (1974): 96–107.

———. *Religion and Respectability: Sunday Schools and Working Class Culture, 1780–1850.* New Haven, 1976.

LaVopa, Anthony J. *Prussian Schoolteachers: Profession and Office, 1763–1848.* Chapel Hill, 1980.

Lee, W. R. "Bastardy and the Socio-economic Structure of South Germany." *Journal of Interdisciplinary History* 7 (1977): 403–425.

Lemoine, René. *La Loi Guizot.* Paris, 1933.

Lockridge, Kenneth. *Literacy in Colonial New England.* New York, 1974.

Lundgreen, Peter. *Bildung und Wirtschaftswachstum im Industrialisierungsprozess des 19. Jahrhunderts.* Berlin, 1973.

———. "Educational Expansion and Economic Growth in Nineteenth-Century Germany: A Quantitative Study," in Lawrence Stone, ed., *Schooling and Society.* Baltimore, 1976.

Marchand, J. "L'Enseignement primaire dans le département de Vaucluse, 1791–1900." *Mémoires de l'Académie de Vaucluse* 19 (1900): 43–130.

Mayeur, Françoise. *L'éducation des filles en France au xixe siècle.* Paris, 1979.

Maynes, Mary Jo. "The Virtues of Archaism: The Political Economy of Schooling in Europe, 1750–1850." *Comparative Studies in Society and History* 21 (1979): 611–625.

———. "Work or School? Youth and the Family in the Midi in the Early Nineteenth Century," in Patrick J. Harrigan, and Donald S. Baker, eds., *The Making of Frenchmen.* Waterloo, Ontario, 1980.

McBride, Theresa. *The Domestic Revolution: The Modernization of Household Service in England and France.* New York, 1976.

McClelland, Charles E. "The Aristocracy and University Reform in Eighteenth-Century Germany," in Lawrence Stone, ed., *Schooling and Society.* Baltimore, 1976.

McClelland, D. "Does Education Accelerate Economic Growth?" *Economic Development and Cultural Change* 14 (1966): 257–278.

McKeown, Thomas, R. G. Brown, and R. G. Record. "An Interpretation of the Modern Rise in Population in Europe." *Population Studies* 26 (1972): 345–382.

Meier, W. "Die Masern Epidemie im Jahr 1823/24 in Karlsruhe." *Annalen für die Gesammte Heilkunde* 2 (1827).

Merlin, P. *La Dépopulation des plateaux de Haute Provence.* Paris, 1969.

Merriman, John, ed. *1830 in France.* New York, 1975.

Meyers, Peter V. "Professionalization and Societal Change: Rural Teachers in Nineteenth-Century France." *Journal of Social History* 9(1976): 542–588.

Midwinter, Eric. *Nineteenth Century Education.* London, 1970.

Modell, John, Frank Furstenberg, and Theodore Hershberg. "Social Change and Transitions to Adulthood in Historical Perspective." *Journal of Family History* 1 (1976): 7–33.

Möller, Helmut. *Die Kleinbürgerliche Familie im 18. Jahrhundert.* Berlin, 1969.

Moore, Barrington. *Social Origins of Dictatorship and Democracy.* Boston, 1966.

Mühlhauser, Dr. "Die Volksschulen in der ehemaligen Markgrafschaft Baden-Durlach." *Zeitschrift für die Geschichte des Oberrheins* 23 (1871).

Musgrave, P. W. *Society and Education in England Since 1800.* London: 1968.

———, ed. *Sociology, History and Education.* London, 1970.

Musgrove, F. "The Decline of the Educative Family." *University Quarterly* 4 (1960).

———. "Population Changes and the Status of the Young," in P. W. Musgrave, ed., *Sociology, History and Education.* London, 1970.

O'Boyle, Lenore. "Klassische Bildung und sozial Struktur in Deutschland zwischen 1800 und 1848." *Historische Zeitschrift* 207 (1968): 584–608.

———. "The Problem of Excess of Educated Men in Europe, 1800–1850." *Journal of Modern History* 42 (1970): 471–495.

Palmer, Robert R. *The School of the French Revolution.* Princeton, 1975.

Pansier, P. *Histoire de la langue provençal du XIIe au XIXe siècle.* Avignon, 1924.

Paulsen, Friedrich. *German Education: Past and Present,* T. Lorenz, trans. London, 1908.

Peaslee, A. L. "Education's Role in Development." *Economic Development and Cultural Change* 17 (1969): 293–318.

Pitt-Rivers, Julien. "Social Change in a French Village," in Charles Tilly, ed., *An Urban World.* Boston, 1974.

Ponteil, Felix. *Histoire de l'enseignement en France: Les grandes étapes, 1789–1964.* Paris, 1966.

Pouthas, C. A. *La Population française pendant la première moitié du XIX-ème siècle.* Paris, 1956.

Prost, Antoine. *L'Enseignement en France, 1800–1967.* Paris, 1968.

Razzell, P. E. "An Interpretation of the Modern Rise of Population in Europe—a Critique." *Population Studies* 28 (1974): 5–18.

Resnick, Daniel, and L. Resnick. "The Nature of Literacy: An Historical Exploration." *Harvard Educational Review* 47 (1977): 370–385.

Reisner, E. H. *Nationalism and Education Since 1789.* New York, 1922.

Rey, R. "L'Enseignement primaires et les écoles publiques dans les états pontificaux de France . . . avant 1789." *Mémoires de l'Académie de Vaucluse* 11 (1892): 9–45.

Roessler, W. B. *Die Entstehung des modernen Erziehungswesens in Deutschland.* Stuttgart, 1971.

Roller, F. "Ein Fall von Variola Vaccinatorum." *Annalen für die Gesammte Heilkunde* (1825).

Sanchez, Josette. "La Culture populaire au XVIIIe siècle." Mémoire de maîtrise, Aix, 1973.

Sanderson, Michael. "Literacy and Social Mobility in the Industrial Revolution in England." *Past and Present* 56 (1972): 75–104.

———. "Social Change and Elementary Instruction in Industrial Lancashire, 1780–1840." *Northern History* 3 (1968): 131–154.

Schafer, J. *Beiträge zur Geschichte des Dorfes Heddesbach.* Mannheim, 1950.

Schäffer, T. "Das Ausbildungssystem in Deutschland in der 1. Halfte des 19. Jahrhunderts," in E. Altvater, ed., *Materielen zur politischen Ökonomie des Ausbildungssektors.* Erlangen, 1971.

Schaffer, John W. "Occupational Expectations of Young Women in Nineteenth-Century Paris." *Journal of Family History* 3 (1978): 62–77.

Schenck, Claudia. "Girls' Secondary Education in the Third Republic." Seminar paper, Ann Arbor, 1973.

Schofield, R. S. "The Measurement of Literacy in Pre-Industrial England," in Jack Goody, ed., *Literacy in Traditional Societies.* Cambridge, 1969.

Schultz, T. W. "Investment in Human Capital." *American Economic Review* 51 (1961): 1–17.

Schumann, H., A. Inkeles, and D. Smith. "Some Social Psychological Effects of Literacy in a New Nation." *Economic Development and Cultural Change* 16 (1967): 1–16.

Scott, Joan. *The Glassworkers of Carmaux.* Cambridge, Mass., 1974.

———, and Louise Tilly. "Women's Work and the Family in Nineteenth Century Europe." *Comparative Studies in Society and History* 17 (1974): 36–64.

Seignour, Paulette. *La Vie économique en Vaucluse de 1815 à 1848.* Aix, 1957.

Sewell, William H., Jr. "Social Change and the Rise of Working Class Politics in Nineteenth-Century Marseille." *Past and Present* 65 (1974): 75–109.

Sheppard, J. F. *Lourmarin in the Eighteenth Century.* Baltimore, 1971.

Shorter, Edward. "Female Emancipation, Birth Control and Fertility in European History." *American Historical Review* 78 (1973): 605–640.

———. *The Making of the Modern Family.* New York, 1975.

Simon, Brian. *Studies in the History of Education.* London, 1960.

Simon, Jules. *L'Ouvrier de huit ans.* Paris, 1867.

Simoni, Pierre. "Un Canton rural au XIXe siècle: Étude de la société et de l'économie Aptesienne de 1806 à 1913." Thèse de doctorat de 3ème cycle, Aix-Marseille, 1976.

Singer, Barnett. "The Teacher as Notable in Brittany, 1880–1914." *French Historical Studies* (1976): 634–659.

Snyders, Georges. *La pédagogie en France aux XVIIe et XVIIIe siècle.* Paris, 1965.

Solomon, L. "Opportunity Costs and Models of Schooling in the Nineteenth Century." *Southern Economic Journal* 37 (1970): 66–83.

Speare, A. "Urbanization and Migration in Taiwan." *Economic Development and Cultural Change* 22 (1974): 302–319.

Stadelmann, R., and W. Fischer. *Die Bildungswelt des deutschen Handwerkers um 1800.* Berlin, 1955.

Steidel, H. *Ortsgeschichte von Daisbach mit Ursenbacherhof.* Heidelberg, 1910.

Stone, Lawrence. "Literacy and Education in England, 1640–1900." *Past and Present* 42 (1969): 61–139.

———, ed. *Schooling and Society.* Baltimore, 1976.

———, ed. *The University in Society.* Princeton, 1974.

Strauss, Gerald. *Luther's House of Learning: Indoctrination of the Young in the German Reformation.* Baltimore, 1978.

Strzelewicz, W., H. D. Roopke, and W. Schulenberg. *Bildung und gesellschaftliche Bewüsstsein.* Stuttgart, 1966.

Thomas, H. "Literacy without Formal Education." *Economic Development and Cultural Change* 22 (1974): 489–496.

Thrupp, Sylvia. "Diachronic Methods in Comparative Politics," in R. L. Holt and T. B. Turner, eds., *The Methodology of Comparative Research.* New York, 1970.

Tilly, Charles, ed. *The Formation of National States in Western Europe.* Princeton, 1975.

———. "Population and Pedagogy in France." *History of Education Quarterly* 13 (1973): 113–129.

———, ed. *An Urban World.* Boston, 1974.

Tilly, Louise and Joan Scott. *Women, Work and Family.* New York, 1978.

———, ———, and Miriam Cohen. "Women's Work and European Fertility Patterns." *Journal of Interdisciplinary History,* 6 (1976): 447–476.

Trapp, Werner. "Liberale Volksschulpolitik in der 2. Hälfte des 19. Jahrhunderts—untersucht am Beispiel des Amtsbezirks Konstanz/Baden." Mimeographed Arbeitspapier, Konstanz, 1974.

Trenard, Louis. "L'Enseignement secondaire sous la Monarchie de Juillet. *Revue d'histoire moderne et contemporaine* 12 (1965): 81–134.

Turner, Ralph. "Modes of Ascent through Education," in R. Bendix and S. M. Kipset, eds., *Class, Status and Power: A Reader in Social Stratification.* New York, 1953.

Valdes, A. "Wages and Schooling of Agricultural Workers in Chile." *Economic Development and Cultural Change* 19 (1971): 313–329.

van de Walle, Etienne. *The Female Population of France in the Nineteenth Century.* Princeton, 1974.

Vaughan, Michelina Clifford, and Margaret Archer. *Social Conflict and Educational Change in France and England, 1789–1848.* Cambridge, 1971.

Vigier, Philippe. *La Seconde République dans la Région Alpine*, 2 vols. Paris, 1963.

Vignery, R. J. *The French Revolution and the Schools.* Madison, Wis., 1965.

Vinovskis, Maris A. "Horace Mann on the Economic Productivity of Education." *New England Quarterly* 43 (1970): 550–571.

———. "Trends in Massachusetts Education, 1826–1860." *History of Education Quarterly* 12 (1972): 501–530.

———, and D. May. "A Ray of Millennial Light: Early Education and Social Reform in the Infant School Movement in Massachusetts, 1826–1840." Multilithed, Ann Arbor, 1975.

Vovelle, Michel. *Piété-baroque et déchristianisation en Provence au 18e siècle.* Paris, 1975.

———. "Y-a-t-il eu une révolution culturelle au XVIIIe siècle? A Propos de l'éducation populaire en Provence." *Revue d'histoire moderne et contemporaine* 22 (1975): 89–141.

Waller, Annaliese. *Baden und Frankreich in der Rheinbundzeit.* Freiburg, 1935.

Wardle, David. *The Rise of the Schooled Society.* London, 1974.

Weber, Eugen. *Peasants into Frenchmen: The Modernization of Rural France, 1870–1914.* Stanford, 1976.

Weber-Kellermann, Ingeborg. *Die deutsche Familie.* Frankfurt am Main, 1974.

Weisbrod, B. A. "Education and Investment in Human Capital." *Journal of Political Economy* 52 (1962): 106–123.

West, E. G. *Education and the Industrial Revolution.* London, 1975.

Wylie, Lawrence. *Village in Vaucluse.* New York, 1964.

Zeldin, Theodore. *Conflicts in French Society: Anticlericalism, Education and Morals in the Nineteenth Century.* London, 1970.

Ziegler, K. *Ortschronik Neidenstein.* Neidenstein, 1962.

Zind, Pierre. *Des Nouvelles congrégations de frères enseignants en France de 1800 à 1830.* Le Montet, 1969.

Archival Abbreviations Used in Notes

ADV	Archives Départementales de Vaucluse. Avignon.
AN	Archives Nationales. France.
BN	Bibliothèque Nationale. France.
GLA	Generallandesarchiv. Baden.
HStA	Stadtarchiv. Heidelberg.
MC	Musée Calvet. Avignon.
MP	Musée Pédagogique. France.
MStA	Stadtarchiv. Mannheim.

Index